Corporate Community Involvement

About the authors

Nick Lakin, a law graduate, worked in Corporate Communications for over ten years, leading external and internal relations. He was then asked to set up the global Community Involvement practice at E.ON, one of the world's largest investor-owned power and gas companies, operating in over 25 markets, including the US, Russia, and a number of European countries. At the time of publishing, he is Vice President, Marketplace & Community, at E.ON AG. It was while here that he saw the difficulties organizations experience in deciding what they should and should not do in the communities where they operate and the importance of inspiring and motivating employees in every part of the business to bring it to life.

Nick can be reached at: lakin.nsw@googlemail.com

Veronica Scheubel originally came from Marketing at Nokia and then built up and managed Nokia's global Community Involvement program in more than 20 countries, including global external and internal stakeholder communications and engagement; cause-related marketing activities; program evaluation and reporting; and capacity building within a global partnership network. Before joining the corporate world, Veronica worked with a number of non-profit organizations in Canada. After leaving Nokia, she acquired a Master's degree in Organization Consulting. Now a self-employed consultant, trainer, and coach based in Germany, one focus of her work is Corporate Responsibility and Sustainability as a strategic, integrated way of doing business and a catalyst for organizational change and transformation.

Veronica can be reached at: veronica@scheubeldevelopment.com
Web site: www.scheubeldevelopment.com
Follow Veronica on Twitter: twitter.com/ScheubelDevelop

If you would like to join a discussion forum around *Corporate Community Involvement: The Definitive Guide*, please access: www.cciguide.com.

Corporate Community Involvement

The Definitive Guide
To Maximizing Your Business'
Societal Engagement

Nick Lakin and Veronica Scheubel

Greenleaf
PUBLISHING

Published in the USA by
Stanford University Press
Stanford, California

ISBN 9780804771740 (cloth)

CIP data for this book is available at Library of Congress.

Published simultaneously in the UK by
Greenleaf Publishing Limited
Aizlewood's Mill
Nursery Street
Sheffield S3 8GG
UK
www.greenleaf-publishing.com

British Library Cataloguing in Publication Data:
    A catalogue record for this book is available from the British Library.

    ISBN-13: 9781906093334

Cover by LaliAbril.com.

Mixed Sources
Product group from well-managed
forests and other controlled sources
www.fsc.org Cert no. SA-COC-1565
© 1996 Forest Stewardship Council

Printed and bound in Great Britain by the MPG Books Group, Bodmin, Cornwall.

Contents

Preface
Why this book,
and how you can use it

We, Veronica and Nick, have been practitioners and team leaders in Corporate Community Involvement for years.[1]

When we started out, no one resource existed to help us understand how to do our job. We scrambled to find the information we needed – mostly by looking at what other people were doing and talking to them. We learned through practical experience (and the occasional mistake!), developing our expertise over time.

When people in other countries started reporting to us, we needed to design a learning process for them. We looked at what we could pass on and how to make it useful and engaging.

Initially, we relied on face-to-face communication. Next, we looked at what materials we could share. Eventually, we each wrote internal "how to" manuals that were passed around the company.

The first manual Veronica developed was so thick that one of her colleagues exclaimed, "Veronica, your manual just landed on one end of my desk and catapulted my computer out the window!" That feedback was a useful learning for us. We made sure that we kept future editions concise and practical. We wanted the manual to be easily accessible on people's desks and not hidden on the shelf above, collecting dust.

After producing a couple more of these manuals, we asked ourselves: "Why are we doing this again and again for different companies? Why hasn't anyone assembled this valuable information for wider use?" We discovered a few booklets and training courses on various topics, and several books with high-profile case studies. Still, no one had written a book from the inside of corporate practice that covered the full journey from A to Z – from how to get started in Community Involvement to how to deliver results-based programs. So we set out to do that, and soon found a publisher who shared our passion.

Corporate Community Involvement is not a business book for you to proudly own yet never find the time to read. We all have enough of those. Keeping in mind your and your colleagues' busy work schedules, we designed this book to be easily accessible. You can open it anywhere and start working. When you have new colleagues or team members reporting to you, the book can also serve as part of their induction.

---

1 In this book, we talk about "Corporate Community Involvement," but for reasons of brevity, throughout the book, we mainly refer to "Community Involvement."

The book's 11 easy-to-read chapters introduce you to every aspect of Community Involvement you will need to cover in your company. Most of the chapters start with an interview with an experienced practitioner who comments on the topic and shares a best-practice example of Corporate Community Involvement in action. Each chapter then elaborates to deepen your understanding, offering tips, tools, and hands-on advice.

Whether you work for a multinational company with a global reach or for a small or medium-sized enterprise in one market, you will learn how to plan and execute a comprehensive and successful approach to Community Involvement for your company.

A few years ago, we received the following message from a colleague at a company in Canada. "Thank you so much for this, guys. We got your manual at the start of our planning and worked through it. It saved us much time and effort and answered many questions. We followed it step by step, and now our community activities are up and running."

This is why we now turned our know-how into this book. We hope it will do the same for you.

To Susi and Penelope with all my love
— *Nick*

To J. C., without whom I would not be
where I am today
— *Veronica*

Acknowledgments

A book like this evolves over many years and countless experiences working in, with, and on behalf of a variety of different organizations – including companies and not-for-profit organizations.

In particular we want to thank our current and former colleagues at E.ON and Nokia who, over the years, gave us the learning and support, encouragement, inspiration, and experiences needed to write it. We also thank our publisher, John Stuart, and his team at Greenleaf for their support and patience. Our personal "writer's support," Sheila Kinkade, provided invaluable input and also deserves our special thanks.

We are grateful to all our interviewees for so generously contributing their time, thoughts, experiences, and insights: Thomas Baumeister, Justine Frain, Celia Moore, Alberto Andreu Pinillos, Rima Qureshi, Ros Tennyson, Ntutule Tshenye, and Dr. Mark Wade. We are also grateful to all the companies whose best practices in Community Involvement we have been privileged to learn from – we appreciate the opportunity to feature them in this book.

It would not have been half as inspiring and productive a process without the contributions from individuals who provided helpful insights as we went along. In particular, special thanks go to the following for being inspiring, sharing ideas and experiences, reviewing copy, or just being wonderfully supportive:

Marcus Alexander, Howard Atkins, Manny Amadi, Martin Blumberg, Amanda Bowman, Erik Brandsma, Andreas Brandtner, Caroline Collard, Christian Conrad, Heike Cosse, Eric Depluet, Suzanne Doxey, Eva Halper, Andy Kenny, Ildiko Kovacs, Jane Linklater, Helen Merrick, Erica Packington, Rob Pope, Joanna Pyres, Dominique Schaub, Catherine Shaw, Thomas Simon, Cristina Sissons, Ed Staples, Marjorie Thompson, Mike Thompson.

Veronica's deep thanks also go to Kimmo Lipponen, an outstanding practitioner and teacher on the topic without whose knowledge and practice this book could not have been written; to the many partners in the International Youth Foundation's global network who always so generously shared their insights; and to the faculty at Ashridge Business School for their wisdom in understanding and working with change.

Finally and most importantly, we are deeply grateful for the patience of family and friends whom we certainly neglected while the book was being written. Nick thanks his wife and daughter, Susi and Penelope, for their continued encouragement, proofreading, smiles, and love, and his parents, Joy and Steve, for their inspiration and support whether near or far. Veronica thanks her partner, Chris, for his love and support, and for so patiently tolerating the stacks of paper lying around for months.

Nick Lakin and Veronica Scheubel, March 2010

Introduction

Corporate Community Involvement: What it is, what it is not

Corporate Responsibility is about a company's responsible and sustainable behavior in *all* company matters, in financial, environmental, and social areas. These areas are also called the "triple bottom line." Corporate Community Involvement is **one subsection** of the third, social area.

This chapter defines **Corporate Community Involvement**[1] in more detail, exploring its origins and related concepts – e.g., Corporate Giving, strategic philanthropy, social sponsoring, and Corporate Citizenship. The upside is that companies have adopted increasingly strategic approaches in their support of important causes. The downside is that a complex vocabulary, including terms that are frequently misunderstood, has accompanied the growth of this expanding field. In this introduction, we provide a brief history of how Corporate Community Involvement developed and an outlook on its future. A Glossary of Terms can be found at the end of the book.

In the beginning: Corporate Giving

> "We do it because we should." – David Ford, President, Lucent Technologies Foundation, 2000

Companies big and small have long contributed to their communities. Beginning in the early 19th century in Western Europe and the United States, companies built housing, schools, and hospitals in the communities where their employees worked and lived. They understood then what the World Business Council for Sustainable Development states in its *10 Messages by Which to Operate*: "Business cannot succeed in societies that fail."[2]

For the longest time, contributions were made as an act of philanthropy – also called "the writing of checks to charity." Such donations frequently went all over the place – to

---

1   See footnote on page vii.
2   www.wbcsd.org/templates/TemplateWBCSD5/layout.asp?type=p&MenuId=MTAyMQ, accessed November 2009.

schools and kindergartens, theaters and museums, hospitals and orphanages, the local fire brigade, and the local swimming pool. Unstructured giving still exists. Nowadays, companies call their donations **Corporate Giving**.

More focus: Strategic philanthropy

Given that companies also look for a return – usually a reputation benefit – in making their contributions, increasingly they are looking to focus their Corporate Giving. This approach is referred to as **strategic philanthropy**.

In their strategic philanthropy, companies seek to align their charitable giving with a cause that connects to their core business. Companies that pursue this path might say, "We only give money to hospitals," or "only to community organizations in our region," or "only to causes that support children's education."

Thinking about a strategic focus for Corporate Giving also means considering the potential reputation value gained from a focused approach to giving. For example, it makes sense from a public recognition and credibility standpoint for a pharmaceutical company to support cancer research, as opposed to arts and culture programs.

Part of Marketing: Social sponsoring

Public recognition and brand image are critical for companies, and the activities of Communications and Marketing departments are directed at continuously improving them. Corporate Giving and strategic philanthropy may accord a company some reputation benefit; however, the main focus is on the charitable giving, and reputation goals are not aggressively pursued. Although one root of today's Corporate Community Involvement is in such Corporate Giving, Community Involvement can also be traced to what is known as **social sponsoring**. What is social sponsoring, and how did it come about?

Consumers care about a company's and a brand's ethics, and are increasingly interested in what is called the **social brand dimension**. Given this reality, companies that prominently displayed their logos at sports events or big concerts thought they could do the same thing in a social context. By sponsoring social causes, they could associate their brand with having a "heart," values, and ethics.

A good example of a social sponsorship was Nokia launching a new mobile phone with a TV spot featuring capoeira dancers on a beach. Parallel to the ad, the company sponsored a charitable initiative in which capoeira dancers taught children in orphanages how to dance to build their physical strength, self-confidence, and team spirit. The capoeira dancers also performed at corporate marketing events attended by VIP customers.

Social sponsoring results mainly in a two-way marketing relationship: an NGO and a cause benefit from funding and, in turn, the company receives recognition as a sponsor. From the company's point of view, the goal is to use a societal cause as a means of achieving a marketing benefit.

By the late 1990s, companies tended to pursue Corporate Giving and some social sponsorships. Was that enough for stakeholders? Let's look at how companies were soon taken to task to do more.

A new role as partner: Corporate Citizenship

"Advertising is on the decline. The future is in Corporate Citizenship."
– Philip Kotler, author and marketing expert

A company is not outside of society. It is a fully participating member with rights and duties, a corporate citizen, if you will. As a member of society, a company has participatory responsibilities – not just "taking the profits and running away with them," but also giving back to society and contributing meaningfully.

In the 1960s, the **social contract** was understood as government providing for the public good. At that time, companies were simply required to obey laws and pay taxes. By the late 1990s, talk of a new social contract emerged. National governments were increasingly losing power and influence, and in 2000 a report on the 200 top corporations by the Institute for Policy Studies established that, out of the top 100 economies in the world, 51 were now companies, and only 49 were nation states.[3] In this context, companies assumed a growing role in helping to solve social challenges related to employment, health, safety, education, culture, and the environment. Acknowledging their role as corporate citizens, they accepted their responsibility to become involved.

As the notion of **Corporate Citizenship** increasingly came to matter, many companies moved the function out of the Marketing department, for example into Public Affairs.

This new role for business asks companies to think together with governments and NGOs on a higher level about finding and co-creating solutions to pressing problems, and to then jointly apply those solutions in local contexts. The new social contract thinking represents a shift in roles, emphasizing the participatory responsibility of all sectors for co-creating societal innovation and change. AccountAbility[4] has named this "collaborative governance."

Doing this work together demands cross-sector commitment, making partnerships increasingly important. It also requires a range of collaboration and partnering skills, which companies need to develop.

And thus began Corporate Community Involvement

As cross-sector commitment grew, people found the notion of Corporate Citizenship confusing. Some companies now use it to describe their philanthropy. Others use it to describe all of their Corporate Responsibility activities.

---

3 S. Anderson and J. Cavanagh, *Report on the Top 200 Corporations* (Washington, DC: Institute for Policy Studies, December 2000).
4 www.accountability21.net

Since the beginning of the millennium, **Corporate Community Involvement** has been the more concrete term most in use for describing the activities that we talk about in this book – though some companies also refer to their Community Relations, Community Engagement, or Community Investment. Corporate Community Involvement is about **active community partnership projects between your company and/or governments and/or NGOs in the countries/regions/communities where you operate.** These are partnerships aimed at co-created solutions, to which the company contributes funding, project management, corporate core competencies, and Employee Involvement.

In such partnerships, you aim for societal impact. You can then leverage the results of your efforts in stakeholder communications or Marketing to also achieve business benefits – e.g., an improved reputation or increased sales.

Comparing the different concepts introduced

To understand the impetus for the development of Corporate Community Involvement, let's look at the different concepts we've introduced and compare them.

How does Corporate Community Involvement differ from Corporate Giving? In Corporate Giving, you simply donate money, and you remain otherwise uninvolved – although you might also contribute employee volunteer hours. You don't expect much in terms of a "return" – perhaps an article in a local newspaper, with a photo of you, or more likely your boss, handing over a check and shaking hands with the recipients.

How do you distinguish Corporate Community Involvement from social sponsoring? In social sponsoring, you provide funds and, in turn, get your logo "out there." Your main interest is your brand positioning and your marketing benefit. It is not a real project partnership, and you tend not to think about societal impact, but mainly about your immediate business benefit.

How does Corporate Responsibility/Sustainability fit in? Corporate Responsibility is complex. As mentioned at the beginning of this chapter, it is about your company's responsible and sustainable behavior in *all* company matters, in financial, environmental, employee, and societal areas. Corporate Community Involvement is **one subsection** of your overall Corporate **Social** Responsibility.[5] Over the past few years, a lot of organizations have become interested in a responsible approach, although governments and NGOs cannot talk about their **Corporate** Responsibility, as they are not corporations. Increasingly, people in the field talk generally about Organization Sustainability. Within Sustainability, Community Involvement is part of the organization's overall Social Performance.

---

5 If you want to understand Corporate Responsibility better, we recommend D. Grayson and A. Hodges, *Everybody's Business* (London: Dorling Kindersley, 2001).

Two phases of involvement

Corporate Community Involvement also came about in two phases. To begin with, in the 1990s many companies still thought: "Let's address a cause in the community that stakeholders want us to get involved with, but that is far enough from our core business, so we won't get accused of Marketing!" At the time, numerous companies jumped on youth and education issues, and those are still popular. They are easy to engage with and tend to be non-controversial. Microsoft, for example, was heavily criticized for tying its Community Involvement directly to its product line, and for being unapologetic about wanting its program beneficiaries to later buy Microsoft products.

All that changed when the United Nations Global Compact was launched in 2000. Kofi Annan, then Secretary-General of the UN, officially asked companies to start thinking hard about the real difference they could make in society by using their corporate core competencies. How could, for example, telecommunications companies bring distance learning content to remote and underprivileged areas in developing countries? How could pharmaceutical companies find solutions for the prevention and treatment of HIV/AIDS? Or how could entrepreneurs contribute to entrepreneurship training and self-employment for the growing numbers of jobless youth around the world?

If the company derived a direct business benefit from that type of involvement – e.g., through having the education solutions they developed within a specific community taken to scale and paid for by governments – that benefit was acceptable to stakeholders.

Enlightened self-interest

The concept of enlightened self-interest was applied to the business context and is now generally accepted. The thinking is: if companies claim that they are doing good for society only out of their ethical conviction, stakeholders won't believe them. If, on the other hand, companies only look for their business benefit and neglect the needs of society, stakeholders will be outraged – and the company will ultimately fail.

What emerged shortly after the turn of the millennium is a balanced, threefold approach to Corporate Community Involvement: (1) striving for real societal impact, based on sound ethics and values; (2) implementing programs by co-creating community partnerships; and (3) leveraging results for improved reputation, brand image, and sales. All of a sudden, Microsoft, with its Partners in Learning program which offers schools access to IT learning,[6] was in just the right spot!

What department is in charge of Community Involvement?

So if you want to work in this area, in which department do you get to sit? You might find yourself in a Corporate Affairs, Corporate Communications, Marketing, or Corporate Responsibility department. It varies, and in some companies, the function itself is still marginal; however, its importance is growing. Many multinational companies now have dozens of people worldwide working solely on the company's Community Involvement.

---

6 www.microsoft.com/education/pil/partnersinlearning.aspx, accessed November 2009.

But are we all talking about the same thing?

We often aren't. People may refer to their CSR when they mean their philanthropy. They may talk of their Corporate Citizenship when they mean their overall Corporate Responsibility. They may talk of their philanthropy when they actually have sophisticated Community Involvement partnerships. We all tend to make meaning in our own ways, using the information currently available to us. So, when you speak with other people, you may want to ask a few questions to clarify how they are involved. Ask more specific questions such as "So what do you do in this area?" to get a more accurate picture of what they're referring to.

What is this book about, then?

Let's be clear. In this book, we engage with strategic philanthropy, but only in Chapter 4. We also engage with Community Involvement as part of cause-related marketing and social sponsoring in Chapter 5. Other than that, we explore Corporate Community Involvement throughout the book as we see it practiced by companies around the world – companies that are co-creating community partnerships with governments and NGOs.

An evolving field

You have seen now how concepts and thinking around corporate contributions to communities have evolved over time. We have not arrived at a final destination yet. You can expect thinking, concepts, and language to evolve and change at least every five years.

Already in 2007, at Ethical Corporation's "Responsible Business in Emerging Markets Summit" in London, none of the speakers referred to Community Involvement anymore. Instead, they spoke of **capacity building**, of enabling social and economic opportunity in communities. Increasingly, mining, oil, and gas companies like Shell and BG Group consider impactful Community Involvement to be part of what they now call **Social Performance Management**, and Social Performance Management is part of overall CR/ Sustainability. Figure I.1 depicts one company's view of this evolution of social performance.

Your company's role

In the countries where you operate, you will be addressing pressing societal concerns. You will build hands-on, local partnerships to which you will contribute funding, project management expertise, your company's core competencies, and the skills – and hopefully, passion – of your employees.

There are countless causes, and none of us will save the world alone. But if you focus on one cause to which your company can make a difference, and if you partner across sectors with the right organizations, your impact will be greater than you can imagine

Figure I.1 **Social performance: increasing value to business and society**

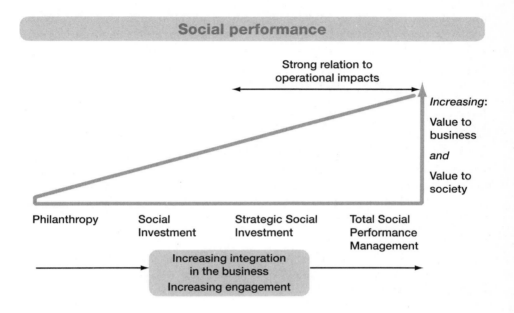

© Royal Dutch Shell plc

right now. You might create a new entrepreneurship model, contribute to systemic societal change, help reshape legislation for the better, change the way children learn, or even alter how people will live in the future. Your company, with all its business competence, has the most powerful means to contribute – and to be seen as a vital player by all relevant stakeholder audiences.

Let's get started.

1

How to develop the right Community Involvement strategy

A Community Involvement strategy defines the long-term direction and systematic action required to achieve a company's goals in both meeting the needs of its communities and achieving business objectives. In short, a Community Involvement strategy is a three- to five-year "how to get there" plan.

The first part of this chapter is an interview addressing how Microsoft successfully created and implemented an outstanding global Community Involvement strategy, and then adapted and implemented that strategy in Sub-Saharan Africa. The chapter then takes you step by step through a process for developing your own Community Involvement strategy.

Interview with Ntutule Tshenye: Accessing unlimited potential

Strategy is often decided centrally; however, countries and regions are unique and different, so strategy implementation needs to be adapted locally. For example, Africa is a large and highly diverse continent, and the needs of its people differ from those in Asia, Europe, or the Americas.

Ntutule Tshenye, Citizenship Lead – West, East, Central Africa and the Indian Ocean Islands at Microsoft, offers his insights into Microsoft's Corporate Citizenship[1] strategy and the ways it is applied in an African context. Ntutule joined Microsoft in 2005, coming from the NGO world, where he had been CEO of South Africa's Youth Development Trust.

---

1 Microsoft groups both Corporate Responsibility and Corporate Community Involvement under the heading of "Corporate Citizenship."

What about the area for which you are responsible? How many countries do you cover?

NT: "We have 13 offices with over 600 full-time and contract staff. And we have worked to create a network of almost 10,000 commercial partners that develop, sell, deploy, and support our software solutions. I work in the West, East, Central Africa, and Indian Ocean Islands subsidiary, also called WECA. WECA sits within the broader Middle East and Africa Region and spans 49 countries. I am based in the headquarters in Johannesburg, South Africa, and have Citizenship managers in each of our four sales locations, including interns in two of the locations. We partner with the student organization AIESEC for our intern program, in order to open up opportunities for students' entry into the job market."

And, just to clarify, at Microsoft, CR is called Corporate Citizenship?

NT: "Yes, we refer to Corporate Responsibility as Corporate Citizenship, because our commitment is more than a responsibility – it's about being an active citizen in the countries and communities in which we operate. Our Corporate Citizenship areas of focus are Responsible Business Practices; Security Privacy and Internet Safety; and Unlimited Potential. In our understanding, addressing all of those three areas is about being a good corporate citizen.

"We have concrete Corporate Citizenship goals. They are to (1) serve the public good through innovative technologies and partnerships; (2) contribute to economic growth and social opportunity; (3) deliver on business responsibilities of growth and value to customers, shareholders, and employees; and (4) approach Citizenship as a core part of Microsoft's business value."

What about your vision and mission for your Corporate Citizenship?

NT: "They are actually not different from our corporate vision and mission. Our vision is: 'To bring the benefits of technology to the next five billion people.' Our mission is: 'To enable people and businesses throughout the world to realize their full potential.' Our specific mission in Africa is: 'Realizing the Unlimited Potential of Africa's people and businesses through the provision of software, services, and solutions toward the attainment of the Millennium Development Goals.'

"We have really thought about what legacy we'd like to leave in Africa. We see an Africa where every school has a computer center where children can practice and use technology. We see every African neighborhood with access to technology and training. We see every government leveraging technology to provide basic services for all citizens. We see every citizen benefiting from technology that supports Africa's transformation to democracy. We see subsistence farmers who are able to realize the true value of their produce on the global market through the use of technology. We see children and families healed by powerful medical expertise. And then we see an Africa at peace with itself and able to contribute to the great endeavors of humanity and compete on the world stage."

What are your strategies then to reach those goals?

NT: "Globally, we have three interrelated strategies: transforming education; enabling jobs and opportunities; and fostering local innovation. Unlimited Potential is the umbrella messaging framework within which these three global strategies are implemented, and it is always a holistic approach; programs never address just one of the three components. Just to give you an example: innovation creates jobs, and you need to be educated for innovation – in 2007, almost 15 million people were employed globally in jobs created by the Microsoft business model. We bring the same spirit of innovation to Corporate Citizenship that we have always applied to our business.

"For Africa, we have adapted the three global strategies to meet local needs appropriately. Our African approach has four core pillars: (1) Coverage – which means expanding our footprint across the subcontinent; (2) Leverage – expanding impact through partnership and capacity building with influential stakeholders; (3) Community Development – citizenship efforts are aligned to national development priorities, and we provide funds to augment NGO impact in the areas of youth and women, entrepreneurship, digital literacy, and employability; and (4) Innovation – here we provide business models and technology innovation relevant for and within Africa.

"We then have three criteria against which to test our activities. They all need to have *local relevance*, offer people *access*, and be *affordable* for people."

What about NGO partnerships?

NT: "Those are absolutely key, just as much as government relations. We want to empower NGOs as key partners and contribute our know-how. If, for example, a government representative or an NGO brings an IT-related community competency issue to our attention, we research what we know and what we can do about it. A small example is that Windows Vista was made available in local African languages like Yoruba, Igbo, and Hausa. We want to also strengthen the NGO sector through ICT, skills development and management, performance for both projects and processes, and business and sustainability models. That's where we have core competencies. Last but not least, we also partner with universities, and that is a huge audience. Those young people are tomorrow's decision-makers!"

And how do you find those partnerships work out?

NT: "With the company's approach to Corporate Citizenship, I have the *space* to really immerse myself in the communities and find out about local needs. What I noticed there initially was a certain level of damage sometimes – an image of the company as 'taking the profits and running with them.' We had to address that, and we did by introducing programs that are aligned to people's needs.

"You have to be seen as part of *building* our countries and markets, and also understand how government works – e.g., understand the continuing influence of previous political leaders and work with that. If you do all that well, the business benefit is that you are earning your loyalty from your stakeholders, and, once they trust you, the lines of communication and interaction are really open both ways."

How are local Microsoft employees involved in your community activities?

NT: "In Sub-Saharan Africa, we have about 500 employees. The company gives them three days of paid leave per year to be active as volunteers, and people do take us up on that. For example, the training centers at Nigeria's Chief Bola Ige Information Technology Center are also enabled by Microsoft funding and volunteers to provide IT skills training to unemployed women, helping them to acquire the skills they need to find employment."

How much do you spend?

NT: "We invest considerable amounts – however, we are careful not to follow a worrying practice that I've seen adopted by some companies operating here. They report even regular local salaries they pay as community investment. We do not do that. Paying local employees local salaries is, to us, part of normal business operations. What we report as investment in the community is uniquely for programs under 'Unlimited Potential.' Microsoft sees incredible potential in Africa. We invest hundreds of millions of dollars in our software, our people, and our partners, in order to transform education, foster local innovation, enable job creation, and support economic development across Africa."

What should companies wanting to implement global Community Involvement themes in Africa be aware of? What should they pay attention to in their approach?

NT: "That is a good question, and to me the answer is actually simple and straightforward. Citizenship to me is first of all about local immersion, and then it is about empowering people. Immerse yourself fully in the local context. Build relationships! That takes time and is so often underestimated. It is a big risk to just start 'doing business as usual' without building the relationships first. And, when you are with people, just talk like one of them – no need to set yourself apart. Then look into what the local needs are and how you can address them, applying your strategy to build local capacity and empower people."

Why strategic Community Involvement?

"Business cannot succeed in societies that fail," according to the World Business Council for Sustainable Development.[2] For societies to succeed, companies need to contribute to the communities where they sell and operate, applying the same rigor and principles that they do to their core business. Such a focused approach calls for a Community Involvement strategy, taking into consideration the current state and needs of local communities, the opportunities the company has to contribute, and the goals the company wants to achieve in society.

Only a sound Community Involvement strategy, fully in line with your company's overall business and, if you have one, Corporate Responsibility strategy, can help you achieve a successful and business-integrated approach to Community Involvement.

2 www.wbcsd.org/templates/TemplateWBCSD5/layout.asp?type=p&MenuId=MTAyMQ, accessed November 2009.

What if you don't have a strategy?

Initially, you may consider that it is difficult to develop a strategy, and that it might be easier to just work without one. You could, for example, try to "keep everyone happy" and support a broad range of philanthropic issues.

While many businesses start with this approach, it has disadvantages. First, it can be difficult to budget support for a broad range of issues. Second, you might face a lack of transparency among the many causes you support. Third, you would likely have limited impact and a low "business return" – e.g., in terms of public recognition. Finally, you would have fewer opportunities to develop deep relationships in the community – and fewer opportunities to contribute real innovation and to stand out as a company making a difference.

In contrast, a more tailored Community Involvement strategy can enable your company to achieve a measurable impact on the community, track spending and results, build better and longer-lasting relationships, achieve more stakeholder recognition, and distinguish itself from the competition.

Of course, a focused approach means that you will have to say "no" to people requesting support for causes or projects that don't align with your strategy. A focused approach also tends to be more resource-intensive, as you need qualified staff to work on your activities. That said, numerous business benefits make the Business Case for strategic Community Involvement, and your company would not want to miss out on them.

Business benefits of strategic Community Involvement:

- Enhancing reputation
- Improving stakeholder relations
- Building credibility and trust
- Demonstrating core competencies and innovation potential
- Exercising leadership
- Enhancing brand image and preference; strengthening brand value
- Improving customer relationships, including increasing customer purchase intentions, retention, and loyalty
- Increasing employee attraction and retention
- Expanding to new growth markets
- Creating a distinct niche for the company
- Contributing to long-term value creation for the company

These benefits are the result of a proactive, impact-driven approach to Corporate Community Involvement – an approach that is essential for corporations that want to achieve integrated business success locally, nationally, globally, or industry-wide.

Figure 1.1 **The journey to Community Involvement leadership**

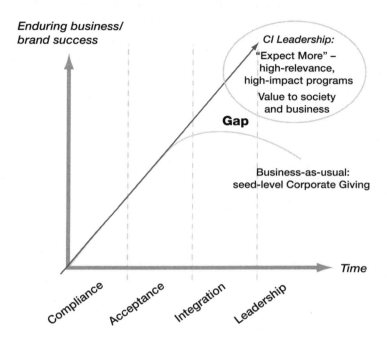

- In your company, strategic Community Involvement may only be entering the phase of "acceptance" (bottom left)
- As expressed by your company's board, the ambition may be to be a leader in CR and therefore also in Community Involvement (top right)
- This requires a corporate Community Involvement strategy aiming to establish acceptance, achieve integration and provide leadership (move from left to right)
- Only then will you be able to bridge the gap "from now to WOW"[3] and ensure leadership.
- A failure to do so risks leaving you "stuck," tailing off without ongoing commitment (line to bottom right)

Source: Manny Amadi, C&E Advisory

As Figure 1.1 shows, achieving Community Involvement leadership is a journey. If your company is new to Community Involvement, you may first need to gain acceptance for your strategic Community Involvement approach. You may need to engage and persuade a number of key internal stakeholders at several levels of the organization. Doing that effectively is described in Chapter 11. You then need to work on business integration.

---

3 The expression "from now to WOW" was coined by Manny Amadi of C&E Advisory.

So what is a Community Involvement strategy?

In the past, corporate contributions to the community often relied on luck and "happy accidents" to create business value. Activities were often chosen at random. To be effective, strategies and programs must be carefully planned.

A Community Involvement strategy outlines how a company systematically participates in meeting the needs of local communities by contributing a value proposition. It entails devising a plan to achieve goals and objectives over the long term – or for at least the first three to five years. It entails creating a sustainable approach that delivers both societal and business advantage. Operational tactics then involve smaller moves to implement the strategy.

An effective Community Involvement strategy usually leverages two aspects in particular:

- The strategic contribution of **corporate core competencies** to achieve real impact in addressing a societal need
- **Strategic cross-sector partnerships** with organizations that are already on location, combining mutual expertise

Developing your Community Involvement strategy: A five-part process

Your strategy is more apt to be accepted if, from the outset, you can involve those people whom you will later need to approve, champion, and implement it. If you give people whose support you need an opportunity to co-create strategy, they will develop a much stronger sense of ownership than if you go away, develop it on your own, and present them with a plan they had no part in developing. For example, if you want country managers to implement future program activities, ask them about what they do currently and involve them in thinking about what the future of your company's Community Involvement could look like.

Defining a strategy involves gathering many ideas and options and then making decisions. For those of you who enjoy models you can use, Manny Amadi of C&E Advisory, one of the World Economic Forum's "Global Leaders for Tomorrow" and a founding adviser of WEF's Corporate Citizenship Task Force, developed the model displayed in Appendix 1.2 (page 35) of a four-part Community Involvement strategy process in detail.

Figure 1.2 depicts a framework for the strategic thinking process that draws from Manny Amadi's model and which we think you will find helpful to follow. Each of its five parts is explained in detail in the rest of this chapter.

Figure 1.2 **Strategic thinking framework**

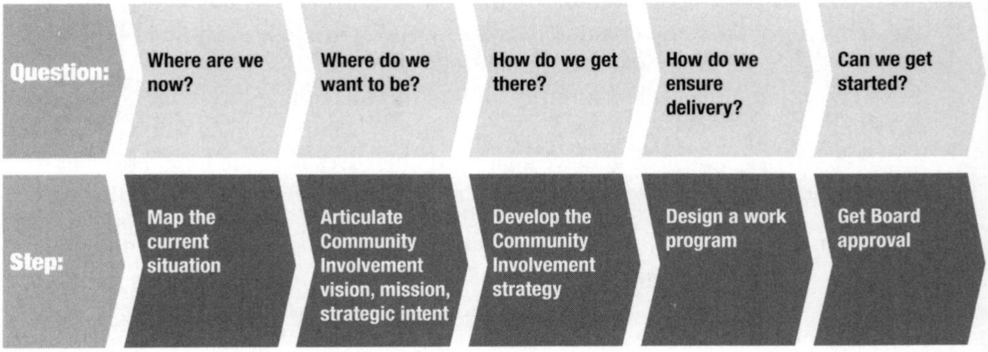

Question:	Where are we now?	Where do we want to be?	How do we get there?	How do we ensure delivery?	Can we get started?
Step:	Map the current situation	Articulate Community Involvement vision, mission, strategic intent	Develop the Community Involvement strategy	Design a work program	Get Board approval

Source: Manny Amadi, C&E Advisory

Part 1: Where are you now? Map the current situation

The most useful approach for you to take is to start with a thorough, in-depth Current State Analysis. Ideally, conduct it in three stages:

1. **External assessment.** Look at the state of the world in which you operate. Develop a good sense of what situation you want to address. Consider your stakeholder demands and other external drivers.

2. **Benchmarking.** Familiarize yourself with the work other companies have done, to learn more about current "best practices." Look at how CR rating agencies have evaluated those companies' programs.

3. **Internal assessment.** Examine what your company has done in the community so far, and identify what you might build on.

There is a lot to these three stages of analysis. Over the following pages, you will gain a more detailed understanding.

Stage 1: External assessment: Societal demands, trends, and issues

Corporations are asked by such bodies as the UN Global Compact and the World Business Council for Sustainable Development to commit to a larger cause and contribute their core competencies toward solving global challenges, particularly in helping provide education, bridging the digital divide, improving health, providing access to water and sanitation, eradicating poverty, creating jobs, and protecting the environment. The rationale for contributing corporate core competencies is well expressed by Michael Porter and Mark Kramer:

> "When a well-run business applies its vast resources, expertise, and management talent to problems that it understands and in which it

has a stake, it can have a greater impact on social good than any other institution or philanthropic organization."[4]

Many CEOs have understood this reasoning and are increasingly committed.

"By using our expertise and skills to address social issues and assist communities, we can create change." – Samuel A. DiPiazza, Jr, CEO, PricewaterhouseCoopers International

Accordingly, ask yourself two questions:

1. What larger cause might your company want to become involved with?

2. What core competencies can your company contribute to such a cause?

First, to identify your cause, it helps to look at what stakeholders – e.g., consumers, communities, governments, NGOs – expect of companies (see Figure 1.3).

Figure 1.3 **Ranking of stakeholders' operational and citizenship expectations of companies**

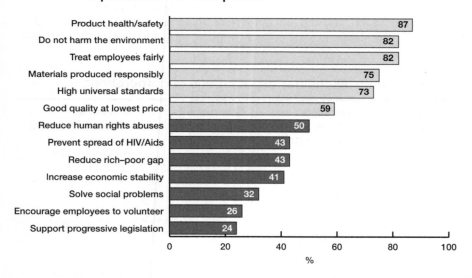

Source: GlobeScan 2005, based on interviews with over 50,000 average citizens and experts from across the world

You can either buy such data (e.g., from GlobeScan, www.globescan.com), or see what surveys your Marketing or Communications department may have already undertaken or have access to. What causes have they determined matter most to your stakeholders? For example, surveys reveal that people tend to connect pharmaceutical companies with corporate involvement in health issues.

For orientation, you can also look at the United Nations Millennium Development

---

4 M. E. Porter and M. R. Kramer, "Strategy & Society: The Link between Competitive Advantage and Corporate Social Responsibility," *Harvard Business Review* 84.12 (December 2006): 56-68.

Goals.[5] Those eight goals form a blueprint, and, according to the United Nations, they have been agreed to by all the world's countries and all the world's leading development organizations. Many companies have committed to contribute as well.

Millennium Development Goals:

- End poverty and hunger
- Universal education
- Gender equality
- Child health
- Maternal health
- Combat HIV/AIDS
- Environmental stability
- Global partnership

If, as a small or medium-sized company, you want to focus on one market, or one region within one market, you can find out as well what each of your respective stakeholder groups in that market expects of your company – e.g., by conducting interviews or focus groups.

Table 1.1 **Example stakeholder expectations of corporations**

Communities	Consumers	Governments	Investors
• Be a good neighbor • Contribute credibly • Make a long-term commitment	• Offer fair prices and good product quality • Treat employees fairly • Show the brand's ethical dimension • Be a good citizen • Support local society	• Do more for society • Help address pressing social needs • Be a good corporate citizen	• Maintain license to operate • Practice Socially Responsible Investment (SRI)
Employees	**NGOs**	**Media**	**Opinion leaders**
• Encourage their pride in the company's involvement • Make Employee Volunteering opportunities available • Offer Matched Time/Matched Funding	• Ensure they are not exploited for marketing • Offer real support, real partnership, sharing of experience	• Offer credibility • Adopt a unique approach • Create tie-in with broader theme	• Be willing to support their causes as needed

5 www.un.org/millenniumgoals, accessed November 2009.

As you can see from Table 1.1, the demands made on a company are varied, yet a strategic Community Involvement program **can** meet them all.

To achieve that, ask yourself and your colleagues what your company's core competencies are. Then match a cause with your corporate core competencies. For example, if your company is a bank, a focus on micro-credit programs in developing countries could be appropriate. If your company is in the food sector, addressing issues related to malnutrition or obesity might make the most sense.

Think about what and how you can contribute. Identify the key area that can drive internal focus and prioritization, as well as external awareness and recognition.

Think also about how you can potentially innovate. How, for example, could your R&D people assist in finding new solutions? Could they think creatively about how your products or services could be applied differently, or in new contexts, to benefit society? An example is IBM's research into how to apply information technology to help children and youth around the world learn in the future – for example, exploring how a child in the Amazon could visit the Forbidden City in Beijing in a 3D experience.[6]

If your company does business in emerging markets, you can find an appendix at the end of this chapter that profiles strategic Community Involvement issues in such markets (page 33).

Stage 2: Benchmarking: Other companies' Community Involvement programs and CR ratings

To inspire you as you consider possible approaches, you might research good practices among other corporations. For assessments of those companies you might also consult international CR rating agencies such as the SAM Group and Vigeo, or indices such as Dow Jones or FTSE4Good. You can turn to Chapter 6 on "How to create and implement leading Community Involvement Programs" for more detailed examples of programs that companies like IBM, Unilever, Rio Tinto, Lafarge, and Accenture have implemented.

What is outstanding about those companies' programs? Each of the companies has committed to a larger cause and uses its core competencies to make a difference in the community that only a company knowledgeable in that specific area can make. Each company also created its program by developing an in-depth understanding of local community needs. While fitting within a strong global strategy and governance structure, each program had the flexibility to adapt to local needs on a country-by-country basis.

International rating agencies such as the Dow Jones Sustainability Indexes (DJSI/SAM), provide regular feedback on companies' Community Involvement performance. Past assessments by these agencies include such comments as the following:

> "This company's involvement focuses on Community Involvement basics and is not yet fine-tuned to social performance indicators." – DJSI/SAM

---

6 www-01.ibm.com/software/uk/itsolutions/soa/virtual-forbidden-city, accessed November 2009.

Benchmarking shows that those companies that are recognized as leaders in Community Involvement achieved this recognition through high-profile programs that demonstrated a number of key aspects:

- Commitment to a larger cause
- Emphasis on **strategic** social involvement
- Contribution of core competencies and innovative solutions
- Effective cross-sector partnerships
- Active involvement of employees
- Achievement of high-relevance, high-impact results for society and the business

> "This company's performance in the community is average due to insufficient group-wide investment in a core cause close to the business and a lack of quantitative information on outcomes related to community activity." – Vigeo

Can you see from these ratings how the company concerned has real potential to further develop its leadership?

Stage 3: Internal Assessment: The company's Community Involvement to date

What has your company done toward Community Involvement so far? What can you build on? You may find that your company has already donated to various causes, encouraged some Employee Involvement, and embarked on one or more NGO partnerships. You may also find social sponsorships or even a cause-related marketing campaign.

Collect as much information as you can about your company's current state of Community Involvement. What has been done on a global level? What have local commitments entailed? Who are the people engaged with Community Involvement? Are there local champions? Is senior management committed? How much money has been spent? How have contributions been allocated? Was the giving systematic or random?

Also look at the resources your company has available for strategic Community Involvement. By now, you have already identified corporate core competencies. Other resources include:

- **Funding.** How much money will your company earmark for Community Involvement? For example, a best practice among multinational companies is to invest 1% of profits before taxes in the community.

- **Management know-how.** How can capable managers contribute to running a program?

- **R&D capability.** How can R&D staff help think about innovation?

- **People.** Is there scope for additional Employee Volunteering in your community activities in general?

Your resources should be relevant and have the potential to create real value in the community.

You can then conduct a SWOT analysis to summarize your assessment of your company's current state of Community Involvement. This strategic planning method is used to evaluate the Strengths, Weaknesses, Opportunities, and Threats involved in a project. Table 1.2 shows a sample SWOT analysis from a fictitious company.

Table 1.2 **Example SWOT analysis**

Strengths	Opportunities

• Available financial resources
• Some local Community Involvement structure in place in most countries
• Local presence/involvement (although philanthropic)
• Positive recognition of local involvement from communities
• Some research of consumers regarding perception of company's CR
	• Introduction of a threefold Community Involvement strategy:
	  – Is close to business and core competencies
	  – Has innovation potential
	  – Balances social and business benefit
	• Effective implementation in each market. Include community responsibilities in objectives
	• Active employee volunteering; participatory, community-focused approach
	• Measurement and evaluation for outcomes and impact
	• Effective leveraging of results through Communications/Marketing
	• Future positioning as Community Involvement leader

Weaknesses	**Threats**
• Lack of strategy and planning; ad hoc and reactive activities • Involvement mainly philanthropic and broad • Confusion regarding sales-related sponsorships, donations, and other Community Involvement activities • Approval structures too decentralized; approval criteria unclear across the group • Sponsorships and arts and culture activities not always leveraging Community Involvement components • Very little measurement and evaluation for outcomes and impact • Little public awareness; limited leveraging of Community Involvement through Communications/Marketing	• Gap between reality and reporting • Lack of significance – not perceived as a Community Involvement leader; other companies setting the pace • Territorial behavior • Internal confusion on what strategic Community Involvement is • High spending without impact data on its contribution • Local dispersion without build-up of central, institutional knowledge

Does the analysis in Table 1.2 look familiar with respect to your company? What might *your* company's SWOT analysis look like?

You can use the insights from your SWOT analysis to plot on Table 1.3 your company's progress in Community Involvement. You will then have a better idea of where you currently stand and also where you want to move to as you start thinking about your vision and mission for Community Involvement.

Having plotted both your existing and your desired future position on Table 1.3, and having carried out your Current State Analysis in full, you should have a thorough understanding of where your business stands today. The next step is to define your Community Involvement vision, mission, and strategic intent.

Part 2: Where do we want to be? Articulate the Community Involvement vision, mission, and strategic intent

It can be helpful to co-create your Community Involvement vision and mission statements with colleagues, to develop shared ownership by relevant functions. In addition, it can be useful to look at your **corporate** vision and mission statements, and to define your Community Involvement vision and mission statements in close relation to those.

We cannot do this work for you, as it is up to you to envision the future for your company and its place in the local, national, or international community. However, we can help you by suggesting a creative approach and by listing a few examples from other companies.

Before you set out to write your Community Involvement vision and mission statements, a helpful approach called "Appreciative Inquiry" can inspire you and your colleagues.

Appreciative Inquiry: Create and describe possible scenarios

In Appreciative Inquiry, you "dream big" and imagine what the world could look like a few years from now because of the breakthrough program your company has created with the best of its social, intellectual, and economic resources. To access your imagination, you can use a number of creative exercises – for example, "Sleep and dream. You wake up in three years to an ideal state! What is your company's strategic Community Involvement like now, and how do stakeholders perceive it? What achievements are you and others celebrating?"

Do this exercise as a team, or with breakout groups that work separately and then come back together to share. Describe to each other your dreamed-up scenarios that show the company at its best in Community Involvement – with all of you proud to be a part of your company's contribution to society. Add sensory details. Describe the scenes, colors, and sounds. Paint a picture of who is there and what everyone is doing. These sensory details will help you build a more complete and powerful mental image of your ideal outcomes.

To visualize such an "ideal state," you have a range of tools to work with. For example, you can create a mood board using images from magazines, or you can develop a "newspaper of tomorrow" with headlines and short articles describing your company's Community Involvement, the vision and strategy behind it, the people involved, and the impact it is having.

Table 1.3 **Stages of Community Involvement: Where we have come from and where we are going**

	Stage 1: Elementary	Stage 2: Engaged	Stage 3: Innovative	Stage 4: Transforming
Approach	Corporate Giving/ philanthropy ✓	Strategic philanthropy* ☐	Community Involvement ☐	Healthy business environment ☐
Motive/ citizenship attitude	Jobs, profits, and taxes; morality on the side ✓	Stakeholder Management; developing self-interest ☐	Long-term partnerships' both societal and business benefits (corporate self-interest); part of CR, Sustainability, triple bottom line ☐	Visionary contributor to society; changing the game; establishment of leadership; corporate self-interest ☐
Strategic intent/ strategy	Legal compliance; ad hoc ✓	License to operate; systematic ☐	Value proposition and Business Case; strategic ☐	Social change and market creation; full organizational ownership ☐
Initiative/ issues management	Passive; generally responsive and reactive to general requests, rather than choiceful and proactive ✓	Selectively responsive and reactive to requests within defined target areas ☐	Proactively initiating; integrated with business ☐	Defining an agenda for the industry; fully integrated with business functions ☐
Drivers	"Chairman's whim" – "what the CEO's wife likes" ✓	Guidelines in place ☐	Linked to business and corporate core competencies; driven by partnership approach ☐	Innovatively part of business strategy ☐
Leadership	Lip service; out of touch ✓	Selective support ☐	Stewardship and championship ☐	Visionary – "changing the game" ☐

* Defined in this book as Corporate Giving with a "strategic" focus aligned to a company's core business. See the Introduction and Chapter 4 for more on the differences between philanthropy, strategic philanthropy, and strategic Community Involvement.

	Stage 1: Elementary	Stage 2: Engaged	Stage 3: Innovative	Stage 4: Transforming	
Structure	Marginal, and detached from business activities	Detached, but linked to business interests	Organizational alignment; cross-functional coordination	Mainstreamed and business-driven; fully integrated with business functions	
	✓	☐	☐	☐	☐
Staff	Any manager	CI manager	CI team in cooperation with business functions	Integrated with relevant business functions	
	✓	☐	☐	☐	☐
Contribution	Mainly cash and/or goods	Cash, goods, Employee Involvement	Monetary funding; business resources – e.g., know-how, core competencies, management competency, Employee Involvement	Visionary, paradigm-changing concepts – in addition to funding, and as part of business resources	
	✓	☐	☐	☐	☐
Community cooperation	Unilateral	Initial interactivity	Mutual partnerships	Multi-organization approach	
	✓	☐	☐	☐	☐
Sustainability	One-offs	Assistance in specific issues	Nurturing and capacity building with NGOs, long-term partnerships, proven societal impact	Part of corporate DNA, ongoing improvement and development, major political player	
	✓	☐	☐	☐	☐
Transparency	Flank protection	Public reporting	External assurance	Comprehensive independent audit	
	✓	☐	☐	☐	☐

Source: Adapted from the "Four Waves" chart of the International Business Leaders Forum and the "Five Stages of Corporate Citizenship" chart of the Boston College Center for Corporate Citizenship.

Make sure that, from such a process, you generate options for the future. Also, take your time. Don't reach closure too soon. Evaluate your options. What are the key drivers? What are potential enablers? Would the organization be ready, willing, and able to act on something like that? What might be barriers, and how could you overcome them?

When you start becoming aware of what might be possible, you may realize that dreams can actually be achieved and challenges can be conquered. This realization may open up a completely new range of possibilities – and that by itself can be a tremendous source of passion and energy.

All the ideas you generate should give you a good basis and food for thought to brainstorm and work toward formulating your vision, mission, and strategic intent.

Defining your Community Involvement vision – writing a compelling vision statement

What is a vision? It is an image of **where you want to be tomorrow and what the future should look like**. A vision statement is a vivid description of a **desired outcome** that inspires, energizes, and helps you create a mental picture of your target – a uniting and inspiring statement about a preferred future. It is for the long term and is probably not easily measurable. It does not talk about concrete targets, but must be durable. A strategy then is a means to *achieve* that vision. It is about bridging the gap between today and tomorrow.

Summarize your vision in a powerful phrase or sentence. Your vision statement should describe the best possible outcome. In fact, you might want to envision something even *better* than what you consider to be the best possible outcome! Someone once said, "You don't get million-dollar ideas from a ten-dollar vision." In other words, the quality of your vision determines the creativity, quality, and originality of your ideas and strategic solutions. A powerful vision statement should stretch expectations and aspirations, helping you jump out of your comfort zone.

An example of a vision is: "Healthy people in a healthy world."

The key to any vision statement is that it is short, concise, and easy to understand. This may be challenging and may require multiple drafts and further refinement over time. If you can, avoid vision statements that could apply to anyone. Try to develop something specific to your company.

Defining your Community Involvement mission – articulating what you will do, and for whom

A mission statement is a statement of purpose: a brief description of what

Tips for writing a Community Involvement vision statement

- Describe your vision statement in the present tense, as if you are reporting what you actually see, hear, think, and feel after your ideal outcome is realized.

- Make your vision statement emotional, describing what you will feel like when the outcome is realized. Including emotion in your vision statement infuses it with passion and makes it even more compelling, inspiring, and energizing.

you want to focus on, what you want to accomplish. It is a way to direct your decisions, behaviors, energy, and actions toward the objectives that matter most to you in your Community Involvement work. While there is no unique format or formula for creating your mission statement, the following tips may be helpful.

To trigger your thinking, we've included a number of anonymous examples of Community Involvement mission statements. Those mission statements can all be mentally preceded by the sentence "We are all about . . .":

- "Recognizing and responding to local needs in partnership with our communities, we address issues of global concern through local implementation."

- "Our company is committed to being an active partner in improving the quality of life in our communities through the sharing of our social, intellectual, and economic resources."

- "Our global quest is to improve the quality of human life by enabling people to do more, feel better, and live longer."

- "To bridge the digital divide and bring access to education to children around the world."

- "To serve the public good through innovative technologies and partnerships."

- "To create the largest public computing grid benefiting humanity."

Tips for writing a Community Involvement mission statement

- Keep your mission statement simple, clear, and brief. Think about specific qualities that would have a significant positive impact on communities in the next three to five years.

- Make sure your mission statement is positive. Find the positive alternatives to any negative statements.

- Make your mission statement emotional. Just as with your vision, including an emotional "payoff' in the statement helps make it more vivid and engaging.

So, your mission statement should express what your company, in its Community Involvement, is all about. It should express generally what you will do, who you will do it for, and what the benefits will be. There should be a stretch in your mission statement, a challenge to take on.

Defining your underlying strategic intent

From a business perspective, your Community Involvement vision and mission will need an underlying strategic intent that is connected to your business. A lot of companies have as their underlying strategic intent, "We want to become the Community Involvement leader in our industry." Their strategic intent is about creating both societal and business benefit. Your company can build business benefit from having made a real difference in the community, together with your partners.

Figure 1.4 **Convergence of social and business benefits**

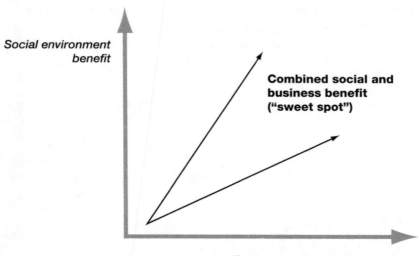

Social environment benefit

Combined social and business benefit ("sweet spot")

Business economic benefit

Michael Porter of the Harvard Institute for Strategy and Competitiveness has defined the achievement of both societal and business benefit as the "sweet spot" (see Figure 1.4). If your activities are highly beneficial for society, but there is no benefit for the company, your Board and your investors will probably be unsatisfied. If, on the other hand, a Community Involvement program results in a high business benefit (e.g., increased sales), but no tangible societal benefit, your external stakeholders will probably be upset. They may consider your activities as "spin" or "greenwashing," and may view the company as exploiting a social cause for its own gain. The sweet spot is about achieving that balance so that everybody perceives they are part of a "win-win" situation. Keep this balance in mind when defining your actual strategy, which is the next part of the process.

Part 3: How do we get there? Develop the strategy

For this part of the process, you may want to consider involving colleagues from your company's Strategy Department. They tend to be good thinkers, and you can use their methods and tools for your strategy development process.

Strategy can address continuity or entail fundamental transformation and change. By this time, you probably have a good idea, based on your Current State Analysis, whether you can strongly build on and enhance existing activities, or whether you need to make a major shift.

Note that, when you're developing your strategy from your existing activities, an **appreciative** approach is recommended. Ask yourself what's **good** about what's already there. How can you and your colleagues build on what you have and achieve more? Often, an appreciative approach is a more effective way of engaging people throughout your company than is telling them that what they did before was of little use.

Often companies focus exclusively on designing *one* strategic, high-profile community initiative. We advise against limiting your thinking that way and recommend pursuing a holistic approach that fully integrates with your company's overall Social Performance Management. Look at aligning *all* elements of your activities in the community in one comprehensive, strategic approach. This means that you can design more than one strategy to realize your vision and mission. Your overall strategy formulation can consist of two, three, or four detailed strategies.

Remember, Community Involvement strategy should seek to accomplish three goals:
- Integrate Community Involvement with the company's overall business strategy and core competencies
- Make a real difference in the community
- Establish, maintain, and enhance relationships of trust with stakeholders

Here is one example of a simple three-phase approach to strategy development:

1. **Put your "house in order."**

   Explanation: Create a Community Involvement governance and implementation structure; build resources, policies, and processes for Community Involvement; and strategically align all elements of your activities in the community.

2. **Fully integrate Community Involvement activities within the business.**

3. **Design an innovative group-wide Community Involvement program** that's aligned with your business strategy and permits you to contribute your corporate core competencies for the benefit of society and your business.

We also value Microsoft's four strategies in Africa as described in the interview earlier in this chapter:

1. **Coverage.** Provide headcount and funding, and expand geographically.

2. **Leverage.** Expand impact through partnerships.

3. **Community Development.** Consider national development priorities and NGO impact.

4. **Innovation.** Create and bring relevant technology solutions to communities.

Your company can easily adopt either of these two approaches, or use them as food for thought in defining your own strategies.

As final inspiration, we give two examples, one from a multinational company and one from a medium-sized national company, of highly successful Community Involvement strategies:

The multinational – how did TNT do it?

TNT is a global transportation and distribution company based in the Netherlands. When TNT's CEO, Peter Bakker, decided that his company would become involved in communities around the world for real impact, he thought about the many needs in society and ways of matching one of those needs with his company's core competencies. What was TNT really good at? The simple answer was: moving things. The company had air and ground transportation fleets. It had logistical knowledge. How about using that ability to address urgency in getting supplies to people who were suffering because of a natural disaster or conflict? That seemed to make sense.

The CEO's next thought had to be about looking for the right partner. The UN's World Food Programme (WFP) seemed to address exactly this kind of urgency, and it looked like it could use some support. Now there seemed to be a strategic fit. TNT had a goal, it could see an opportunity, the World Food Programme seemed to be an appropriate partner, and TNT was certain it could contribute the needed resources. This strategic assumption was tested, and there was a match.

So the CEO's goal of contributing meaningfully to communities internationally was translated into a straightforward strategy: Use TNT's core competency in "moving things" to partner with and support the World Food Programme and get urgently needed food supplies quickly to areas stricken by disaster and conflict.

The joint program was called "Moving the World," and the partners have received significant praise for it. Every year since 2003, TNT and WFP have had a presence at the World Economic Forum (WEF) annual meeting held in Davos, Switzerland. TNT attends the WEF to increase awareness of public–private partnerships, and of WFP in general. TNT has been able to influence the transportation industry and motivate other companies to make similar commitments.

The medium-sized company – how did Betapharm do it?

Betapharm, a German generic pharmaceuticals company with only 350 employees, faced about 60 competitors in its national market. Initially competing via price, it reached a stage where prices could not be lowered any more without destroying profit margins. So Betapharm looked for other opportunities to set itself apart in the eyes of its key stakeholders – doctors and pharmacists.

Adopting the cause of long-term home care for chronically sick children, Betapharm partnered with NGO "Bunter Kreis" to provide support and training for caregivers. Recognizing a larger need, Betapharm also successfully lobbied another stakeholder group, the German parliament, for legislation ensuring that long-term at-home care for chronically sick children would be covered financially by the health care system.

With these initiatives, Betapharm created a strategic approach to Community Involvement that helped it stand out from its competitors. It won considerable market share through influencing its key stakeholders positively and creating strong brand preference among them. The approach has been featured at international conferences on ethical branding and CR Communications. When Betapharm was later bought by India-based pharmaceuticals company Dr. Reddy's, the value of the company's Community Involvement had increased its price by 35%.

If you apply the methods and tools introduced in this chapter, you should be able to identify a strategic Community Involvement fit for your own company, no matter how big or small your company is or where in the world you are based.

Test your strategy

Once you have defined your strategy, you may want to pursue a due diligence process and test it. From among a number of models you can use for this purpose, we introduce two here.

One simple model you can use is depicted in Figure 1.5.

Figure 1.5 **Process tool to improve strategic alignment**

Source: Adapted from: M. Alexander, *Models and Messages for Strategic Decisions*, materials from the Strategic Decisions course at Ashridge Business School, Berkhamsted, UK, 2004.

From all the work you have done up to this point, next to the respective circles in Figure 1.5, write in your responses to these three questions:

1. What are your **goals**?

2. What **opportunities** for involvement and contribution of core competencies have you identified?

3. What **resources** are available in the company to realize your goals and follow through on your opportunities?

The model then allows you to check for consistency. Goals, opportunities, and resources need to be appropriate to each other. You may see a wonderful opportunity yet not have the resources to seize it. Or you may find that you have plenty of resources to apply but have not defined your goals well.

Another optional model to use to test your strategy is displayed in Figure 1.6.

Figure 1.6 **Four criteria for a strategic fit**

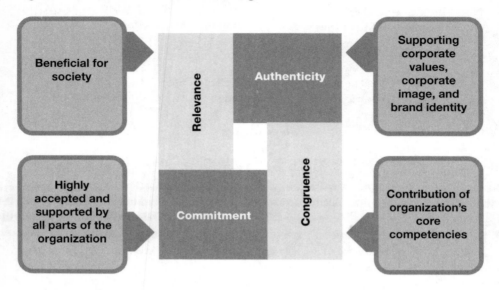

Source: Adapted from M. Blumberg and C. Conrad, *Cause Related Marketing: Key Success Factors* (Germany: brands & values GmbH, 2006).

Using the criteria in Figure 1.6, we've given some examples of how a strategic fit would be missing:

1. It would not be helpful if your company identified a compelling issue to engage with that had little or no **relevance** for society.

2. Nor would it be helpful if you and your team identified a cause that you think would be great to address, yet all the relevant parts of your organization that need to "buy into it" think it is, for example, too risky to engage with. In that case, you would be lacking internal **commitment**.

3. If you look into supporting a cause to which you cannot contribute any of your corporate core competencies (e.g., a car company addressing healthy eating), **congruence** would definitely be lacking, and stakeholders might wonder: "Now what has *that* program got to do with *that* company?"

4. Following the same line of thought, a program that does not fit with your corporate values, your corporate image, or your brand identity would also confuse stakeholders and be viewed as lacking **authenticity**. For example, one beer company advertised, "For every case of beer you buy, we donate *x* amount to save the rainforest." Stakeholders turned this line into "getting drunk to save the rainforest."

Ensure your strategy's internal consistency and authenticity

Make sure that your Community Involvement strategy is well aligned with all, some, or any of the other corporate strategies – specifically:

- Overall business strategy

- CR strategy

- Brand strategy

- Marketing and sponsorship strategy

- HR strategy

The more closely your Community Involvement strategy is aligned, the greater the potential for the whole organization to champion and implement it – and the greater the potential for external stakeholders to see an integrated, credible approach.

Last, but certainly not least in this part, undertake both a critical success factors analysis and a risk analysis. Critical success factors are areas where "things must go right." Risk analysis is a technique to identify and assess factors that may put implementation of your strategy in jeopardy. This technique can also help you define preventive measures to eliminate constraints ahead of time, or at least reduce the likelihood of these risks occurring.

Part 4: How do we ensure delivery? Design a work program

You have now developed a strategy for becoming involved in the community that will create value and impact, both for society and for your company. The next step is to design a program to deliver that value proposition. That's what the chapters of this book are about:

- Chapter 1 outlines a process for developing your Community Involvement strategy.

- Chapter 2 introduces you to setting up internal governance and structure, policies, and processes.

- Chapter 3 aims to assist you in planning your Community Involvement budget.

- Chapter 4 gives advice on aligning your Corporate Giving.

- Chapter 5 looks at how to integrate your Community Involvement activities into the business (e.g., with Marketing initiatives).

- Chapter 6 shows you how to develop and implement a leading Community Involvement program.

- Chapter 7 engages with the art and science of engaging in cross-sector partnerships.

- Chapter 8 outlines a comprehensive process for setting up your company's Employee Involvement.

- Chapter 9 shows you how to approach measurement and evaluation of your Community Involvement work.

- Chapter 10 deals with how you can successfully communicate your Community Involvement activities to a wider audience.

- Chapter 11 engages with the specific challenges of effecting the in-company change that is needed for successful Community Involvement work, through internal engagement, influencing and persuasion.

Bring all of your work programs together into a realistic timeline, so you know what, especially for the next 12 months, you need to do to get you on the way. Build in regular review points to make sure you take a step back and check that your strategy and work program are still meeting your business needs.

Part 5: Can we get started? Get Board approval

Once you have tested your strategy, carried out an analysis of success factors and risks, and developed a realistic work program, the final, most important part will be to get Board approval and commitment.

You need to be able to show convincingly how you arrived at your proposal. Show the results of your Current State Analysis, and explain your strategy process. Map out the opportunities you see, and identify clear business benefits. Cover the critical success factors analysis and the risk analysis. Show your intended workplan and timeline, and present a financial projection.

If you have applied the process introduced in this chapter, incorporating elements from the rest of this book, you will have something sound and robust to show for your efforts.

A useful final tip

Test out what you want to present on some individual Board members, getting their buy-in and support ahead of time before taking it to the Board meeting.

Appendix 1.1. Community Involvement strategy in emerging markets: Understanding the interrelatedness of causes

Among the issues companies are being asked to address, health, education, and jobs are closely interrelated (see Figure 1.7). They are all constituting elements of the concept of capacity building.

Figure 1.7 **Societal issues are interrelated**

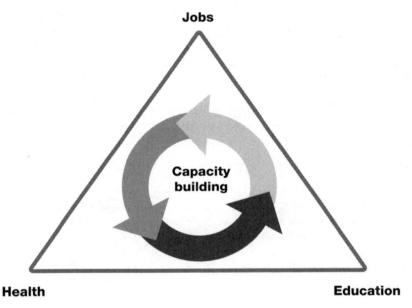

Jobs

Capacity building

Health   **Education**

People want to be healthy so they can go to school or to work. They want to have an education so they can find gainful employment. This interrelation can be highlighted by two examples:

1. Jeffrey Sachs[7] has pointed out that the simple act of giving mosquito nets to people across Africa can increase both literacy and gross national product considerably.

2. Morocco's King Mohammed VI ran a highly successful initiative to make sure more women would receive an education and could study at university. The number of women with academic degrees increased considerably. However, adequate employment for these women was missing – with the result that only 30% of them found jobs, and the remainder had to stay at home.

---

7 J. Sachs, *The End of Poverty: Economic Possibilities for Our Time* (New York: Penguin, 2006).

These two short examples show how such strategic issues are related and need to be looked at as one big picture when you want to decide on a larger cause to adopt. Building on the second example above, if you want to contribute to young people's education, you need to think about the bigger picture. For what purpose do you want to do that? What opportunities will these young people then have? What else may be needed?

From a strategic perspective, it is important to ask the right questions when setting out to make a difference in the community. Bono of U2, who has become just as known for his international development work (together with Bill Gates and Jeffrey Sachs) as for his music, famously pointed out: "We thought that we had the answers, it was the questions we had wrong."[8]

We already spoke about the 2007 conference on "Corporate Responsibility in Emerging Markets" in London at which the presenters spoke of capacity building, rather than Community Involvement. You also saw capacity building referred to in the interview on Microsoft's strategic involvement in Africa. By committing to a larger strategic cause, your company, through its Community Involvement, can contribute to local capacity building.

If your company operates in emerging markets and you are interested in reading more on opportunities for local capacity building, we can recommend two excellent books:

- Jeffrey Sachs, *The End of Poverty: Economic Possibilities for Our Time* (New York: Penguin, 2006)

- C. K. Prahalad, *The Fortune at the Bottom of the Pyramid: Eradicating Poverty through Profits* (Upper Saddle River, NJ: Wharton School Publishing, 2006)

---

8 N. Gibbs, "Persons of the Year: The Good Samaritans," *Time* 166.26 (December 26, 2005): cover.

Appendix 1.2. Detailed Community Involvement strategy development process

Source: Manny Amadi, C&E Advisory

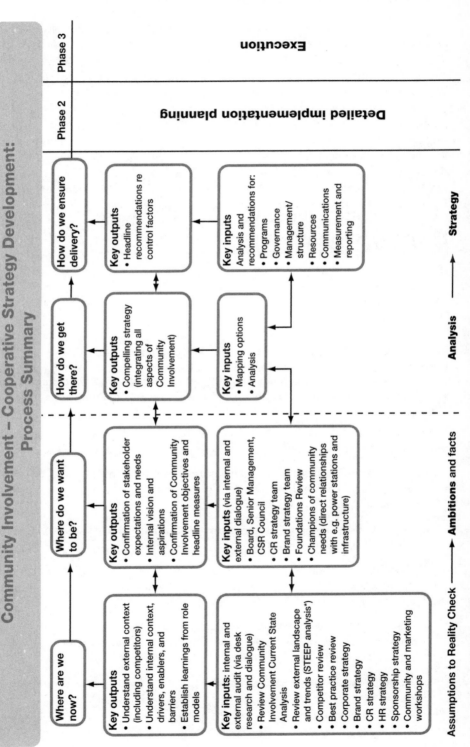

Community Involvement – Cooperative Strategy Development: Process Summary

Phase 2	Phase 3
Detailed implementation planning	Execution

Where are we now?

Key outputs
- Understand external context (including competitors)
- Understand internal context, drivers, enablers, and barriers
- Establish learnings from role models

Key inputs: internal and external audit (via desk research and dialogue)
- Review Community Involvement Current State Analysis
- Review external landscape and trends (STEEP analysis*)
- Competitor review
- Best practice review
- Corporate strategy
- Brand strategy
- CR strategy
- HR strategy
- Sponsorship strategy
- Community and marketing workshops

Where do we want to be?

Key outputs
- Confirmation of stakeholder expectations and needs
- Internal vision and aspirations
- Confirmation of Community Involvement objectives and headline measures

Key inputs (via internal and external dialogue)
- Board, Senior Management, CSR Council
- CR strategy team
- Brand strategy team
- Foundations Review
- Champions of community needs (direct relationships with e.g. power stations and infrastructure)

How do we get there?

Key outputs
- Compelling strategy (integrating all aspects of Community Involvement)

Key inputs
- Mapping options
- Analysis

How do we ensure delivery?

Key outputs
- Headline recommendations re control factors

Key inputs
Analysis and recommendations for:
- Programs
- Governance
- Management/structure
- Resources
- Communications
- Measurement and reporting

Assumptions to Reality Check ⟶ Ambitions and facts   Analysis ⟶ Strategy

* STEEP analysis is a tool to evaluate various external factors impacting a business or organization. STEEP is an acronym for Social, Technological, Economic, Environmental, Political.

2

Company roles, responsibilities, and skills in Community Involvement

In this chapter, we explore internal roles, responsibilities and skills in Community Involvement from two perspectives. One perspective is that of the multinational company, where you need to look at what your business does across a number of markets. The second is that of the smaller company that is based in one country, or even one community.

For both perspectives, the chapter addresses the "people" side of a company's Community Involvement in the following five sections:

1. **Championing and overseeing Corporate Community Involvement.** How best to structure, lead, and manage your Community Involvement team for your company.

2. **Identifying the responsible departments.** As many parts of your business will affect the community, it will rarely be one department.

3. **Building the team, both internally and externally.** The team or partnership approach is appropriate for the Community Involvement function, especially when you consult with the community too.

4. **Recruiting the right people.** Community practitioners hail from a variety of backgrounds; however, some personal qualities will distinguish your team members.

5. **Learning new skills.** Because nobody's perfect and we all need to keep growing.

1. Championing and overseeing Corporate Community Involvement

Few businesses are in the same position as TNT in having their CEO identify an opportunity and champion a community program to take forward (see Chapter 1, pages 27f.). However, you do need senior management who will support you from the start. Make sure that you have some form of CEO or Board member support. As a relatively new discipline, Community Involvement must establish credibility throughout the business and ensure it receives sufficient support. You do not need to report directly to the CEO or a Board member, but whoever your boss is, make sure that he or she:

- Has a passion for what you want to do

- Understands what strategic Community Involvement entails

- Is willing to champion Community Involvement at all levels, and in particular at the most senior level

If you are to lead Community Involvement at an international level, you will also need the support of senior management at head office when convincing local country management to engage in Community Involvement. You will need them to communicate to local markets that you are in charge of this work, and that those markets need to identify Community Involvement managers or specialists (ideally, together with you) who are to report in a matrix structure to you.

Part of good Community Involvement governance is the setting-up of Community Involvement steering groups within the company, at both the global and the local level. Besides the Community Involvement lead, members of such groups typically include the heads of Communications, Marketing, HR, and potentially Business Development, and, depending on your business, a representative from the operational side(s), such as the production manager or site manager.

A good Community Involvement steering group will also draw on change facilitators. If your business has them, ask for their advice on how to implement community activities, both internally and externally. They should know a lot about changing a company's culture and engaging people in new ways of working.

If your company already has a CR steering group or CR council, you may not need to set up a separate one for Community Involvement. In that case, make sure that Community Involvement issues are put on the agenda when the CR group meets. Ideally, such a group should meet about every three months.

What should the head office do?

With multinational businesses, the key is to define the head office's remit in the company's community work and then identify the country's (or region's) role. Head office responsibilities can include developing strategy, leading programs, overseeing teams, challenging/changing/training the business, reporting, and managing group community communications. Setting strategy and leading programs are elements of a senior role. Most multinational companies have somebody at vice president or director level in this position.

We covered setting strategy in Chapter 1. This is a key responsibility of the head office. Involve your senior-level sponsor and someone from the strategy department, or at least engage people who are good strategic thinkers.

The Community Involvement function at head office is expected to oversee program direction and implementation around the world. Often, it involves managing a central budget. Other activities are likely to include leading the management of a global Employee Involvement initiative; convincing leaders in countries to support Community Involvement; identifying local Community Involvement employees; helping to find NGO partners; and providing guidance on program implementation and partnership management as needed and requested by local colleagues.

The key to doing this successfully is appreciating and balancing the profit-making and Community Involvement sides of the company.

Leading community work in diverse global operations

Unfortunately, there is no easy way to ensure every country in a multi-country initiative achieves 100% success in its community work. Pay close attention to each country, its culture, and its way of doing business. What works in South Africa does not work in Thailand. What works in the US does not work in Poland – and vice versa.

Spend time locally and immerse yourself in the country and the culture, and your company's local operations. If you find you are puzzled about the way things are done, ask an expatriate colleague who has done business in that country about what works and what doesn't.

Even with the luxury of teleconferencing, you need to visit locations in person. If you want to fully understand local needs in your company's markets around the world, there is no better way than exploring local realities yourself. The local businesses will value your openness and engagement.

Pay attention to developing good individual relationships of familiarity and trust, especially with the local Community Involvement manager and the country CEO. Make sure that you devote sufficient time to relationship building. Cooperation within the company is essentially about good internal partnering. For advice on partnering and collaborating, turn to Chapter 7.

Once you have established a good community operation locally, then work on aligning local Community Involvement activities with corporate strategy, and helping local managers develop their community projects, partnerships, and processes. Often, you need to find the balance between having a global community strategy/programs/projects and addressing a business' desire to meet local market needs. Both parts are critical.

Without local business involvement in a wider purpose aligned to your company's global business strategy and values, your country-specific or region-specific work will not contribute to overall group reputation. On the other hand, without the country- or region-specific work, you will not always meet local stakeholder needs, which can be potentially restricting or, worse still, damaging to local business prospects.

Being aware of this need for balance, the head office's role is to give ongoing support to country Community Involvement managers. The support may include offering training or coaching and being a sounding board for local challenges – for example, bringing local management on board or working with challenging partners. At the same time, head office should not be overly controlling and should ensure country Community Involvement managers have sufficient autonomy. They know their local situation best. A capable head office function will balance guidance and supervision with appreciation of what colleagues bring to the role.

2. Identifying the responsible departments

Areas of the organization typically active in your communities besides the operational side of the business will include Communications, Marketing (or Brand, Area Management, Sales), HR, Corporate Responsibility (if you have such a department), and Public Affairs. Depending on the company, this remit could be decided centrally or could be the choice of each market. For example, at a corporate head office, Community Involvement could be part of the CR department, whereas in country offices whose operations are potentially too small to have a dedicated CR department, Community Involvement could be taken on by Communications, Marketing, or HR.

In being responsible for the Community Involvement program, each department has its strengths and its challenges, which we have summarized in Table 2.1.

In short, there's no right or wrong answer for the best department to take on responsibility for Community Involvement. Again, the answer for you will also depend on your organization. Where will the program fit best? Who will ensure it has the right level of buy-in throughout the business? Who can be most effective in handling cross-sector partnerships and achieving societal impact?

Tip for managing multiple countries

Devise some form of "traffic-light" system to keep track of different countries' performance, progress, and needs – for example:

- Greens – countries that are confident performers and that rarely need you to check in with them

- Yellows – countries that perform adequately but benefit from more frequent monitoring

- Reds – countries that require intensive, ongoing support, be it with a program start-up, a developing partnership, or an ongoing project. Can also indicate a country where the Community Involvement manager just left or changed role, and where a replacement needs to be found and trained

Review countries' progress at least every six months.

Table 2.1 **Benefits and potential weaknesses of Community Involvement responsibility, by department**

Department	Benefits	Potential weaknesses
Communications	• Good for a strategic focus; will concentrate on community activities with reputation benefits • Closeness to senior management helps ensure legitimacy of the work • Can maximize internal and external communications of Community Involvement, and align it with other business issues	• Risk of community work being done for PR value alone • Accusations of "greenwashing" in Communications activities can be common in environmental initiatives • Ultimately, can run risk of losing credibility if insufficient concentration on long-term societal impact, as well as business benefit
Public Affairs	• Similar to Communications • Often, the Public Affairs function covers political relations and so has a stronger focus on government as a key stakeholder	• Also similar to Communications, particularly where work is being done for political or "lobbying" value alone
Marketing	• Good for a strategic focus • Can strongly align community activities with your customers' interests and brand positioning • Has the expertise to apply robust research process to any community project plans • Will be most effective for cause-related marketing initiatives	• Need to ensure whatever is done is not seen as purely for marketing purposes • Accusations of "greenwashing" in Marketing activities can be common in environmental initiatives • Need to ensure any activities are not over-promoted (or advertised) before they are ready
HR	• Instinctively strong employee focus on activities • Great for engaging and motivating existing and prospective employees	• Can be seen as being too detached from the business • Community activities may be seen as purely for employees' benefit, and not as contributing to the wider business (license to operate, reputation), or to societal issues
Corporate Responsibility	• Will ensure it is part of the company's overall CR strategy, ensuring strong credibility among stakeholders • Allows for a neutral approach without pursuing one business area's interests to the detriment of the wider organization • Depending on the wider remit of CR, may strengthen cross-functional initiatives (e.g., working with environmental, R&D, or marketplace teams)	• Can be seen as being too detached from the business • Dependent on legitimacy and acceptance of CR department within the company compared to more established corporate functions

→

Department	Benefits	Potential weaknesses
Business Development	• Good for aligning community involvement with existing and future business opportunity • Likely to have a good connection to corporate strategy function • Increased likelihood of results-/numbers-driven senior managers buying into it	• Can be too detached from day-to-day local business • May risk turning Community Involvement into a sales support/development function, undermining credibility of what could otherwise be worthwhile initiatives
Local Operational Business	• Perfect for closely aligning work to business needs • Should ensure strong support from senior manager who has most to gain from effective local community work	• Can become too detached from the wider organization • Depending on senior manager, may run risk of local pet projects being pursued

From our business experience, our preference is to place the Community Involvement function in the CR department, with strong ties to all other functions mentioned. This placement should help build the function's credibility and ensure its alignment with your company's overall CR issues. If your company has no CR department, or if the remit of CR in your business means Community Involvement would not fit, bring the program into Communications. At the country level, Communications people often manage community activities, to ensure sufficient alignment to other communications and maximum reputation benefit.

Finally, make sure within your company that the community person/function participates in relevant internal groups or forums. Apart from being a member of the company's CR council, the overall head of Community Involvement should also be involved working with other areas of the company – such as Marketing (e.g., community sponsorship programs), HR (e.g., employee engagement projects), and business operations (e.g., new site developments).

Coordinating multiple business units in your community

Sometimes, a company has different interests, maybe even multiple business units, that are working in the same country or community. A number of local giving projects could be under way – maybe a sports sponsorship, a children's program, and even an employee fundraising initiative. The local government could be a customer, or you may have production activities with a community impact – for example, a local factory. A common problem, especially for larger companies, is deciding which of these interests or business units is to lead the Community Involvement work.

In solving this problem, you need to address three questions:

• How will you ensure a coordinated approach to your communities?

• Who has overall responsibility for your key regions?

• Who should local stakeholders go to if they have a problem?

The answers will likely vary by region. We believe the lead should be the business unit (and person) whose financial performance is most affected by having those strong local relationships.

While this business area should have primacy in your coordinated approach to Community Involvement, you also have an opportunity to test your company's skills at matrix working. Bring together all the company actors in the community to build a holistic view of their activities. Work out how they can complement and support each other's interests across the subsidiaries.

3. Building the team, both internally and externally

Depending on how many markets your company covers and how big your community activities grow, you will need to explore staffing needs. If your program is in its infancy, one person leading at head office and part-time employees in local markets will suffice. As your community activities grow, so will your team.

At head office, you may want to assign responsibility for large projects or key partnerships to specific individuals. Depending on how the program grows, you may also want to have one or two people exclusively responsible for Employee Involvement, and one person exclusively devoted to internal and external Community Involvement communications. As your need for measurement, evaluation, and reporting increases, someone will need to be dedicated to those aspects.

At the country level, one person may start out with Community Involvement at just 30% of her or his time – for example, as an add-on to a Communications, Marketing, or HR job. However, do not rule out employees from other areas. Our experience indicates that a sales manager or an IT person can be highly committed to this work and can do an excellent job.

Make sure that part-time commitment does not turn into or become perceived as a "volunteer" job in the company. It needs to be appropriately addressed in that person's job description and bonus scheme. Once again, as activities grow in scope and scale, the part-time commitment may turn into a full-time position. A specialist may be promoted to manager, and she or he might have the support of an additional part-time or full-time specialist or assistant.

When assessing staffing requirements, answer these questions:

- What role is each person needed for?
- What do we want that person to achieve and deliver?
- What time commitment will that person need to carry out the role?
- To justify the additional costs, how will that person's activity add value to our business?

Ultimately, the number of people you need will be decided by the scope of the work and, especially, the scale of any project. If it is a multinational, multi-million-euro initiative, then more people will be involved, usually supported by a wider indirect network whose members are often working for the partner NGOs of the company.

But rest assured, lots of people are not necessary. A small team composed of motivated, talented individuals who are well networked within the business can accomplish great results. Let them do what they need to and, if their approach is successful, your company will want to build on it.

Bringing the team together

Figure 2.1 shows an example of a multinational company operating in a number of countries. The head office should have direct relationships with community practitioners in all markets. These practitioners can be brought together globally or in region-specific working groups.

Figure 2.1 **Bringing the regions together**

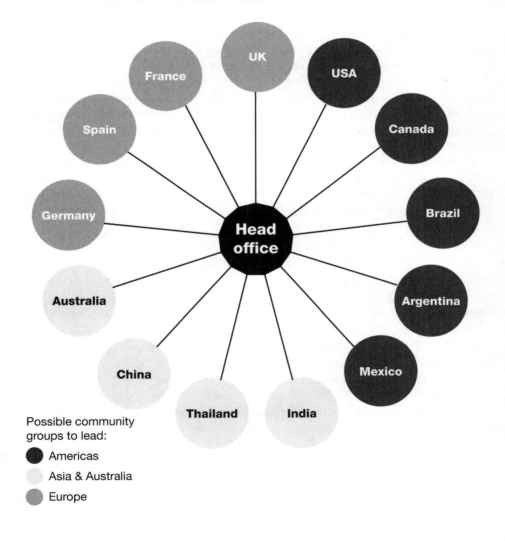

Possible community groups to lead:
- Americas
- Asia & Australia
- Europe

Ideally, you will help each country or region appreciate and learn from the skills and experiences elsewhere in your group. An annual global Community Involvement workshop provides an opportunity for collective learning and exchange. If a global meeting is not possible (owing to cost or time limitations), consider periodic regional meetings. The format will, of course, depend on the size and complexity of your business.

For inspiration, bring in external people to your meetings or workshops. Representatives of multinationals, governments, intergovernmental organizations, or NGOs can be excellent guest speakers, sparking valuable discussions.

Some companies run such meetings for their Community Involvement practitioners together with their NGO partners. They can result in fruitful exchange, fostering better partner relations locally as NGOs feel fully included. The joint presence also allows local partners to better showcase their work, and in turn to learn about other countries' experiences. In addition, this practice helps to connect NGOs across countries.

Remember, it takes time to establish teams, and people inevitably change roles. What's important is that people appreciate that they are not alone with the challenges they face. Team retreats can also contribute to cost savings down the line, as people will often adapt successful projects from elsewhere in their group.

In one international education program at E.ON, countries adapted an existing best practice from one market, resulting in a cost saving of over €1 million (about $1.5 million). Instead of each country manager spending money and time creating a new but comparable education tool, they simply adapted the successful approach to their country's needs.

When bringing such a group together, decide how you want to structure the experience to maximize benefits for participants, as well as the company. Make sure you develop terms of reference for the group, so that everyone is clear on its purpose, targets, constitution, and legitimacy. Ideally, co-create the terms with the people you want to take part; it will help generate buy-in.

Running local community forums

With all these internal machinations, it is easy to lose sight of your external stakeholders. In order to keep the "community perspective" in focus, think about setting up local steering groups or community forums that engage external as well as internal participants. The potential benefits of such groups or forums include generating buy-in for your projects from the community or just from within your business, and over the longer term building trust and understanding in your company and the community.

Figure 2.2 depicts the community forum model E.ON uses when building new power stations. Note the variety of participants and key influencers in the region – NGOs, local government, religious organizations, unions, and other local businesses. A community forum is an effective way of bringing together all relevant parts of the local community.

Figure 2.2 **Structure of community steering group for Datteln power plant project, Germany**

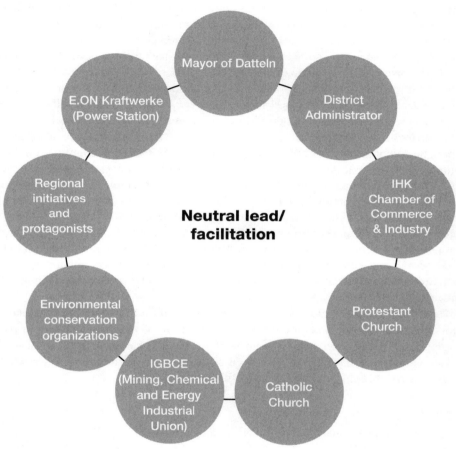

Source: E.ON Kraftwerke, 2008

However, do not underestimate the challenges and time involved in organizing a community forum. As with all relationships, building such forums takes time. Again, see Chapter 7 for more detail on how to engage in cross-sector partnering.

One route, particularly if participants have widely differing views, is to use an external mediator to bring the groups together. Also, as a golden rule, never view such a forum as a PR tool. This approach will destroy all credibility before you even get started.

We will pick up the issue of community forums again in Chapter 5 as part of integrating Community Involvement into your business.

4. Recruiting the right people

People are the key to a company's success. Nowhere is that more so than in Community Involvement. So much of the work is about more than its cost; it's about having the right people with the passion, commitment, and skills to see things through. Having the right people is critical for success in your community activities. So who can do this work?

As we saw when we looked at which departments are typically responsible for Community Involvement, some parts of corporations – in particular, Marketing, Communications, Business Development, and HR – tend to provide more community practitioners than do other departments. This is not to say that people from these areas will always be the best; however, they do bring a number of complementary skills and experience.

So let's look at what key qualities are required for a community role. Our research and experience point to a number of core qualities – both professional skills and personal competencies – that are likely to predict Community Involvement excellence.

In terms of experience, it is similar to recruiting for any other role. You cannot simply say "at least five years of Community Involvement experience" for a manager role. Some people may have built up ideal experience much earlier than that. Equally, other people may not have any direct community experience, but you realize as soon as you meet them that they have all the transferable skills to suit the role. We know of individuals who started out as administrative assistants or sales managers and who then sought to expand or change their careers, and who within only a few years excelled in community leadership roles.

Unlike surgeons who need to know all the essentials of the human body before starting to operate, new colleagues coming to Community Involvement do not have to know

---

Desired personal traits and skills for Community Involvement practitioners

- Ability to:
  - Communicate well, both internally and externally, in an interdisciplinary way, beyond individual areas of expertise
  - Express ideas in a clear and accessible manner
  - Bring people together and generate trusting relationships
  - Participate as a team player
- Listening skills and receptiveness to new ideas
- Persuasion skills – ability to motivate and inspire others at all levels of the organization
- Passion, motivation, and enthusiasm
- Patience, staying power, and "frustration tolerance" – i.e., doesn't give up easily
- Openness to and understanding of societal issues and other parts of society beyond the core business
- A degree of entrepreneurship and ability to act as a catalyst for new ideas and initiatives in the business

all the community management tools. Such skills can be developed through "learning by doing." In particular, community practitioners learn through experience that helping to integrate Corporate Responsibility and Community Involvement thinking with colleagues throughout a business requires significant time and effort – and lots of patience.

While our discussion so far has emphasized the "soft" skills, you will see from the core community activities this book covers the type of business skills that are also needed. For example, delivering community programs requires project and budget management skills, communication ability, and measurement and evaluation competence.

The European Academy of Business in Society has developed the "Management Competency Model" displayed in Figure 2.3, to remind people recruiting in this area to be aware of what candidates have to offer and how they need to interact with stakeholders and partners, both internally and externally.

Figure 2.3 **Management competency model**

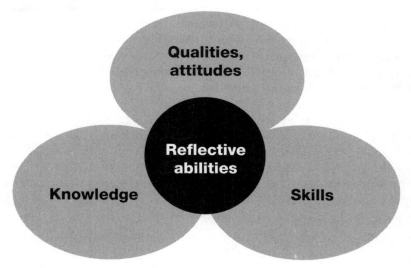

Source: European Academy of Business in Society (G. Lenssen)

At the end of the chapter Appendix 2.1 provides a sample role description for the position of Community Involvement Manager and also lists the required skills and experience in more detail.

Looking beyond your organization

When recruiting outside the company, you can search in a number of places. Agencies specializing in PR, cause-related marketing, or internal communications, or other companies whose work involves bringing cross-functional groups together are likely to contain people with the right kinds of skills and experience.

You can also look to NGOs and government agencies. Your company will already be working with a number of NGOs. Do their culture and employees' skills complement those of your company? Some companies love a fresh, outside perspective; for others, the different perspectives, particularly from other sectors, are too wide a gap to fill.

The perspective of Ntutule Tshenye from Microsoft (interviewed in Chapter 1) is useful to consider, as someone who transitioned from the NGO to the corporate world:

"For companies, processes, systems, professional approaches, and measurability of success are important. It is helpful to speak that language and work with those concepts. My advice would be, immerse yourself fully within your new environment – albeit without losing your sense of the unique contribution you are bringing! Never lose what brought you to the company in the first place: your unique knowledge of community development and your sense of mission to make a difference in the community. If you lose that, then you fail. You might feel a bit alone at first, especially if the company you enter is a huge 'sales engine.' However, if you speak of what you know, you'll be surprised at the recognition you will get."

Ntutule also talked about using interns to support community projects. The intern role offers people, particularly students, an opportunity for work experience and the chance to decide if a corporate community role is right for them. Speak to local universities or student organizations. While those studying business or Corporate Responsibility may be a good fit, as we said before, finding people with the right character, motivation, and soft skills is most important.

Corporate Responsibility websites for posting Community Involvement job vacancies

To recruit outside the company, consider posting your job description on one or more of the following websites:

- BSR (www.bsr.org/resources/jobs/index.cfm)
- CSR Europe (www.csreurope.org/jobs.php)
- Ethical Corporation (www.ethicalcorporation.com/jobs_listing.asp)
- Ethical Performance (www.ethicalperformance.com/recruitment/index.php)
- Lifeworth (www.lifeworth.com/search-jobs)

Conversely, if you happen to be looking for employment in Corporate Community Involvement, you might just find your future dream job there!

5. Learning new skills

Every person in Community Involvement can benefit from developing certain skills. Given the range required to be an excellent Community Involvement practitioner, rarely will one course (or, indeed, one book!) give you all you need to know.

You may want to consider taking a course covering any of the topics below. The relevant chapters of this book that we advise you to read before considering further training in a specific topic are given in brackets.

- **Strategy**. Most major business schools offer training of a few days to help improve the quality of your strategic thinking and strategy development (Chapter 1).

- **Partnering**. The right partnering skills will be more likely to guarantee success for your projects. The Partnering Initiative, a global program of the International Business Leaders Forum (IBLF), is an excellent source of insight and advice and runs training programs including PBAS (Partnership Brokers Accreditation Scheme; see www.partnershipbrokers.org (Chapter 7).

- **Measurement and evaluation**. Market researchers in your business or in external agencies working with your company are an excellent starting point. NGOs you work with may also be experienced at measuring the impact of their activities. See what metrics they track. Speak to the people who developed the metrics about your community work. A training course in evaluating and measuring Community Involvement is offered by the Boston College Center for Corporate Citizenship (Chapter 9).

- **Communications**. Speak with colleagues with this expertise in your company or with external advisors. In addition to PR agencies, a number of external training organizations cover all aspects of communications. Seek advice from people who have already taken such courses (Chapter 10).

- **Influencing and change facilitation**. Your HR department may be able to point you to specialists in this area; alternatively, look to external HR consultancies. Business schools also offer a variety of "business change" or "consulting in change" education programs that will give you some understanding of this area. Also speak with visiting professors at the business schools who can give you more tailored, personal advice (Chapter 11).

More learning opportunities

For larger companies, where you have people undertaking community roles in different parts of the business, whether in the same country or internationally, you may want to investigate job rotation or job swap opportunities. Job swapping only works if both people want to make the switch, but it can be an excellent way of accessing fresh perspectives and experiences.

A further development path to consider, particularly when looking at becoming a well-rounded Community Involvement practitioner, is coaching or mentoring. It is time- and resource-intensive, taking place over months and maybe even lasting a year or longer. However, it can be a highly relevant experience. You can either find a coach or mentor within your company or connect with an external professional coach. Consider carefully your development needs with the coach or mentor, and ensure that your personalities fit well.

You may also want to check with your business industry body or with specialized Corporate Responsibility associations to see what learning opportunities they can recommend. Of course, many will only be too happy to offer their own programs! And, indeed, membership in such an association may prove to be beneficial for both your learning and the company's development. For the truly dedicated who are looking to develop a greater depth of community expertise, rather than just training for specific skill sets, a limited number of more formal qualifications are available for community practitioners to gain.

Table 2.2 lists some US and European organizations with Corporate Responsibility and Community Involvement expertise that are offering courses, workshops, and other avenues for networking and information.

Table 2.2 **Educational opportunities in Corporate Responsibility including Community Involvement**

Institution	Offerings

Boston College Center for Corporate Citizenship (www.bcccc.net)	• A number of management development programs and an annual conference. Programs include:
	  – Certificate in Corporate Community Involvement Management
	  – Advanced Certificate in Corporate Community Involvement Leadership

BSR (www.bsr.org)	• Consulting, research, networking, and conferences. Also has offices in China (website available also in French and Mandarin)
Business in the Community (www.bitc.org.uk)	• Offers a "CR Academy" with a few introductory courses
The Conference Board (www.conference-board.org)	• CR conferences across the US
CSR Europe (www.csreurope.org)	• Facilitation of a number of business-to-business working groups in which members exchange practical solutions to specific CR challenges
Ethical Corporation (www.ethicalcorp.com)	• CR conferences across Europe
European Academy of Business in Society (www.eabis.org)	• Case studies and research findings online, as well as an annual colloquium
International Business Leaders Forum (www.iblf.org)	• Development and leadership work. Setting business standards, developing partnerships
LBG (www.lbg-online.net)	• Workshops, training, networking, and support, mainly around measuring Corporate Community Involvement

If your interest in or need for academic development is really strong, you can also consider earning yourself a formal Corporate Responsibility accreditation – for example:

- Ashridge Business School in the UK offers an MSc in Sustainability and Responsibility (www.ashridge.org.uk)

- The University of Nottingham offers an MA in Corporate Social Responsibility (www.nottingham.ac.uk)

- The University of Bath offers an MSc in Responsibility and Business Practice (www.bath.ac.uk)

In addition, nearly all of the leading business schools in Europe and the US now routinely incorporate Corporate Responsibility as part of their MBA or Executive Education program.

Remember that expertise and the ability to teach are two different things. Always check that whoever is going to teach you or your colleagues has the right skills to train people effectively. Make sure he or she understands your industry, the challenges facing you and your Community Involvement colleagues, and your specific training needs.

It seems likely that community learning and development opportunities will grow along with the roles in this evolving sector. And, whatever the range of options on offer, there is no one path to excellence in Corporate Community Involvement.

Appendix 2.1. Role profile template: Community Involvement manager

Points to consider

- Is the role global, pan-regional, national, or community-specific?
- For a Community Involvement specialist or coordinator role, refine the profile to reflect more junior responsibilities.

Job purpose

- To develop, manage, and deliver the strategy for Community Involvement in [define scope of role]. The Community Involvement strategy will address the following areas: providing benefits to society; developing cross-sector partnerships; driving employee engagement; supporting [Company X]'s overall Corporate Responsibility approach; enhancing [Company X]'s reputation; and communicating, building, and supporting [Company X]'s brand among key stakeholders.

Key activities

- Develop and deliver a coherent strategy for all [Company X] Community Involvement activity that builds the company's impact in society and reputation among stakeholders in [country/region] and supports the company's business needs.
- Build close connections to senior [Company X] management to identify and maximize positive Community Involvement opportunities, and to identify and manage any potential risks.
- Provide consultancy on Community Involvement throughout [country/region/business unit] where appropriate.
- Undertake day-to-day management of the Community Involvement team and wider Community Involvement network in [country/region/business unit].
- Appoint, review, and manage all external Community Involvement support. Lead on relationships with key community NGOs.
- Evaluate all Community Involvement activity, including its impact on the development of [Company X]'s overall Corporate Responsibility approach, brand, and reputation in [country/region/business unit], with a special emphasis on demonstrating measurable ROI and tracking success for similar businesses in [respective country/region/market].
- Represent [Company X] at appropriate external Community Involvement forums and internationally within the group.

Skills requirements

Business experience

- Graduate or similar level of academic experience
- Demonstrated understanding of the not-for-profit sector; experience in Community Involvement/Corporate Responsibility and in the community/charitable arena would be an advantage
- Comprehensive understanding of the entire business
- Budget management experience
- Project management experience
- Good strategic thinker with strong analytical skills
- Openness to and understanding of issues beyond the core business

Relational/personal skills

- Drive, enthusiasm, and determination
- Passionate belief in the importance of Corporate Responsibility and the social dimension of the [Company X] brand
- Client focus, both internal and external customers
- Team management skills
- Strong communicator, written and verbal, both internally and externally
- Ability to operate and influence at a senior level, both internally and externally
- Appreciation of market, customer, industry, and stakeholder dynamics
- Empathy with internal and external stakeholders
- Stakeholder management skills

3

'How much does it cost?'
How to budget for Corporate Community Involvement

You have identified the strategy, and the company wants to increase its Community Involvement, but after "what is it you want to do?" the second question people ask is, "and how much does it cost?" We can't tell you the actual figure, but in this chapter we will do the next best thing – give you the tools to work it out yourself.

We first look at your company's community expenditure from the holistic perspective of its overall financial contribution to its communities – which needs to be reported to your stakeholders – before taking the operational view, looking at what you, as the head of the department responsible for Community Involvement, should be budgeting for.

The appendix to this chapter summarizes how much to budget in each area and issues to look out for (pages 67f.).

From basic philanthropy to multinational programs

When you start to think about budgeting for Community Involvement, your first challenge is to define what activities you want to cover. As the previous chapters have shown, what a company can do for its communities covers a wide spectrum and it is likely that different areas of community activity will be run by different departments and will not always be under your budgetary control.

When looking at your company's community expenditure, there are two areas to address:

1. The 'holistic' view

This is the comprehensive part of Community Involvement, where you need to see, in full, what financial contribution your company makes to its communities. The primary purpose of this is for CR or stakeholder reporting and communications.

The more you can show that your company is making a substantial, positive, societal impact through as many of its actions as possible, the better. But this is not just about the money spent. Expenditure without quality impact lacks credibility. Chapter 9 on Community Involvement reporting, measurement, and evaluation, will help you avoid this.

A question that may come up internally once you have found out how much your company really does spend is, "that's great, but are we spending too much?" There are ways to benchmark this externally, to answer those internal questions. Asked in confidence, many companies will reveal the size of their community budget or program, especially if there is little competitive risk in sharing figures. You can also look at annual CR reports, but use them for guidance only because, unfortunately, Community Involvement reporting is prone to inconsistent methodology.

The UK's Business in the Community (BITC) used to run the Per Cent Club for companies that spent 1% or more of their profits before taxes on Community Involvement. It helped to set a benchmark, but was open to different interpretations of what could be counted as community expenditure. Were, for example, salaries of Community Involvement managers included? BITC has since developed the CommunityMark,[1] which takes a much more holistic, and not just financial, view of what community programs do.

It will always depend on what you want to count. On expenditure, our own guidelines are: if you are spending more than 0.5% of profits before taxes on Community Involvement, it's a start. Over 1% is better still. But regardless of the amount, it's *what you do with it* that ultimately matters.

2. The 'departmental' view

As the head of the department responsible for Community Involvement, what budget do you need for your operations? The key areas range from Community Involvement projects to membership of relevant organizations but, before going into detail, we want to share two simple mechanisms to help guide you when considering how much to budget on community activities.

Fewer, bigger, better

For all your community activities, whether run by your own team or somewhere else in the business, always champion this mantra: the fewer and bigger the projects, with more effort put into them, the better they will be.

They will be easier to understand from inside and outside the company and easier for you to explain to stakeholders what you do and why. This principle applies whether your company is just one small business in one region – in which case don't spread too thinly across lots of community organizations; or a large multinational – when you should identify a limited number of core themes to focus on.

---

1 www.bitc.org.uk/community/communitymark/about_the_communitymark/about_the.html, accessed November 2009.

Create an investment profile

When looking at where to direct your community investment, develop an investment profile. This will enable you to break down your community expenditure into different areas to see if you have the balance right. For example, how much does your company spend on each of these three areas?

- Leading, strategic community programs – those that will make your company truly stand out. How to develop these is covered in Chapter 6.

- Integrating Community Involvement into business as usual

- Corporate Giving

Once you have this perspective, consider whether you are satisfied with how your company's community investment is split between the different areas. Ask yourself how much should you be spending in each area? Can you create any investment profile rules?

For example, for a multinational company with a mature approach to Community Involvement, operating in a number of countries (some rich, some developing), we would expect to see spending split somewhere along the lines of 50% on Strategic Partnerships, 30% on integrating Community Involvement and 20% on Corporate Giving.

But this will vary by country. For example, investment in Bulgaria may require a lot less expenditure on leading, strategic community programs (maybe only 10–15%) and a lot more on Corporate Giving (perhaps as much as 40–50%) because of the broader, more basic societal needs that your company should address.

It will also vary by industry. If your company is a sports business, you would expect to focus on more sports-related activity with a community impact and have a strong sponsorship connection, whereas a pharmaceutical business would probably focus more on strategic Community Involvement and Corporate Giving (particularly in donating medicines to developing countries) but a lot less on sponsorships.

There is no single rule or spending split for a company's community investment profile. Ultimately, it will be what is appropriate for your company. But the investment profile can be a good sanity check for your expenditure to see if your community strategy is going in the right direction.

Head office and subsidiary budgeting: who pays for what

The final aspect to consider from an overall company perspective is what community investment needs to be undertaken by the head office and what by the local subsidiary. This is particularly relevant for companies operating with a lot of divisions in one country or operating in many countries.

Head office's role is to set the strategy and framework that Community Involvement needs to operate within. It is then about helping the business, wherever it operates, to have the right skills and practices to achieve that strategy.

This means that the head office should budget for Community Involvement. This needs to cover strategy development, training, and reporting and to fund any global high-profile community initiatives. To engage its local businesses in certain projects, it may also want to offer a funding arrangement that its local subsidiaries can tap into – of which more shortly.

For the local subsidiary, the requirements differ. It needs to manage its local stakeholder relationships and Community Involvement while also supporting the overall group-wide strategy. It will need trained personnel to do this and may also need to implement its part of any multinational flagship program(s). The subsidiary will also need a budget for Corporate Giving and other local projects, depending on the market (as well as having the right processes in place, such as having a Community Investment decision-making body).

This means that neither the head office nor the local subsidiary should have sole control of a company's Community Investment budget. Each side needs to understand its role and recognize its limits. This will vary depending on the culture of the organization – does the head office rule by "command and control," or is there a more collaborative process between the business areas? It will also depend on the need for local community relationships: the stronger the involvement required, the greater the local autonomy should be.

Co-funding for success

For the head office, consider whether to co-fund any community programs with your local businesses. This is particularly useful if you have identified a community flagship program or theme that you want to see implemented.

It is also important that the local subsidiary of the business should "put its own skin in the game." If everything is funded by head office, the local business will be less engaged and put less effort in to making a community program a success.

The amount each part of the business contributes should be realistic and guided by head office. We know of a company with a global community program in which its local subsidiaries could propose projects that they and the head office would co-finance. The subsidiary in Peru got very excited and came up with an excellent project. Unfortunately, the program would have cost around $200,000, and the local subsidiary had only $20,000. It expected the rest to come from head office. The project could not go ahead on that basis.

Engagement will not happen overnight because local businesses need time to buy in to the project and to adapt or change current activities. You need to develop a long-term co-funding model so subsidiaries can get engaged and, if it works for them, be happy to take it on completely. Table 3.1 shows how costs could be shared over several years:

Table 3.1 **Example of community project cost sharing between head office and local office**

	Year 1	Year 2	Year 3	Year 4
Head office funds percentage of project costs	75%	50%	25%	0%
Local office funds percentage of project costs	25%	50%	75%	100%

Another aspect of co-funding to consider is between different departments of the same business. For example, the CR (or Community Involvement) department could jointly fund with Marketing a cause-related marketing or sponsorship program with community impact, or with HR an employee development initiative with community benefits, or with Business Development a micro-finance program.

This approach to co-funding can be particularly useful when, for whatever reason, the central community budget is limited. And, remember, "co-funding" may not be just about the euros or dollars. One department could provide the money, the other the project management resources.

Using a little entrepreneurial sales flair, the astute Community Involvement manager will need to hustle just a little harder to sell the benefits of a community program to his or her colleagues in other parts of the business to get their support, engagement, and budget.

Community Involvement: areas to budget for

Let us now look in more detail at the different areas of Community Involvement a manager needs to budget for. Please note any numbers we feature carry a health warning on accuracy. Our caveat is that it will always depend on the country you are operating in and the projects you want to do there.

The figures we provide are from the viewpoint of being based in a Western European or North American market, so we will use euros and dollars. With some exceptions, these figures would need to be revised, probably downwards, for running Community Involvement in Eastern Europe, Russia, Africa, Asia, or South America.

Whether you run a small Community Involvement team or a large department responsible for one or many countries, the nine key areas you need to oversee budget for are:

1. Community Involvement projects

2. Corporate Giving and In-kind Donation

3. Employee Involvement – including Employee Volunteering, Matched Time and Matched Funding

4. Personnel

5. Consultants

6. Communications

7. Evaluation

8. Membership of community organizations

9. Developing your organization's Community Involvement

1. Community Involvement projects

These are the most important part of community activity. Budgeting for projects can be split into two areas: (1) Budgeting for leading, strategic community programs run by the Community Involvement department, and (2) Budgeting for "integration" of Community Involvement to support other parts of the business, such as the examples of projects with other departments such as HR, Marketing, or Business Development mentioned earlier.

When budgeting for any kind of community project involving other partners, such as NGOs, take into account the management costs for your NGO partners as well as the cost to deliver the societal benefit. In any organization, projects need administrative and management time to deliver them. What you need to look out for is how much this eats into the budget that could have been spent on benefiting the community.

Avoid getting into a distillation process where an NGO charges a management fee to pass the money on to another NGO that takes a further management fee before passing it on to the organization actually doing the work in the community. This can easily happen if your partner is an international grant-making organization that distributes funds to national grant-making organizations, which in turn grant funds to local implementing organizations. What may have started as a €1 million (about $1.5 million) project to support single-parent families may end up providing only half that amount in actual help!

Also take this context into consideration when you make disaster relief contributions – when you contribute to the Red Cross or to UNICEF, how will your contribution be spent?

In terms of how much to spend, community projects tend to range from €50,000 (about $75,000) to several million euros or dollars a year. Wherever you find your organization is spending more than €50,000 on a community initiative, work with your colleagues and the receiving partner organizations to get the most out of it as an impactful community program – it's too much money for a simple donation.

In terms of an overall budget, it is difficult to give guidance, as it really depends on the kind of community activity under consideration. For serious flagship projects aiming to deliver credible impact in one country, somewhere from €250,000 (about $370,000) upwards per country per year is realistic. In countries with a comparatively low cost of living, that starting amount might be lower, at around €100,000 (about $150,000) per year. An important consideration is whether you start a program in just a few specific locations or make it a nationwide initiative. Nationwide programs will obviously cost more.

For flagship multinational programs, the budget will depend on the number of countries, but you are likely to spend several million euros or dollars per year. However, it really depends what you want to do – we know of very successful flagship multinational programs that are delivered for €500,000 (about $750,000) per year, but this is rare, and many programs cost much more.

Finally, you may also want your business to invest some type of Community Involvement development cost where it provides start-up funding to develop a leading profile program. When Nokia developed BridgeIt,[2] the CEO made a considerable amount of start-up funding available to R&D so the team there could develop the technology solution needed.

Anything is possible; however, there will be a limit below which charities will not want to work with you or just may not take you seriously. But while there is only so low you can go, the *more* you spend, the greater the societal and business return needed to correspond to the millions you invest.

2. Corporate Giving and In-kind Donation

You should be aware of these two types of giving (Chapter 4 explains how they work in more detail), although it is possible that neither will actually fall within your budget area.

Corporate Giving, or the writing of checks to charity, may also be handled via the CEO's office or the Communications department. Businesses typically receive little benefit for Corporate Giving money spent so the Community Involvement manager's role is to help the business not to spend too much on mere Corporate Giving and to spend more on Community Involvement projects.

Individual charitable donations will depend on the size of your business and what charitable initiative you are thinking of supporting, but, as a guide, somewhere from hundreds of euros or dollars up to €25,000 (about $37,000) is acceptable. If a business is thinking of giving more money than this to a charity, it should be looking to create a much more substantial partnership – for instance, getting its employees and customers to take part in charitable fundraising.

In-kind Donations, or Gifts in Kind, is when a business makes a non-monetary contribution of equipment, supplies, or other items to the community. This may be used computers or office equipment or some of its products, e.g., pharmaceutical companies distributing free or discounted medicine in the so-called developing world. Most Gifts in Kind are unlikely to come from the Community department's budget, but this type of giving should be identified and the value of any items tracked for the purpose of CR reporting and informing other stakeholders what the company has spent in this area.

3. Employee Involvement

There are three types of Employee Involvement to take into account: Employee Volunteering, Matched Time, and Matched Funding (Chapter 8 explains how to organize them). The beauty of much Employee Involvement is that it is comparatively low-cost, with high benefit to the company.

Employee Volunteering

This is volunteering organized by the company, typically, but not always, on company time. While the budget for this will always increase if you have more and more people

---

2 www.nokia.com/corporate-responsibility/society/universal-access/bridgeit, accessed November 2009.

getting involved (which is a sign of success!), the cost to organize any one team volunteering exercise is only around a few hundred euros or dollars for materials.

If you are running a volunteering day for 50 or 100 people and, for example, need building materials to renovate a school, then the sum may go up to a few thousand euros or dollars. But it will be very difficult to spend much more than that unless, as part of the volunteering, you want to pay for additional investment at the location where volunteering takes place, for example where employees are working to replace a children's play area and fund a new playground.

For individual volunteering, the costs are lower still – typically just the travel costs for the employee to get to the volunteering activity – for example, an employee traveling to a school as part of a student-mentoring program.

The only other item to consider for Employee Volunteering is any "marketing collateral" to support the volunteering activity, e.g., promotional information to engage employees, a PR budget if you want to communicate about your activities externally, company-branded t-shirts, etc. Overall, even if your company is actively engaging several thousand employees in volunteering, there is little need to spend more than €100,000 (about $150,000) a year, and it can be done for much less. For a small or medium-sized business, you could engage several hundred colleagues for less than €5,000 (about $7,500) in total.

The exception to the low costs for Employee Volunteering is if you organize a flagship volunteering program: for example, running an international disaster-relief program in partnership with the United Nations, or running a volunteering partnership where you are placing employees with a charity partner, possibly in other countries, for a sustained period of time, say between one and three months. TNT and Ericsson are two companies that have followed this path (see Chapter 1, pages 27f. and Chapter 4, pages 72ff.).

These kinds of program will reach relatively small numbers of employees, but can be by far the most powerful type of volunteering you do. Costs to run such programs are typically in the hundreds of thousands of euros or dollars, with costs increasing depending on the duration of the activity, the location and the number of employees you want to involve. Always consider additional logistical costs as part of this – for example travel, accommodation, and employee insurance – so you are able to consider the project costs in their entirety.

Matched Time and Matched Funding

These areas are the more employee-driven side of Employee Involvement. Matched Time is when employees spend a certain amount of personal time volunteering, e.g., 50 or 100 hours a year, and a company matches those hours by donating to the charities the employees work with. Matched Funding is when the company matches in some form the employees' charitable fundraising. In both cases, you need the skill both to manage your budget to meet employee and community needs and also to ensure the company is deriving public recognition benefit worth the money involved.

We recommend investing more in Matched Time, as this requires a significant personal ongoing commitment from the employee and strengthens the relationship between employee and employer.

For example, if you set a minimum threshold of 50 hours (or more) a year of volunteering with a charity in personal time for the employee to claim the Matched Time financial support from your company, then you are supporting only those employees who are truly dedicated and making a real difference to society with their charity work.

If 50 employees spend more than 50 hours a year volunteering with a charity and you offer to give each charity €500 (about $750), then you need to budget €25,000 (about $37,500). Managed correctly, you should be able to derive employee goodwill and external PR for your company worth much more than that. Sometimes it is important to "do the math" like this if, for example, you need to convince your company's head of HR of the value of the expenditure.

For Matched Funding, we advise you to be much more cautious. Only support those activities that employees can really engage in. You could offer to support a team of employees running a marathon for charity. If between them they have raised €5,000 (about $7,500), your company could offer to double it so their charity receives €10,000 (about $15,000).

As you can see, the problem is that sums for Matched Funding can increase rapidly with relatively little benefit for the company. The charity gets the extra money, maybe you can get one internal and one external news story out of it and some employee goodwill, but was it really worth €5,000?

There are ways to focus this investment. You can have a "charity of the year" to direct the giving towards, perhaps aligned to a cause-related marketing initiative of your company. Another route is to run a form of Payroll Giving that the company can contribute an additional sum towards. In many countries, such Payroll Giving includes tax benefits, so the charity gains additional benefits. Simply, our advice is: do not ignore Matched Funding, but do limit how much you want to spend.

4. Personnel

The salary range of your country and company will affect how much you will have to pay for community employees' salaries and benefits packages. Typically, a company could have up to three different grades of community roles:

- A director, vice president or head of department, equivalent to a senior manager role

- A Community Involvement manager or Employee Involvement manager, equivalent to a middle manager position

- Community Involvement coordinators or specialists, equivalent to a more junior role

Speak with your HR department for guidance and to find out the mid-point salary range of the employee grade for your budgeting. If you have no equivalent roles in your company, compare to Communications or Marketing salaries, or do some external benchmarking. Speak with external recruitment firms, or with companies that already have such posts – or check out other online recruitment sites such as Monster (www. monster.com).

Remember to set aside some money for training and development. External one- or two-day training programs cost between €500 and €2,000 (about $750 and $3,000) per person. Alternatively, use an expert training organization and develop a tailored in-house program. As well as being more relevant to your organization (if you are not looking to pick up best practice from other companies), these can be much cheaper and you benefit from bringing colleagues together who are in similar circumstances. The external trainer's costs are likely to be between €5,000 and €15,000 (about $7,500 and $22,500) (for preparation, travel, and delivery) and typically a program can reach between 15 and 30 people.

5. Consultants

You may want to use CR or Community consultants for external challenge and perspective. They can help in developing strategy, planning, and implementing projects or to support specialist areas – for example, in building dialogue with NGOs or in undertaking Social Impact Assessments.

You can pay consultants a monthly retainer, a daily rate, or by project. As specialists in this area are usually self-employed rather than part of a larger organization, there will always be some flexibility in their fees that can be negotiated, particularly if you are able to offer a longer-term contract for three or six months or even longer. Expect to pay a fee based on their experience and the skills they offer: between €750 and €2,000 (about $1,100 and $3,000) per day for someone with a good level of expertise, and more for specialists in high demand.

6. Communications

How you communicate your Community Involvement activity is key for the image and reputation benefits it brings and Chapter 10 will expand on how to go about this.

Communications may be handled by your colleagues in house. This is much cheaper than going to an external agency, provided they have sufficient time allocated to support you. Most likely you will be looking at the cost of one full-time employee and bought-in costs such as photography and printing of materials.

Alternatively, or even with the in-house team's support, you may prefer to use an external communications or PR agency. This can have benefits such as having an outside perspective challenge what you think is newsworthy, and it ensures people are always dedicated to supporting your project. Sometimes in-house communications resources will be stretched dealing with other issues.

However, ensure that PR agencies are able to deliver what they pitch and that they do not put too junior people on the account. Also look out for extra costs for handling fees or mark-up where they have to buy something in. It will be cheaper if any suppliers that they use invoice you directly.

Whichever way you go, a guideline is to spend around 5–10% of your community budget on communication. Spend less and you will not be able to do much. Spend more and it distracts from the purpose of the project and risks becoming more about PR than about the societal or community impact – something your stakeholders, and especially any critics of the company, will quickly see through.

7. Evaluation

Evaluation is as integral to successful Community Involvement as communication. It is vital that any project you undertake has a budget to measure and evaluate what it is doing for both the community and the company. Otherwise, how can you, independently, demonstrate the value of what the project is delivering? See Chapter 9 for all you need to know about measurement and evaluation.

You may want to use a market research agency, academic institution, or other external supplier to carry out evaluation for you. But whether evaluation is done externally or internally the important thing is that it must be done. Set aside a percentage of a project's budget similar to that for communications – around 5–10%, and speak to your company's market research colleagues for guidance.

8. Membership of community organizations

There are a number of CR or community organizations out there that you should consider joining to keep in touch with the latest thinking, build your network, benchmark, and be inspired.

Organizations such as the Boston College Center for Corporate Citizenship (particularly relevant for America but also with excellent academic materials relevant internationally), the International Business Leaders Forum, Business in the Community (if you are based in the UK), or CSR Europe in Brussels all offer excellent contacts and information for relatively little money. For a large corporate, you should set aside between €5,000 and €15,000 (about $7,500 and $22,500) per year for working with such organizations. For smaller companies, you can set aside less.

9. Developing your organization's Community Involvement

Finally, there are a couple of further areas to consider for developing your organization's Community Involvement.

Community Reporting

This may be your role alone or part of a wider CR Reporting process. Consider whether you need to buy in specific IT tools to help support Community Reporting in your company.

Bringing multinational teams together

If you want to bring colleagues and perhaps their NGO partners together from around the world, e.g., for an annual workshop, consider whether head office needs to set funds aside for meetings, travel and accommodation costs, etc. While this will not require big sums – a few thousand euros or dollars should suffice – it will help to have head office support for this.

Law, tax, and accounting

For the "average" Community Involvement practitioner, this area might be considered "boring" or even "incomprehensible." After all, you did not take a job in Community Involvement to become an expert on the arcane intricacies of your country's tax law – even if it does help you maximize the amount of money you can spend on your community projects.

And that is the important point, because how tax is handled can make a big difference to how much you have to spend. In some countries it could be the difference between spending 5% of your budget on tax and over 30%.

Tax laws are complicated and neither you, we presume, nor we have spent sufficient hours studying the subject to know enough. And even if we had been accountants or lawyers in a previous existence, that knowledge would be out of date. Therefore our advice is simple:

Speak to the experts!

That is what they are there for – either within your own company or outside. Any time you spend with them will add greatly to what your company gets out of the project. This applies both in ensuring the project achieves what you want within a legally enforceable framework and in making sure the money goes to the right place rather than in to government tax coffers or worse, where corruption is involved, offshore bank accounts.

This needs to be looked at country by country. Laws and tax systems vary considerably between different markets, so always see what the consequences are locally. For example, in Finland, Matched Funding is seen as a taxable benefit for employees, which typically is not the case in other countries. This may affect what Employee Involvement activity you want to offer there. If you work for a professional services firm, look into how any pro bono work that you contribute is viewed in each country.

The use of Foundations by companies for Community Involvement purposes (see Chapter 4) also involves taxable benefits. Foundations are also subject to different country laws so, again, get expert advice on each local situation.

Managing your community partners' expenditure

The final part of this chapter might appear to be provocatively headed because, as any good partnering expert will tell you, it is not your job to manage the expenditure of your partners but theirs. However, when you have created a leading Community Involvement project, it *is* your responsibility to make sure your company's money goes where you told your Management Board it would be spent.

There are a number of financial controls you should consider putting in place in your community projects, and the more you plan to spend, the more thorough you should be. It is vital you work *with* your partners on this. If necessary, offer to bring in your finance specialists or use external ones to advise them how best to establish principles and procedures.

With your partner, agree and lay down clear principles for how you manage your community projects' budget forecasting and review process. It is almost inevitable with community projects, especially when they are doing something new, that the sums of money actually spent will be different from what was predicted. That is not necessarily a problem, but both parties need to know how to handle the changes and, from the company's side, you need to understand and be happy that any changes in the budget are appropriate.

There are two key principles that you should apply to all community partnerships: financial transparency and, not just for budgeting, trust. You need to be able to trust your partners to deliver what they promise. If you do not, that is an entirely different problem and you cannot use financial controls to address a fundamental issue in your relationship. However, financial transparency is an important part of the overall relationship. For example, does your community partner use external auditors to verify its expenditure as part of its annual reporting, similar to any company?

Setting up rigorous financial structures is part of good business management. Regardless of whether you are building a factory or running a community project, the same principles for how your company spends its money should apply. Unsurprisingly, if your projects are active in developing countries, the more important, and challenging, it may be to have good financial processes in place.

What to do if anything goes wrong

We hope it never happens to you, and thousands of community programs run without this ever having to be addressed. But there is always the risk of financial abuse, particularly if your project is in a country notorious for corruption.

What happens if one of the parties in your community project is embezzling funds? You and your community project partners should be prepared to act swiftly to suspend suspected parties while an investigation is undertaken. Perhaps bring in accounting experts to trace what has happened to the money and, if necessary, involve the authorities.

In the worst case, you may have to decide if you want to continue with your partner and the entire project. Exiting a project in such a situation requires careful planning, management, and preparation for crisis communication to manage the news externally.

Do not assume that you will be able to redress whatever has gone wrong through the courts. Even if your partner has been in clear legal breach of the contract you both developed, any legal process to recover funds or to sue for damages will take time and assumes your community partner has the resources in place to compensate you. Few NGOs do, and it never looks good for a big multinational to be seen to be "picking" on a small charity, regardless of what your company perceives as the rights and wrongs of the situation.

Obviously this is a very bleak perspective to finish on, but one you need to keep in mind. The better your due diligence and the financial transparency and processes you have in place, the more likely you will avoid these situations. But if you suspect financial abuse has happened, act fast, openly, and comprehensively to stop it from contaminating the rest of the project or, worse still, your company's reputation.

Appendix 3.1. Summary of Community Involvement areas to budget for and guidance on costs

Figures are based on typical expenditure for a Western European or North American medium-sized to large company (from 1,000 employees upwards).

	How much?	Useful tips
Community Involvement Projects	• From €50,000 (about $75,000) to millions per year • Consider whether your business also needs to invest development funds to create a leading project, e.g., in R&D	• Get community and business value equivalent to the sum invested. Calculate return on investment in terms of image and reputation gain
Corporate Giving and In-kind Donation	• Individual Corporate Giving from the hundreds of euros/dollars to no more than €25,000 (about $37,500) • Make sure any Gifts in Kind (typically not budgeted in your department) are tracked	• If your company spends a lot on giving, look to get more out of it – turn it into a strategic community partnership, do more to engage employees and customers
Employee Involvement	• Corporate Volunteering: between €10,000 and €100,000 (about $15,000 and $150,000) per year • Several hundred thousand for any leading volunteering partnerships • Matched Funding: €25,000–€200,000 (about $37,500–$300,700) per year • Matched Time: €10,000–€30,000 (about $15,000–$45,000) per year	• Set clear parameters around the Matched Time and Matched Funding activities to limit expenditure reasonably

Personnel	• Consider at three possible levels for calculating salaries and benefits packages:
	  – Director, vice president, head of Community Involvement
	  – Manager
	  – Coordinator, specialist
	• Remember to budget for internal or external training: up to €2,000 (about $3,000) per person
		• Benchmark with similar-level roles in your company and also with external businesses. Roles in Marketing and Communications are good for comparison

Consultants	• Depends on the consultant and the expertise required. Typically between €750 and €1,500 (about $1,100 and $2,250) per day. More for high-demand specialists, e.g., for a Social Impact Assessment	• Try to avoid paying day rates. Use retainers or employ on focused projects to keep costs down

→

	How much?	**Useful tips**
Communica-tions	• Depends on the support required. With in-house Communications support, it will be employee costs plus photography, materials, etc. Allow €10,000–€25,000 (about $15,000–$37,500) per year for additional costs • Communications or PR Agency support is typically between €50,000 and €500,000+ (about $75,000–$750,000) (for multimillion-euro/dollar community projects), depending on what you want them to do. Can be higher if marketing and especially advertising is involved • Guideline budget between 5% and 10% of the community project's total cost	• Set clear project parameters • Make sure you have Communications people with appropriate expertise; do not end up with the office trainee • Measure and evaluate Communications results • Ask other agencies as well as the incumbent agency to put in new proposals to run the account every 2–4 years for fresh thinking
Evaluation	• Between 5% and 10% of the community project's costs	• Be clear what you are trying to measure and evaluate before starting • Get input from Market Research experts in your business • Consider different forms of evaluation experts, e.g., agency, academic
Memberships	• €5,000–€20,000 (about $7,500–$30,000) per year	• Ensure you receive benefits from the organization • Ask for a trial membership first • If you are not using your membership, cancel it

4

How to manage Corporate Giving, foundations, and disaster relief

In this chapter we present the various forms of charitable or philanthropic spending that a company can pursue. For many companies, this can be quite random and thinking about mutual benefit for both the charity and the company when making a donation is not always part of decision-making. But at least some of it should be strategic, and certainly all of it should be a worthwhile investment for both your company and for society.

We have divided the chapter into three main sections:

1. Managing your company's Corporate Giving. How do you make it more strategic than simply "writing checks to charity"?

2. Company foundations – the why, what, and how of creating one. What are the pros and cons of this means of giving?

3. Managing disaster relief on behalf of your company. How can you best get involved?

These three areas can all be addressed as separate from your company's core business. However, especially in times of financial crisis and budget cuts, a planned, structured, well-organized, and well-managed approach is always best. Before we discuss the details, Table 4.1 summarizes the key elements of these three forms of contribution to the community, and a corporate best-practice interview will highlight an exemplary approach.

Table 4.1 Corporate Giving, foundations, and disaster relief: summary of key elements

	Corporate Giving	Company foundation	Disaster relief
Definition	Philanthropy; checks to charity. Can be random with no focus or more strategic and aligned to business interests	One or more organizations set up separate from the business to support the development of society. Areas may be broad ("make society better") or focused ("support the participation of teenage girls in sports") and strategic	The actions of a company when a natural or human-made disaster occurs. Two areas to consider: • What happens if the disaster is in a country where you operate? • What if it takes place in a country where you have no operations?
Commitment required	Minimal, often devolved in organizations as part of a manager's usual role. If centralized, one person oversees it	More substantial, long-term commitment from Board level down. Expert resources required to set up, as well as ongoing personnel and reporting requirements	Intensive, including Board-level time. Requires a senior manager to lead it, but limited to duration of disaster relief program (unless this turns into a longer-term strategic community initiative)
What should a large company do?	Set an overall strategic framework aligned to the business with flexibility for regional managers to meet local needs	Ensure a strategic approach to the foundation's purpose. Ideally just have one global foundation, led from head office	Ensure local business is empowered to react quickly. Offer additional support in partnership with NGOs including personnel and expertise from across the group
What should a smaller company do?	Focus on your business interests – support activities that benefit the region in which you operate or work with customers and use that to strengthen the relationship	Ensure the foundation has focus and a close connection to the business	Focus on your region; devote what resources and finance you can. If these are limited, partner with other small companies, NGOs, or even local/national government to make a difference
Personnel	One full-time employee to oversee, maximum	At least two full-time employees plus external support (legal, accounting, tax). Could require much more, depending on size of foundation and opportunities for other company employees to provide part-time support	Senior manager, perhaps as part of existing role, e.g., CR manager, plus junior support

→

	Corporate Giving	Company foundation	Disaster relief
Structure – local or global	Can be either. Often highly local. For larger and multinational companies, a global strategic focus to direct local giving will help	One foundation with an international remit is ideal; however, its giving may be restrictive, e.g., it may only be able to give to other foundations and not end-beneficiaries in another country. Ideally aim to have only one foundation per country	Usually locally driven and led by the representative office in the country. Head office or sister companies in other markets may also want to support depending on severity of the disaster
Investment required	The less the better! Company money designed to improve society should be spent elsewhere, e.g., on strategic Community Involvement projects, sponsorships with a community impact, cause-related marketing campaigns, or employee-nominated charity initiatives	Depends on country and remit of foundation. Start-up costs can be low, particularly for less affluent countries, but then ongoing financial support may be needed. For larger foundations wanting high relevance and visibility, in Western countries, a regional long-term commitment may require €10 million (about $15 million); a national commitment over €50 million; an international commitment €100 million plus	Usually one-off project costs, maybe longer-term for lasting project (maximum 1–5 years). Depends on country and scale and whether your company can contribute resources in kind. Could be €50,000 to €5 million (about $75,000 to $7.5 million), or more. As with all projects, the more spent, the greater impact it should have, and the more the professional approach required
Some general benefits	Good to address local issues; strong for local relationship building if executed properly. Don't just send a check: follow through on commitments, e.g., what happened to the money?	Brings a certain level of independence to a company's giving. Can be good for ensuring long-term commitment to address societal issue(s), regardless of financial fluctuations	Time for the company to step up. Need to do what's expected of you. When you say you're committed, this shows you mean it
Reputation benefit	Limited, local, rarely more	Potentially significant, subject to scale of foundation, focus, opportunities for branding, alignment, and connection to your company. Planning and set-up are key	Potentially significant. Key is to identify how to stand out from other companies active at the same time. Do not just give money and not follow up. Ideally make longer-term societal restoration commitments

→

	Corporate Giving	Company foundation	Disaster relief
Risks	Can run out of control if managers donate at random. Company might miss out on establishing strategic focus and real community partnerships. Depending on country, need to be careful that your charitable giving doesn't turn into local bribery	Can be too detached from your company, creating suspicion you've outsourced your Community Involvement. Equally can be legal issues regarding "mutual benefit" e.g., the company using a foundation for marketing	No real risks as such, but some "don'ts"– don't give money to organizations if you have no idea how your money will be used, don't just hand over money and walk away, don't be insincere – just doing it for the PR
Employee Volunteering possible?	Often combining giving with volunteering is possible, with potential for a more strategic relationship to evolve	Depends on terms of foundation. Ideally, yes	Yes, but make sure they're safe

Interview with Rima Qureshi: One of the most amazing experiences of their life

Currently a Senior Program Manager with Ericsson in North America, formerly Global Head of Customer Support reporting to the Head of Business Unit Global Services. Rima has over 15 years' telecommunications experience and has also been head of Ericsson Response since June 2006.

Setting a benchmark for company involvement in disaster relief, Ericsson Response is a global initiative aimed at developing a faster response to human suffering caused by disaster. It provides rapid deployment of communications solutions using Ericsson technologies and skills, providing equipment and employees to support relief efforts. It partners with the United Nations (UNICEF, World Food Programme, Office for the Co-ordination of Humanitarian Affairs), the International Federation of Red Cross and Red Crescent Societies, and the Swedish Rescue Services Agency.

How did you get involved with Ericsson Response?

RQ: "Ericsson Response is now in its tenth year so you could say it's been around since before CR became 'fashionable.' I first heard about it when I was head of our Technical Assistance Center in Montreal in 2001. It was just after the US deployment in Afghanistan and an employee asked, 'What can I do?' He was very quickly on a plane to Afghanistan and soon we had an Ericsson Response mission.

"As my former boss said to me when I was considering taking on the role of leading Ericsson Response, you have to really want to do it. I did then and I still do. The catalyst for me was the Pakistan earthquake in December 2005. I lost members of my family and I'd heard about the work we were doing with the UN. I just had to lead it when the opportunity came up six months later."

Ericsson's headquartered in Sweden. You're in Canada. Ericsson Response is all over the world. Is the geography a challenge?

RQ: "The geography can be challenging at times but there are some advantages – I am closer to the volunteers and our partners. The UN offices in New York are only an hour away by plane."

What advice would you share from your experiences of working with NGOs?

RQ: "Patience is most important. We've also found that bringing volunteers in who have had on-the-ground experience is excellent for both sides to really build understanding.

"Speaking more generally, NGOs can be a little wary of private enterprises, because of limited interaction with the private sector. This will become easier as interaction between the public and private sector increases.

"Also, it's important to understand how NGOs are organized. Their priorities and ways of operating can be quite different than those of a private company. There are different agencies to get together and it's important to identify who has the power. And then we have our own questions. How should we get engaged? How do we get an agreement?"

In what way?

RQ: "A specific example. If you're sending an employee into a disaster zone where there's no Ericsson office, they must be safe. If we're working with the UN, we need to ensure they'll be treated as a UN employee. If they have any medical issues when they're out there, they'll be treated by the UN. Meanwhile, we cover those employees' personal costs, salaries, and expenses. And, if they need to go home, we ensure there's a way to get them back fast via our partners."

What projects are you involved in?

RQ: "It depends how you define a project. Obviously there are the big disasters but there's also a range of ongoing activities. For example, basic training for the volunteers, joint exercises with our partners, and ongoing relief projects. One place where we have people currently is refugee camps in Sudan [June 2009]."

And how many employees are involved?

RQ: "We usually have 10% of Ericsson Response volunteers out on assignment at any one time. That's 10–15 people from around 150 fully trained. We also have other colleagues providing important back office support – for example, communication, volunteer communities, and updating web pages."

How do employees get involved and what do you expect of them?

RQ: "This has evolved. People nominate themselves with line manager agreement (a line manager also has to commit to pay their salary and benefits while they are on a mission). The people that are accepted as volunteers get a great message from the company: 'We value you enough to offer you this, and we'll be here for you when you get back.' Given that there are relatively small numbers involved, it definitely has a certain kudos within the company.

"Once trained, they need to be willing to go on a 1–2 month posting. Some of our partners would like longer but in those cases we'll rotate participation. Originally, we said we'd take everyone who volunteered. But, as it's gone on, we've found that, although there are key personal qualities, the right technical capabilities are really important. With the best will in the world, a non-technical person may be perfect in every other way but they won't have those technical skills. In that case, we'd look to get them involved in other volunteering activities.

"When volunteers go out, they may set up one of a number of telecommunications systems. For example, getting a complete telecom network (GSM system) running in the refugee camp or a system we developed with the UN called WIDER (a wireless LAN system connected to satellite that provides a basic email system locally). We're now looking at a complete 3G system (QuickLink) that you can connect up to satellite. Once they've set the communications up, they then get involved wherever they can help. If there are sacks of flour that need moving, they move sacks of flour."

Is it popular?

RQ: "People who have participated in missions say it's one of the most amazing experiences of their life so, yes, we're oversubscribed. Managing the interest is part of the challenge but you've got to balance that with having a large enough pool of volunteers ready to get involved.

"I work on the basis that, if I need one person, I may have to ask ten volunteers. Not everybody has the right skills and, even if trained and willing, may not always be able to drop everything and go owing to personal or work circumstances. For all our volunteers, not just Ericsson Response, we then check on a yearly basis the status of our volunteer pool and ask if anyone wants to leave the program."

How do you manage it and what resources do you need?

RQ: "I have a full-time job, so this is my passion, my 'volunteering' if you will. We have two full-time employees: one oversees the training and volunteering – he is a former UN employee with an operations background who can be an operations director in the field; and another who looks after our inventory: phones, telecommunications systems, etc.

"We then have a network of regional Ericsson Response volunteer heads who'll be active volunteers (they also have other full-time jobs). For example, there's one in Montreal whose role is to look after volunteers in Canada and North America. Another in South America, others in Europe and, right now, I'm also further building our Asia capability – especially given the increase in disasters there."

How much does it cost?

RQ: "Since we have been working with Ericsson Response for ten years, the foundations and the network with partners are in place. The cost is insignificant under the circumstances. What matters is the deployment process with a short lead time to reduce suffering and, as I mentioned earlier, the job satisfaction for the volunteers."

Are there areas you won't get involved in?

RQ: "First, we make sure this is done in a completely non-commercial context. If someone calls us and says 'can you get involved in X country as we can then set a network up for profit,' we would refuse.

"We also stay out of any conflict where we might be obliged to take sides or could be perceived as doing so. For example, after bombings in Palestine and Israel the UN wanted us to get involved, but we stayed out.

"More recently, one area we've reconsidered is donation of our equipment. We now prefer to offer a complete solution with our equipment and resources. We do not leave equipment behind after our mission is complete."

What's been its impact for Ericsson?

RQ: "Very positive. Internally, it's a huge motivator. Externally, there's always been a lot of interest in the media to explain what we're doing."

How does it fit with Ericsson's other CSR activities?

RQ: "It has varied over time. My role is purely with Ericsson Response but I'm in close contact with our group Head of Corporate Responsibility.

"It should and does perfectly complement our core values: perseverance, respect, professionalism. This is a living example of them in action but it has to be a part of the business, not the other way round. Ultimately, we do this for our employees. They want to do it, they want to use their skills to help people.

"For any business generally, I fundamentally believe that there are all sorts of ways to empower employees that do not mean a bigger pay check. Employee volunteering is a differentiator for companies, for our employees and definitely for Ericsson."

1. Managing your company's Corporate Giving

The term "philanthropy" can be traced to ancient Greece, where it meant "to love people." In the context of what companies usually do, this may seem a little incongruous. Philanthropy involves the giving of money, goods, services, time, or effort to support a socially beneficial cause, with a defined objective, and with no (or little) financial or material reward to the donor.

Corporate Giving – or corporate philanthropy, corporate donations, or "writing checks to charity" – is very similar. It is the act of corporations donating some of their profits, or their resources, to non-profit organizations. Typical recipients include artistic, religious, sports, charitable, and humanitarian causes and educational institutions.

Businesses often support charitable institutions through financial gifts, equipment, supplies, or other contributions. Giving is often handled by the corporation directly, or it may be done through a company foundation (see section 2, pages 82ff.). Companies or foundations may also set up Employee Volunteering groups that get involved by giving their time and skills.

How does Corporate Giving fit with strategic Community Involvement and Marketing activities?

As we explained in the introduction, many businesses give money at random to a variety of local "good causes." Nice as this is, if you want your work in the community to be taken seriously, there should be a stronger case than that. After all, few business plans are passed by the Board on the "it just felt right" test!

These days, leading organizations undertake a more sophisticated and strategic approach to their involvement in their communities. Which is what this book is all about.

So, instead of Corporate Giving (checks to charity with little other benefit, no long-term relationship, etc.), you see Marketing or Communications departments sponsoring initiatives that have a societal impact, or offering their customers products that include a charitable benefit (cause-related marketing – CRM). All of these are much better ways to be involved in the Community than pure Corporate Giving.

Strategic Community Involvement may have some sponsorship or CRM elements, but it should have much more than that. It should come with a strong societal focus, be designed around a long-term partnership for mutual benefit, and be closely connected to the company's core business interests. Chapter 6 covers in detail how to do this well.

LBG comprises over 100 international companies working together to measure Corporate Community Investment. It offers valuable information about measurement and evaluation, as well as being a useful resource on Community Involvement generally. Their model (see Figure 4.1) shows the relationship of charitable gifts to other activities a business may have in the community.[1]

Why bother with Corporate Giving?

To understand the importance of Corporate Giving, it's helpful to think back to the roles of some businesses in 19th-century industrialized society. Corporate Giving, known then as philanthropy, was often an integral part of how companies supported their employees' existence, for example by funding their housing or setting up schools for their children (which also benefited the company as it ensured they could come to work and do their jobs). However, as business became more market-oriented and as government's role, especially in Western society, grew, motivation for Corporate Giving changed.

Sometimes Corporate Giving was cut out almost completely, or it was sidelined to an obscure part of the organization. Commonly, it was (and often still is) not "managed" at all. Some managers do it; others don't, depending on personal tastes. What a company gives to could even depend on what causes the spouse of the Managing Director or the CEO wants to see supported.

Giving money is still an important initial basis of how you support the communities where you operate – but it is only a basis. Sometimes it may be in your company's interest to support an issue or cause that is not aligned to your business – for example, when a particular cause (like helping to rebuild the town library when you don't sell books) is very important to a local stakeholder (the town mayor) whose support you need.

---

1 www.lbg-online.net, accessed December 2009.

Figure 4.1 **The LBG model showing the relationship between charitable giving and other community activities**

Charitable gifts — Intermittent support to a wide range of good causes in response to the needs and appeals of charitable and community organizations, increasingly through partnerships between the company, its employees, customers, and suppliers

Community investment — Long-term strategic involvement in community partnerships to address a limited range of social issues chosen by the company in order to protect its long-term corporate interests and to enhance its reputation

Commercial initiatives in the community — Activities in the community, usually by commercial departments, to support directly the success of the company, promoting its corporate brand identities and other policies, in partnership with charities and community-based organizations

Mandatory spend — Community investment required by contract or regulation

Business basics — The core business activities in meeting society's needs for cost-effective goods and services in a manner that is ethically, socially, and environmentally responsible

Source: LBG: www.lbg-online.net

While you still need to make sure your company does it right, we advise you to keep the sums involved relatively small. You can make your donations more beneficial by aligning them to your business. In other words: "strategic" Corporate Giving.

Getting more strategic, even in giving

The focus here is on structuring how you provide basic support to communities and to ensure this process is properly managed. However, be aware that the right approach will always vary according to the company, industry, country, and, to an extent, community concerned.

First, make the donation requests that your business receives subject to a clearly defined and rigorous review process. Where your company operates in many markets, you may want to create an overall framework; however, each country may still need more specific guidelines for its local circumstances.

Then put in place two key elements:

- Set the right criteria
- Create an appropriate giving framework

Set your criteria for causes to support

Barclays'[2] website gives a good example of their Corporate Giving criteria. Having this online, with a simple process so people know where to go to make requests, can save your company a lot of time and give a much more professional impression to outsiders, even if the end result is still "Sorry, but we cannot fund your request."

You can even set up an online application process, which can help to weed out time wasters and identify those organizations most relevant to you. Sponsorium is an online evaluation tool you can buy that does this for sponsorships and has been adapted by some companies to manage their community enquiries as well.[3]

In order to properly evaluate what causes are appropriate for your company to support, first consider some basics.

Look at your company's business strategy or, if it has one, CR strategy. Are there some specific themes that you could follow in your giving? For example, the majority of Avon's customers and employees are women. It therefore makes sense for them to be actively involved in charitable initiatives around breast cancer and domestic violence.[4]

Similarly, you may want to build on your themes and develop focused charitable partnerships, or select a "charity of the year." If you go down this route, consider involving employees in the cause as a way of moving your charitable work away from Corporate Giving and towards Community Involvement. A "charity of the year" is very popular in the UK but less so in the US.

A "charity of the year" can be one way to focus your giving. Other companies run successful initiatives for much longer. British Airways' very successful Change for Good fundraising initiative, begun in 1994 in partnership with UNICEF, encourages customers and employees to donate any spare change or foreign currency.[5] Another route, not uncommon, is to take a seasonal initiative. For example a Christmas fund where employees raise money, supported by the company, that goes to help individuals or families in urgent need. The UK-based Charities Aid Foundation has a wealth of ideas and case studies of how different companies have brought their giving to life.[6]

In July 2008, British grocery chain Waitrose launched a locally focused giving program, enlisting customers' help in identifying issues close to home. Waitrose's Community Matters program assigns each store £1,000 (about €1,100, $1,600) each trading month to donate among three local organizations such as community groups, schools,

---

2   group.barclays.com/Sustainability/Responsible-global-citizenship/Community-investment/ Programmes, accessed December 2009.

3   www.sponsor.com, accessed December 2009.

4   Interestingly, run both via the corporation and through the Avon Foundation; responsibility. avoncompany.com/page-20-philanthropy, accessed December 2009.

5   www.britishairways.com/travel/change-for-good/public/en_gb, accessed December 2009.

6   www.cafonline.org, accessed December 2009.

or local divisions of national charities. Customers nominate the organizations to benefit, and Waitrose's local funding bodies (known as PartnerVoice forums – based on the approach of parent company, John Lewis Partnership) make the final selection. Customers are then offered a token each time they shop that can be inserted in any of three Perspex tubes—one for each of the selected charitable groups. At the end of the month, the pile of tokens donated to each organization is weighed and the beneficiaries receive a corresponding proportion of the cash.

A similar program is also in place in the US at the grocery chain Whole Foods, where customers who bring their own bags are rewarded with wooden nickels that can be deposited in boxes assigned for donation to select local charities.[7]

If the organization fits your criteria, you should then pay attention to its profile. Make sure you are only ever involved with organizations that have:

- An excellent reputation

- A good project track record

- Sound financial management (equally applicable to both big and small organizations)

You can find out about the first two by doing some background research. Speak to other parties who know the organizations or have worked with them in the past. For the third, get access to their (audited) financial report and accounts.

Identify your funding exclusions

The more you can focus your areas of giving, the easier it will be to build a reputation for your company in this area, not as a company that gives to anyone and everyone. You may want to establish an internationally applicable list of the kinds of causes and organizations you won't support. Common ones include:

- Activities related to the promotion of religious or political interests

- Charities that support, work with, or fund terrorist organizations (obviously!)

- Profit-making organizations

- The repayment of debts or retrospective grants (for work that has already been undertaken)

- Individuals, including athletes, artists, political candidates, or political office holders

There are a range of others that you may want to rule in or out depending on your business – for example, you may support animal charities if you are a pet foods company, or medical research if you make pharmaceuticals, or even veterans' organizations if the military is a key customer.

A common example for ruling out a cause is with faith-based groups and initiatives. If your company is religiously neutral, you probably won't want to get involved in causes

---

7 trendwatching.com/trends/generationg, accessed December 2009.

specifically designed to fulfill or further a particular faith-based goal (e.g., to increase the membership of a faith-based organization). However, if your company has very strong religious roots, maybe even a clear association with a particular faith, its societal interests and focus could drive all your business' community activities. If so, you will want to create a stronger community partnership, not just give money and walk away. In that case, turn to Chapter 6 to find out more about strategic Community Partnerships.

A common problem is that you know your employees are passionate about many more causes than you can back, and you may not want to support all of those causes through your Corporate Giving. One solution is to have tight Corporate Giving criteria for requests from external stakeholders, but broader criteria for other causes your employees want to get involved in – and to support those through, for example, Matched Time or Matched Funding as elements of your Employee Involvement (see more on this in Chapter 8). This way, employees who are really passionate and make the effort to contribute to society are supported (and motivated). Meanwhile, your company stays focused in its giving.

Non-monetary Giving

It is usually, but not always, about the money. A non-cash gift, also called an In-kind Donation, is a non-monetary contribution of equipment, supplies, or other property. Non-cash/in-kind gifts are often offered by Corporate Giving programs along with, or instead of, cash grants.

Support can include products, supplies, and equipment (e.g., furniture, computers), or the use of corporate services/facilities (e.g., meeting/events space, mailing services, computer services, printing, and photocopying). Make sure whatever non-monetary donations you do give are appropriate for the recipient organization and the situation they have.

Create your giving framework

When you have set your criteria for giving you can establish the framework. First, set levels for who decides how much local Corporate Giving can take place without wider authorization in your company. This may be especially relevant for companies spread over many locations, or with a devolved management structure where local managers are fairly autonomous.

For example, you could say that below €500 (about $750), or whatever seems appropriate in your company, is solely the responsibility of the manager/department doing the giving. It still needs to be transparently reported to one central office. However, any higher amount must then be approved by the person responsible for local Community Involvement or a wider (management-staffed) giving team (see below).

Someone in your company needs to oversee this, usually the Community Involvement Manager, whose role includes:

- Ensuring understanding of the company's Corporate Giving framework throughout the business and towards organizations requesting support

- Ensuring that Corporate Giving is carried out within that framework

- Putting in place processes to track, monitor, and transparently report what has been given

It's important to set a maximum threshold (e.g., €/US$50,000) per individual donation. You should never (or at least very rarely) go above this figure for Corporate Giving. Higher amounts are more appropriate for Community Involvement partnerships.

What if my competitors are already supporting causes I'm looking at?

It is not unusual for companies in the same business to support similar causes, especially when the cause is aligned to their core business and they share the same key stakeholder audiences. It would be a mistake to avoid supporting the most relevant cause for your business simply because others are already active in the same space. As Simon Zadek of AccountAbility has pointed out, [8] corporate platforms dedicated to one common cause can often be highly effective, as they can achieve more scale in their support.

When you select your causes, it is a good idea to look at activities that other corporations in your region/country, as well as your competitors, support. Do some benchmarking. The key is to find causes that will be distinct, or perhaps create opportunities for wider cooperation and greater impact. Consider:

1. What could make your contribution stand out from others already in the marketplace?

2. Are there any opportunities to work together with other companies to jointly support the cause and demonstrate a focused effort (without compromising your commercial position)? Would that be beneficial for the cause? Could it even be beneficial for your company?

Making Corporate Giving credible

There are two more things you should do: (1) Engage management, and (2) Be transparent.

To help give credibility to your Corporate Giving policy and to get senior management buy-in, set up a Corporate Giving Committee (of which the Community Involvement Manager is a member and probably coordinator). The Cause Evaluation chart in Appendix 4.1 on page 94 is a tool that can help committees or individuals to choose the right causes to support. And to make it easier for you to turn down requests for financial assistance we have given you a sample "Sorry, but we cannot support you" letter in Appendix 4.2 on page 95.

Finally, be transparent, especially when you are operating in developing countries. There can be a fine line between Corporate Giving – helping society develop while benefiting your business – and bribery. Make sure the projects being funded are for the benefit of society and not just certain local individuals. As seen in the case of Siemens

---

8 In a speech at a CR conference run by the Conference Board, New York, February 2002.

in 2008, such scandals can be very far-reaching.[9] We've always found that the guiding principle of transparency works well. If recipients don't want to report or promote your contribution, or if you are not seeing the impact of money spent, there's probably something fishy. If recipients do report and promote your contribution, it's probably going to an "OK" cause.

All your company's contributions to the community through Corporate Giving need to be counted towards total donation amounts you disclose in your Corporate Responsibility Report.

Useful sources of further information

- Boston College Center for Corporate Citizenship (www.bcccc.net)
- Business in the Community (www.bitc.co.uk)
- Charities Aid Foundation (www.cafonline.org)
- International Business Leaders Forum

2. Company foundations: The what, why, and how of creating one

At some point in setting up your Corporate Community Involvement, you may come across the question of whether it would make sense for your company to establish a foundation. Many companies go through the process of evaluating the pros and cons of such a move; however, active Community Involvement still needs to be driven directly from within the company.

Many companies have foundations – from classic corporate foundations at the likes of Vodafone, Citigroup, Shell, or UPS to others that have become powerful societal institutions in their own right, such as the Ford Foundation and the Bertelsmann Foundation. There are even foundations that own the company, as in the case of the Bosch Foundation.

There are tens of thousands of foundations around the world. The European Foundation Centre groups them into four broad categories:

- Independent (or individual) foundations – founded by one, or a group of individuals, or a family
- Corporate foundations
- Government-linked foundations
- Community foundations and other fund-raising foundations

---

9 Siemens, beginning in the mid-1990s, offered bribes and kickbacks to foreign officials to secure government contracts for projects. The company is estimated to have paid $1.4 billion in bribes to government officials in Asia, Africa, Europe, the Middle East, and Latin America; www.nytimes.com/2008/12/16/business/worldbusiness/16siemens.html, accessed December 2009.

Over the last few years, we have seen foundations return to their roots – driven by an individual's philanthropic commitments. While many of these individuals (e.g., Bill Gates) may have made their money in the business world, they are now some of the highest-profile philanthropists. Think of the Gates Foundation's massive resources, ambitions, and highly professional approach, such as its campaigns to eradicate malaria and river blindness; or billionaire investor and Berkshire Hathaway Chairman Warren Buffett's donation in 2006 of $31 billion to the Gates Foundation.

Entire books are devoted to this area. Here we provide the basic information you will need to see if setting up a foundation could work for your company.

Why do it?

This is the most important question to ask and one not to lose sight of when having the discussion in your company. Consult relevant internal decision-makers in answering the following:

- What are the objectives driving the creation of a foundation (or foundations) in your company?

- What alternative options exist for the delivery of the objectives?

- Are these objectives long- or short-term in nature, and what is their hierarchy in terms of importance?

- What added value could a foundation potentially offer that other forms of giving or Community Involvement in your organization could not?

Fundamentally your key questions to ask are: Why do we want a foundation? What do we want to achieve by having it? Consider this from two perspectives: the societal perspective – to make grants to causes that need support – and the company perspective: for example, we are interested in image gain or in tax deductions.

What are the pros and cons of foundations?

The pros

Foundations can:

- Provide a structure and focus for Corporate Giving
- Bring a certain level of independence to a company's giving
- Address a specific social need or challenge or "kick-start" a new initiative
- Sometimes provide a company with a more credible way of engaging with the voluntary sector by being seen as separate from business interests
- Provide core funding over a sustained period, ensuring continuity of giving, rather than just making one-off charitable donations
- Take the administrative burden of coordination away from the company

→

- Provide focus and identity for Employee Involvement, but only in some markets, and it does create an administrative burden as people are required to run and coordinate it, as well as external supporting resource (e.g., auditors and advisors)
- Act as a legitimate and less risky way of supporting difficult and unpopular social issues through a less close connection to the company
- Provide clarity for charities seeking funding, as foundations are governed by deeds that state their purpose, as opposed to company-internal criteria, which can be difficult to access from the outside
- Provide some tax benefits; however, always get expert advice about this as some companies have found the tax benefits hard to realize
- For many companies, foundations also provide good visibility for raising your company profile; demonstrate a consistent and enduring commitment to the community; and serve as a responsive, reactive, local philanthropy presence in the community.

The cons

- Foundations are complex and time-consuming and require very solid, transparent governance structures if they are to be credible.
- There is a risk that stakeholders could perceive a foundation as "outsourcing" Corporate Community Involvement, as opposed to it being more of an integral part of the business.
- Some companies feel strongly that community activities should be more aligned with the core business than a foundation would allow them to be.
- A strategic approach to Corporate Community Involvement should achieve the same results in-house.
- In some countries there can be very severe tax restrictions on what a foundation can and cannot do. Make sure you understand these limitations so the foundation can still meet your objectives, especially in connection with how much it can support projects aligned to your business and the reputation benefit you can get from it.
- Starting a foundation is certainly not the easiest road. A foundation can require a sizeable financial commitment to set up and also requires a serious commitment of personnel, both in its own administration and within the supporting company, to make it a success.
- Foundations last forever. Once set up, they are difficult to dismantle. So, like a marriage, make sure you know what you are committing to.

How do we do it?

Only once the "why" questions have been addressed can you start thinking through the "how" questions. Once you have determined how a foundation could work for your company and how you will get around the risks, there are practical questions to consider when setting one up. These include:

- How to create a corporate foundation. In each country, the laws in this area can vary considerably. Get expert advice.

- How to align the foundation with your company's CR, corporate, and/or brand strategies

- How to maximize fiscal and reputation benefits for the foundation and, especially, for your company

What is the best structure for a foundation?

A Business in the Community report[10] suggested that, while many corporate foundations are set up and operated slightly differently, the key differentiator is the integrated versus independent set-up of the foundation and most corporate foundations sit somewhere between these two poles. Table 4.2 shows the different attributes offered by the two kinds of set-up.

Table 4.2 **Comparison of the attributes of integrated and independent foundations**

Foundation attributes	Integrated	Independent
Governance/trustees	All trustees are employees of the company	Trustees are all non-employees (or a mix)
Committed funding formula	No	Yes
Giving focus	Linked to business strategy or business locality	Not linked to business
Foundation staff	Seconded from the business	Not linked to the business
Link to Employee Volunteering	Yes	No
Senior management involvement	Yes	No

Source: Business in the Community, *Corporate Foundations, Building a Sustainable Foundation for Corporate Giving* (London: BITC, 2003)

10 Business in the Community, *Corporate Foundations: Building a Sustainable Foundation for Corporate Giving* (London: BITC, 2003; www.bitc.org.uk/resources/publications/corporate. html, accessed December 2008).

As a "best fit," the BITC report recommended a hybrid model, indicated by the shaded boxes in Table 4.2. It is both independent from but integrated with the parent company values and facilitates Employee Involvement.

BITC concluded that, particularly from a UK perspective, corporate foundations are a "good thing," providing a formal structure for large-scale company giving. As we advocate more strategic Community Involvement and less Corporate Giving, you will see why we have some reservations about the use of company foundations. This can be complicated further depending on which country you are operating in.

The question of integration versus independence is a long-running one. It is further complicated as the distinction between an integrated and independent model may not be clear-cut.

Key points to look out for include who identified and appointed the trustees. For complete independence and transparency, it is also important to have completely separate banking and legal arrangements and to consult specialists when setting these up. Funding can also affect actual or perceived independence. A large, one-off endowment helps the foundation to be self-determining, whereas a funding arrangement based on annual, negotiated corporate donations may require more compromise in terms of the foundation's operation as an independent entity.

Ways to fund foundations

There are two basic types of funding for foundations: donations or endowments. The source, amount, and schedule of payment varies for these:

- Regular, agreed amounts (e.g., annual "promise" donations) from the company. The Vodafone Foundations in various countries receive an annual donation from the local Vodafone business. The Body Shop Foundation receives an annual donation of roughly £660,000 (about €660,500, $1.1 million) from Bodyshop International.[11]

- Endowment linked to percentage of pre-tax profits. The Northern Rock Foundation used to receive 5% of Northern Rock's annual pre-tax profits. With Northern Rock's implosion in the financial crisis in 2008, this could have been unfortunate, but the British Government has committed that the Foundation will receive £15 million (about €16.5 million, $25 million) a year in 2008, 2009, and 2010 as part of the arrangement under which the bank was taken into temporary public ownership.[12]

- Periodic, but not necessarily annual, donations from the company

- Endowed foundations – the foundation receives a single "set-up" donation from the company and only spends the annual interest earned. The Shell Foundation was set up with an endowment of $250 million (about €165 million) from Shell in December 2000.[13]

---

11 thebodyshopfoundation.org/what-we-do/faqs, accessed December 2009.
12 www.nr-foundation.org.uk/important_message.html, accessed December 2009.
13 www.shellfoundation.org/images/origins/Shel_Foundation_origins.pdf, accessed December 2009.

- Foundations can use up their capital over a predetermined period of time. In 2007, the Home Depot Foundation (US) announced a ten-year, $400 million (about €264.8 million) commitment to improve local communities through building homes for working families.[14]

- Money raised by a company's customers or employees. Zurich Financial Services Group employees raise over £0.5 million (about €550,000, $831,000) each year through "Give as you Earn" schemes for the Zurich Community Trust.[15]

Skills, structure, capacity, and cost

A foundation is a complex body that needs to be well managed, with very solid, transparent governance structures. Beyond that, to achieve public credibility and a unique positioning, a company foundation has to commit to a lengthy process of creating a profile for itself by taking on specific social issues and showing tangible impact. Direct Community Involvement from within a company's business may offer quicker returns in terms of recognition of engagement.

A foundation with an endowment requires a large-scale initial investment. For a foundation in a Western European country operating at the national or international level to really stand out, an investment of about €100 million (about $150 million) or more is needed. For a less high-profile national foundation, a capital endowment of about €10 million would get the ball rolling. A recent example comes from Siemens who founded the Siemens Stiftung (Foundation) in 2008 to manage the company's corporate citizenship activities with a capital investment of €390 million (about $575 million).[16]

Setting up a foundation on a large scale is a lengthy, complex, and time-consuming process. It will involve your legal department, the identification and engagement of the suitable members for the foundation's executive and advisory boards, and the recruitment and hiring of capable administrators. There are complex reporting processes in addition to your company's regular Corporate Responsibility reporting. This can ensure real credibility and buy-in to your company's charitable giving, but it requires as much, if not more, commitment than managing giving only inside the company.

A company intending to set up a foundation on a large scale needs to ask itself whether it is equipped – or intends to equip itself – to undertake such an endeavor. The process of creating an appropriate structure requires a certain level of skill that – if unavailable in house – needs to be accessed externally.

Finally, as with any Community Involvement activity, always look at how a foundation's effectiveness can be measured, both regarding the support of individual projects and overall. Once you have made all the effort to establish a foundation, the same principles of having robust measurement and evaluation processes in place still matter. See Chapter 9 for more on measuring and evaluating community projects, but also look holistically at the overall purpose the foundation serves. If you want it to, the existence

---

14 www.homedepotfoundation.org/pdfs/08_thdf_fact_sheet.pdf, accessed December 2009.
15 www.zurich.co.uk/home/aboutus/Community/introduction.htm, accessed December 2009.
16 www.siemens-stiftung.org/en/siemens-stiftung/about-us.html, accessed December 2009.

of a separate body can be a powerful force in its own right. Does it achieve that potential?

Profile and reputation gains and limits

In some countries (especially in Western Europe) foundations are limited in the levels at which they can profile and involve the companies that fund them. This means that in these countries a company may not be able to support social causes through direct involvement and then strongly market and promote its association with such causes through, for example, cause-related marketing and media events.

Consider the following questions relevant to your company's reputation:

- How will news about your company's foundation be communicated?

- How will your stakeholders know about it?

- How will you keep stakeholders close, building reputation and trust over a long period of time?

Final thoughts on foundations

Ultimately, the distinction between a corporate foundation and delivering Community Involvement through the business is rarely an either/or choice.

The motivation behind starting a corporate foundation on a large-scale, country-wide level (or eventually even on an international level) would be largely the desire to create an independent body, sufficiently funded (either endowed or funded regularly) to "do good" for society.

The image of foundations is largely connected to philanthropy, and with recent paradigm changes in the focus of corporate involvement in communities, the question has arisen whether a foundation is still the appropriate instrument to express a company's commitment to society and undertake the company's involvement on its behalf.

The increasing contribution of management know-how to community projects, with a growing emphasis on companies contributing their core competencies to finding solutions to significant societal challenges, is best made directly from within the business. There is therefore a growing school of thought that it is more effective to deliver significant social impact from within the company than through corporate foundations.

Strategic community investment and foundation-based giving are not mutually exclusive. It is possible and thoroughly acceptable to undertake both. However, both should be firmly embedded as part of a company's holistic, strategic Community Involvement program.

This is reflected in a 2007 SMART Company report for the Charities Aid Foundation:

> As companies continue to strategise their corporate responsibility activities, corporate foundations become more popular as a way for companies to continue with charitable and philanthropic commitments . . . On the other hand, if companies want to distance themselves from philanthropy entirely, foundations might become less

popular, with those already in existence either wound down or shifted towards a totally independent model.[17]

If you decide your company does want to go ahead with setting up a foundation, the most successful company foundations have structures that work for their audiences, not their founders. They also are driven by a clear societal purpose. Their local decision-making is enabled since they know best, after all, where they can focus their work to make a difference.

Set up and run the right way, a foundation can work for the company, its employees, and the community. This is a win-win-win situation, but it takes time, effort, and serious commitment to get there.

Good luck deciding the best route for your company!

Useful sources of further information

- The European Foundation Centre (www.efc.be)
- Business in the Community (www.bitc.co.uk)
- The Boston College Center for Corporate Citizenship in the US (www.bcccc.net)

3. Managing disaster relief on behalf of your company

The term "disaster," applied in a broad sense, can cover both natural and human-made catastrophes.

Natural disasters fall into three categories:

- Meteorological disasters, including hurricanes, hailstorms, tornadoes, typhoons, snowstorms, droughts, cold spells, and heatwaves

- Topological catastrophes, including earthquakes, avalanches, landslides, and floods

- Biological disasters, including insect swarms and disease epidemics

The most notorious example of a natural disaster of recent times was the Tsunami in the Indian Ocean in December 2004 in which over 200,000 people died. Individuals, NGOs, governments, and corporations responded immediately with generous contributions for disaster relief.

---

17 The SMART Company, "The Changing Nature of Corporate Responsibility: What Role for Corporate Foundations?" (A report by the SMART Company for Charities Aid Foundation; London: The SMART Company, 2007; www.cafonline.org/PDF/CorporateFoundations.pdf, accessed December 2009).

Human-made catastrophes can include:

- Accidents, including transportation, mining, pollution, chemical, and nuclear incidents

- Refugee crises involving the forced movements of people across borders; civil disturbances such as riots and demonstrations

- Warfare-related upheavals, including those created by guerrilla activity and terrorism

The most high-profile example from the past decade would be the attacks in the United States on September 11, 2001. Again, countless individuals, NGOs, governments, and corporations reacted immediately and contributed generously to disaster relief for families affected.

Disaster relief efforts are typically a government-coordinated activity, as local, regional, and national governments take on varied responsibilities. Government statutes define appropriate procedures for disaster declarations and emergency orders.

Government efforts are supported by leading disaster relief organizations such as the International Federation of Red Cross and Red Crescent Societies, Save the Children, CARE International, or the World Food Programme. Government statutes empower relief agencies to be "first on the ground" and take immediate action, such as arranging for medical relief and temporary housing during an emergency. This is why it is appropriate to support the relevant appointed relief organizations with corporate contributions and, most importantly, not get in the way.

Useful sources of further information

- Red Cross and Red Crescent Societies (www.ifrc.org)
- CARE International (www.careinternational.org)
- Save the Children – International Save the Children Alliance (www.savethechildren.net/alliance/index.html)
- World Food Programme (www.wfp.org)
- Center for International Disaster Information (www.cidi.org) provides information and guidance to help appropriate international disaster relief. It includes guidelines for companies.
- Centre for Research on the Epidemiology of Disasters (www.cred.be) promotes research, training, and information dissemination on disasters, with a special focus on public health, epidemiology, and structural and socio-economic aspects. It aims to enhance the effectiveness of developing countries' disaster management capabilities as well as fostering policy-oriented research.
- Disaster Management Alliance (www.padf.org) is an initiative of the Pan American Development Foundation and the Office of Foreign Disaster Assistance (OFDA) of the US Agency for International Development (USAID), which is the primary donor. It serves as a channel to leverage private sector resources for all phases of disaster management.

To provide financial assistance when disasters occur, it can be easiest to cooperate with well-recognized relief organizations that offer a sound track record. They may have subsidiaries in your country, or can recommend one of their local partners. When you have selected your recipient organization, decide together with them how your company's contribution can be directed in a targeted way.

What should your company do?

Disaster relief should be a cornerstone of your company's Corporate Giving. If a disaster occurs in a region or country where your business operates, your stakeholders in the communities there will be in urgent and immediate need of support. At the very least, your company needs to do its part.

It may seem a little inappropriate given the situation, but it is important to acknowledge that this could also be an opportunity for you to prove to society that your company can be counted on when it matters. The priority must be to help alleviate suffering and to do it sincerely. But there is no denying that, done right, your standing in that community and with key stakeholders can improve. However, that outcome requires much more than just wiring over the money.

In a region where your company does not operate, you need to consider if you want to get involved and for what reasons. This is clearly different from when you, your customers, or your employees and their families are affected. Do you want to contribute because it seems like "the right thing to do" in an atmosphere of public concern (e.g., with many companies around you, including competitors and peers, contributing)? Or, do you want to contribute because your company has many employees who happen to be from that country?

You also need to consider what would be the best way to get involved. Do you simply donate money, or perhaps support your employees as they donate? Or is there more to it than that? Perhaps through your community strategy, there is a theme directly relevant to your business that you could focus on, as there was for the Ericsson Response program featured in the interview with Rima Qureshi (pages 72ff.).

The latter would be the most credible way, and you could even take it further, offering opportunities for your employees (working with the right aid organizations, of course) to get directly involved. This can be a great motivator and it can also broaden employees' social competencies. A good example is TNT's work with the UN World Food Programme. Chapter 8 on Employee Involvement covers this aspect in more detail.

Prioritizing the situation

By following several steps, you can gauge how much you need to get involved.

First, ask if your employees are directly affected. If so, do what it takes to ensure they and their families are safe.

Second, what about your wider stakeholders, especially your customers and key business partners? If their business is dramatically affected, what would be the right response for you, and what risk does the situation pose to your organization? For example, should you postpone or cancel customer bills while their business recovers? Are there other ways you can help or work with them to support relief work?

Then, looking to the communities where you operate, the two most effective ways to get involved are by:

a. Using your expertise to help

In an emergency, how can your business provide support directly related to your company's core competency?

We have already talked about telecommunications and logistics. What about utility engineers reconnecting power, clothing manufacturers providing items to keep people warm, pharmaceutical firms providing free vaccines against disease, or caterers providing food?

There are more options than you may initially think. Two recent examples are FedEx's response to Hurricane Katrina, where the company used its expertise in distribution systems and logistics to provide support and supplies to hurricane victims, or Pfizer's response to the Tsunami, where it mobilized its health and disease experts and environmental health and safety professionals to work with NGOs in recovery efforts.

b. Making donations to support relief efforts

Beyond the company's own competency, prompt financial aid may be needed to alleviate the suffering of disaster victims in many ways.

Your company can make charitable contributions in support of disaster relief efforts to finance: humanitarian services; transportation; the provision of food, clothing, medicine, beds, and bedding; temporary shelter and housing; the provision of medical material and medical and technical personnel; and making repairs to essential services.

Depending on the relationships your business has in the country affected, the head of your operation may want to speak to a senior representative in government to offer support and discuss appropriate actions. If your business is not headquartered in that country, you may also want to work with the diplomatic representatives from the country of your parent company.

However, giving money, while good and sometimes vital, is rarely enough, or even what is really needed. Think of the 2009 earthquake in Italy, a wealthy country. Within two days of the event, the government announced that it did not need any more immediate support. It said that instead organizations should look to get involved in addressing longer-term clean-up and restoration efforts.

This is an important aspect: often, immediate support is heaped on an area, and, once the frenzy dies down, a region is left alone with long-term restoration problems. To give you an example: many children lost their parents in the Tsunami. What about their long-term education? Who takes care of and pays for it? Especially in light of sustainability, your company may want to look into such longer-term issues in an area affected by disaster.

Regarding the effects of civil disturbances such as riots and demonstrations, you will need to decide on the right approach for your company. Should you get involved? And, if so, how?

In countries with unstable political situations, how can you make sure your company is not supporting a corrupt regime or getting involved in regime change? If ever that happened, it would be a sure way to attract controversy and international condemnation. In such cases of uncertainty and risk, it is especially important to work with credible NGOs to find the right approach for your company. This is true not just in disaster situations but, as companies from the extractive industries will tell you, also when operating in such communities on a day-to-day basis. We look at this further in Chapter 5.

You should also check how local donation law affects your contribution, and it is always better to get a written agreement between your company and the recipient organization.

Direct volunteering

Opportunities for employees to volunteer may include cleaning up forests, parks, or beaches after heavy storms; renovating schools or community centers after floods; or planting trees to support reforestation after a tornado.

Getting your employees involved in disaster relief

In many cases, your people will also want to help, especially if they are living in the country affected. Chapter 8 outlines Employee Involvement in more detail. The two most obvious ways to engage employees is through your company matching any money they raise and by direct volunteering, as outlined in the Ericsson Response interview (pages 72ff.).

However, with employees volunteering in a disaster relief context, you need to be much more careful than with other volunteering activities. This may require proper training and planning for involvement, together with local disaster relief organizations, and potentially some time before a disaster happens. It takes more effort to organize, but could generate many new and exciting community relationships for your business and the people involved. Your employees' safety is paramount, so you will need to attend to employee safety issues (potentially also in dialogue with local disaster relief organizations) before deciding what they can really do.

Appendix 4.3 (page 96) gives a sample approach to disaster relief.

Appendix 4.1. Cause Evaluation Chart

This chart can help you evaluate your choices. The criteria give you a basis on which to decide which requests to support. They also make it easy to communicate to colleagues what causes your company supports through its Corporate Giving – and why.

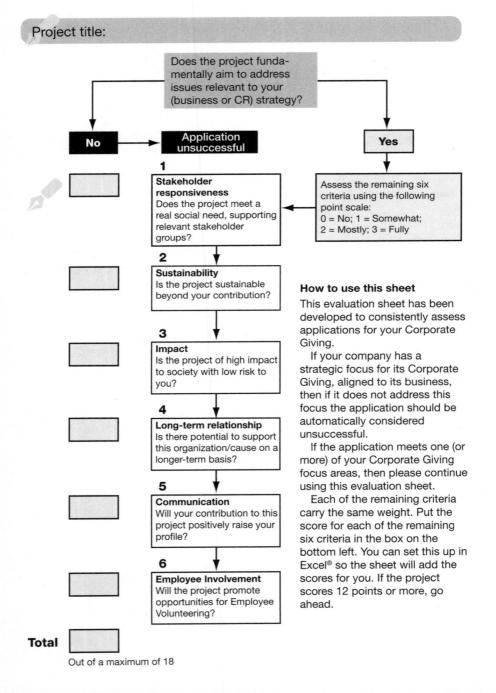

Project title:

Does the project fundamentally aim to address issues relevant to your (business or CR) strategy?

No → **Application unsuccessful**

Yes

1 Stakeholder responsiveness
Does the project meet a real social need, supporting relevant stakeholder groups?

Assess the remaining six criteria using the following point scale:
0 = No; 1 = Somewhat;
2 = Mostly; 3 = Fully

2 Sustainability
Is the project sustainable beyond your contribution?

3 Impact
Is the project of high impact to society with low risk to you?

4 Long-term relationship
Is there potential to support this organization/cause on a longer-term basis?

5 Communication
Will your contribution to this project positively raise your profile?

6 Employee Involvement
Will the project promote opportunities for Employee Volunteering?

How to use this sheet

This evaluation sheet has been developed to consistently assess applications for your Corporate Giving.

If your company has a strategic focus for its Corporate Giving, aligned to its business, then if it does not address this focus the application should be automatically considered unsuccessful.

If the application meets one (or more) of your Corporate Giving focus areas, then please continue using this evaluation sheet.

Each of the remaining criteria carry the same weight. Put the score for each of the remaining six criteria in the box on the bottom left. You can set this up in Excel® so the sheet will add the scores for you. If the project scores 12 points or more, go ahead.

Total

Out of a maximum of 18

Appendix 4.2. Sample 'Sorry, but we cannot support you' letter

Dear [name of addressee]

Thank you for your letter of [date] to [name of addressee] requesting support for [purpose of grant].

At [Company X] we are committed to investing in the communities where we live and work. We do this through structured community investment activity alongside Employee Volunteering and Matched Funding opportunities for our colleagues.

We focus our community investment in line with [outline your CR or community strategy here] and have a series of existing community programs in place to do this. Our Employee Volunteering initiatives are geared to support our community involvement in this way. We also support charitable organizations nominated by our employees through our Matched Funding and Payroll Giving initiatives. [assuming you do, of course!]

Approaching community and charitable activity in this way means we can deliver long-term support to structured projects, while also helping the charities that mean the most to our employees.

As such, we regret that we are unable to offer any financial assistance in support of your request.

We wish your [organization/charity] every success in the future.

Yours sincerely

[your name]
Community Involvement Manager, [Company X]

Appendix 4.3. Sample approach to disaster relief

Situation	There is a severe flood in your country, due to heavy rains, causing considerable damage
Relief effort	Relief workers from well-known disaster relief organizations in your country are out there, trying to help, evacuating people and setting up temporary housing
Media response	The media report on the disaster, on the relief organizations at work, and on money needed to support the victims
Corporate response	The media report about corporate disaster relief donations being made (e.g., to the Red Cross/Red Crescent Societies)
Stakeholder requests	Your company is being approached by stakeholders (these can also be your own employees) to contribute – or your own country management might already have decided that it would be appropriate to make a donation
Community Involvement Manager/ Management Board	As the country's Community Involvement Manager, it is your role to cooperate with the Management Board to assess the situation
Caution: don't let decisions be guided by emotion	Be aware that the atmosphere post-disaster may be emotionally charged, also in the media. Avoid making any quick decisions guided by emotion or for pure PR benefit. Strive to make decisions that will still stand as a "best practice" in response to disaster when you look back three years later

Decision-making	The Community Manager and Management Board need to decide jointly:
	• What is the appropriate organization to support? (e.g., your country's Red Cross/Red Crescent Society, or is there another renowned disaster relief organization that you consider appropriate?)
	    Make sure you are fully aware of that organization's:
	    – Reputation
	    – Project track record
	    – Financial track record
	• What is the appropriate amount to contribute? Is it in the range of:
	    – €20,000 ($30,000)?
	    – €200,000 ($300,000)?
	    – €2,000,000 ($3,000,000)?
	    You may want to research the giving range of other corporations (your competitors, your peers).
	    You may want to communicate with your chosen relief organization to discuss appropriate amounts and how your contribution would be used.
	• Are there opportunities to do more and work in partnership with NGOs in the area affected?
	Note: When making a disaster relief contribution, ensure that you have a written agreement with the recipient organization and that you receive detailed information on how your contribution will be allocated, so you will have proof both for internal and external stakeholder reporting about what happened with the money given

→

Involving your employees	Employee Involvement is important, and it is up to you to decide the best approach. It may be easiest to support employees' own spontaneous fundraising in response to the disaster through Matched Funding (see Chapter 8). If employees have relevant skills, can they contribute practically to relief efforts with paid time off? e.g., your logistics people offering their distribution expertise. Inquire with local disaster relief organizations, and always consider employees' safety first
Matched Funding from Corporate Center	If yours is not the head office, see if head office can provide additional support. It may not happen, but it's worth asking. Some corporate head offices match local disaster relief contributions 100%

5

Integrating Community Involvement into your core business

How to work with Operations, Marketing, and HR

For Corporate Responsibility leadership, it is critical to integrate Community Involvement into all parts of your business. This chapter covers this from three perspectives:

- From the operational side, the part of your business that manufactures, produces, or refines

- From a Marketing angle: how excellent Community Involvement can be integrated into and enhance cause-related marketing or sponsorship programs

- From a Human Resources standpoint: where Community Involvement can play a part in building employee pride with the company, and contribute to employee recruitment and training

Integrating Community Involvement can easily overlap with what some companies may see as overall CSR or CR. It depends on how your company looks at it. We believe excellent Community Involvement can and should be a part of many areas of business in your company (and it matters less what you call it). This brings us to our best-practice interview with one of the world's leading telecoms companies and a recognized leader in (what they call) CSR.

Interview with Alberto Andreu Pinillos: Create a trustworthy atmosphere within the company

Telefónica is one of the world's largest telecommunications companies. With over 250,000 employees, it operates in 25 countries with over 260 million customers globally. Telefónica's growth strategy is focused on the markets in which it has a strong foothold: Spain, Europe, and Latin America.

Alberto Andreu Pinillos (AA), Managing Director – Corporate Reputation, Identity, and Sustainability, has been responsible for developing Telefónica's CSR for the past eight years. In 2009, Telefónica was the best-performing telecommunications company in the Dow Jones Sustainability Index (DJSI). With a background combining academia, the oil industry, and banking, before joining Telefónica Alberto was with Santander, the major Spanish bank, as Managing Director of Corporate Identity and Culture. He is also an associate professor of Organizational Behavior and Corporate Identity and Culture at the Instituto de Empresa.

In 2008, Telefónica invested €114 million (about $171 million) in social and cultural activities, €69 million of which was undertaken by the Telefónica Foundation, which forms one important part of Telefónica's Community Involvement. The foundation, established in 1998, has the purpose of coordinating long-term social and cultural projects of the Telefónica Group of companies.

What is Telefónica's overall approach to CSR and how does Community Involvement fit in that?

AA: "For the general public, CSR can be misinterpreted as being only about philanthropy. It's not; it's about much more. For Telefónica, our overall approach to CSR has placed a lot of emphasis on building transparency, trust, and good, effective relationships with all our stakeholders. A particular emphasis is on our investors, local and global NGOs, and key organizations for our employees. In effect, we focus on all groups who have a way to reach our final end-customers and to influence their opinion.

"The key to our overall approach has been our focus on being recognized as a leader in the DJSI. From that, our CSR strategy covers three main aspects and how they relate to our business: environmental sustainability, societal, and economic issues.

"For the environment, the focus is on climate change and energy efficiency. The economic approach is about how we manage risks, corporate governance, and relations with our customers. The societal issues cover a range of areas – from attracting the right employees, to working with stakeholders, to the impact our products and services have in the community. It also includes ethical issues in our supply chain and supporting human rights. This is where our Corporate Community Involvement and its link to our foundation's philanthropic work comes in."

And how do you work with the Telefónica Foundation?

AA: "In the last three years, how the business and the foundation work together has really moved on. Historically, and I think this can often be the case with corporate foundations, the foundation focused on worthy not-for-profit programs, but rarely connected with our business. This was a missed opportunity, and together we decided we should be able to find some links. As with any partnership, it's always challenging to define boundaries and play to each other's strengths, but we've made good progress.

This year, for the first time, we have brought our CSR and Foundation Reporting processes together, which works very well. As an example, we package together Telefónica's CSR Report and the Telefónica Foundation's Annual Report.

"Although the foundation's work is really important, we see that Telefónica's overall societal impact is economic as well as social. Our company spends €30 billion [about $45 billion] per annum on procurement. Not looking at all of our company's impacts on the community does not make sense and so, for example, we work with our Procurement department. If we fix a target of 0.7% of overall annual procurement expenditure to have a clear societal consideration linked to our foundation's work, then we impact the community with €182 million [about $274 million] expenditure a year. That is how our commitment to develop our responsible supply chain would lead directly to sustainable community impact. We help the foundation to secure societal change and, at the same time, we improve the way we do business."

What areas is the foundation active in, and how do those connect to the business?

AA: "The foundation has four main fields of action. The biggest is its Proñino program, helping over 150,000 children in 2009. The second, called 'EducaRed,' is about improving education through new technologies. Here the business side brings in content for child protection, helping children to use mobile phones safely and to be careful and responsible on the Internet. The third area is on the use of ICT [Information Communication Technologies] in the community – here we linked the foundation with our work around climate change and issues on social and digital inclusion. Finally, the foundation manages Telefónica's employee volunteering program. Here our role is about helping the foundation identify potential volunteering areas that link to core business aspects of the company: for example, employee volunteers helping the elderly benefit from Internet services."

And how does your department work with the business?

AA: "We see ourselves as facilitators, helping our business understand what society is demanding of ICT services and then working with them to figure out how to improve lives and generate business out of that – for example, by supporting the elderly or helping customers with disabilities.

"Let me give an example. For deaf people, our CSR and innovation departments formed a relationship with CNSE,[1] the national federation for deaf people in Spain. In Telefónica, we had developed a platform with a sophisticated form of video-conferencing connected to a call center with sign language interpreters. This way a deaf person can go to a hospital and talk to a doctor or, in an emergency, contact the police. But when we went to the hospitals to offer them this technology, they all asked whether we had a joint venture with CNSE. Without such a relationship, our product would not have had the legitimacy it needed. Now we're selling the platform to public and private hospitals."

---

1   The Confederación Estatal de Personas Sordas.

What advice do you have on how to engage the business?

AA: "Most important is to create a trustworthy atmosphere within the company. It's also about finding the right rhythm and speed. Sometimes it helps to go slowly. If you move slowly but with confidence, things happen. If you try to run, people may pull back and wonder what your agenda is, even whether you are trying to take over their work!

"It's not about being at the front; often it's rather about working as a facilitator, spotting the trends, identifying possible market opportunities, and being prepared. In the example I spoke of earlier, when the business said 'we need to work with an association for deaf people,' we were already there. So part of our role is about opening doors, making the right connections for our business with society.

Telefónica operates in some very diverse regions. How has the international nature of the business shaped your CSR and Community Involvement strategy?

AA: "Every part of the planet has its own view, public agenda, and priorities, so I believe it's impossible to have just one theme to suit the world. Initially, our focus on 'achieving leadership in the DJSI' was a simple message to transmit throughout the organization. Now, as we have built up over eight years, we have evolved into a three-step approach.

"First, using Global Compact and GRI[2] Indicators, our businesses report on these all over the world. Second, we identified what were the main areas of priority for a telecoms company. We did this through our involvement in the global telecoms sustainability forum, GeSI,[3] which had identified the hot topics our industry faces in the coming years – accessibility, child protection, climate change, and electro-magnetic fields. A real mix of CSR and community issues.

"Finally, each market can then also focus on its local projects. With this perspective, each country identifies their focus areas and projects relevant to their community. The reality is that child protection is a hot topic in Europe, but less so in some Latin American countries. Meanwhile, climate change is a big issue in Northern Europe, it's middle agenda in Spain, and lower down in South America. This way, each country can then put the right emphasis on its locally relevant issues.

"This does not mean every market does only what it wants. Our CSR Strategy has 13 key projects that must be implemented in every market by 2012. These cover areas such as human rights, child protection, supply chain, and climate charge."

Isn't it complex to have so many projects going on?

AA: "This is one big umbrella focused on building a trustworthy relationship with our stakeholders to reduce business risk.

"Expectations change. Six years ago no one talked about child protection. Now they do. In the future, it will be a must-have. Where it comes to energy efficiency with mobiles, today it's a nice-to-have. In three years, it could be a must-have. The main challenge is about being transparent and showing stakeholders that we are evolving every year."

---

2 Global Reporting Initiative, www.globalreporting.org/AboutGRI, accessed December 2009.
3 Global e-Sustainability Initiative (GeSI) dedicated to information and communication technologies (ICT) sustainability through innovation; www.gesi.org, accessed December 2009.

What support do you get from your senior managers?

AA: "We have had a role devoted to CSR and reputation in the Board of Directors since 2002. When we started work in this area eight years ago, no one had any official responsibility assigned. Now, in every country, we have a team of two or three people. This is great progress, but there are still challenges. I'm satisfied that our top managers' belief in the importance of CSR is deep enough but I still want to improve our company culture regarding CSR and Sustainability issues. Of course we manage this via formal processes, but it's also about the informal side, and there you have to influence and work on it every day.

"I think this is the nature with all 'intangible' functions. Getting to the top of DJSI helps us so much as it's a key argument for our investors. Linking CSR and Sustainability to our investors means you can speak the language that any Board of Directors, not just ours, will understand. That will always guarantee their support, and this is our responsibility and our main challenge: to be an enabler for our business units and a tool to create confidence in Telefónica in our markets."

Engaging and working with your core business

It is possible for you to sit behind closed doors in your own department, create some good Community Involvement projects for your company and be happy. We believe this is not enough. You need more. You need business integration. Why?

From a CR perspective, a company will never be a leader if, although it has solid community activities, Community Involvement is not integrated into the company's core business and operations. Moreover, if there is no Business Case behind what you do, why should the company bother doing it? Real leadership in Community Involvement means it is integrated into all parts of your business, rather than remaining on the periphery.

Start by focusing on the societal impact

Companies exist to make a profit but, in doing so, they can no longer ignore the consequences of their actions. They need to proactively manage their societal, including their community, impact on the core regions where the company operates. The difference between Community Involvement and societal impact is that societal impact is about the bigger picture. It covers a company's overall impact on society – for example, through its products, the taxes it pays, and how it manages its supply chain, as well as the relationships it has in its communities.

When looking at your company's impact on its communities, consider both the positive and negative. Look at where the risks are, but also ask: What are the business and societal-enhancing opportunities that Community Involvement can contribute to?

Cover all areas of your business. While every company is different, this chapter covers what we consider to be the three areas common to almost every business. These are where existing activities have a community impact already, or where almost any business could benefit by doing more. The three areas are:

1. **The impact that building and running company operations has on local communities**

This covers not just production, manufacturing, and industrial operations, but also where your company has its office-based workers. Your company will have a community impact, and it will need to take responsibility for it. In short, it needs to be a "good neighbor."

From the community perspective, this can be relatively straightforward. For example, your business could be building new offices employing 1,000 people in a business park on the outskirts of Manchester, England. Or your company could be poised to enter Equatorial Guinea in Africa to set up a gas exploration and production operation – a far riskier proposition.

2. **Marketing your company's products or services**

There are two key areas for Community Involvement: cause-related marketing and sponsorships. If your company already does either of these activities, how can you bring as sophisticated a Community Involvement approach as possible to them? If it does not do them yet, can you develop Community Involvement ideas that would excite your Marketing and Sales colleagues enough to want to work with you to create something?

3. **The 'people' side, otherwise known as Human Resources**

Community Involvement can increase employee pride in and identification with the company, enhancing recruitment efforts and contributing to the personal development of your employees.

Please note that you may also wish to engage your Business Development and R&D colleagues. However, work with those departments is not about a need to integrate Community Involvement into their day-to-day roles, but rather to get their input when developing community strategy and profile projects. See Chapter 6 for more on this.

Business benefit is critical

Your objective should be that your CEO or the vice president or director of the business area you want to work with are fully supportive of whatever Community Involvement initiatives you want to undertake. This should not be just because they have a personal passion for it, but because you have shown them how it will contribute to their business.

Start by thinking from the perspective of those departments that you want to engage with. Think about what priorities occupy their minds and how you can bring your Community Involvement context to those. Ask yourself: What's in it for them?

Consider this on both a departmental and personal level for the people you want to work with (including the CEO, vice president, or director). If you can't answer this question – ideally from both perspectives – then do not be surprised if they do not seem interested in working together.

In engaging any business area, follow these six steps:

1. **What's the issue?** What stakeholder or community-related issues does a particular business area need to address? Is there some controversy, perhaps nationally or in the local community, that could put business operations at risk?

   Research the national or local press and go online to see what's being discussed. Alternatively, see if there is any feedback from the local community. Has your business met with any local councilors or politicians (perhaps through your political lobbying department)? Are there any local NGOs that someone should speak to (and may not have done)? Before you go out and meet any stakeholders, coordinate your approach with other colleagues from your business. If you do not have a close relationship, now is the time to invite your Communications, Public Affairs, and Strategy department colleagues for a cup of coffee.

2. Then ask, **what's the opportunity?** Are there things your business could do that it's missing out on? Look at what your competitors do and companies with similar challenges in other industries. Whether in your market or in another country, it is likely someone, somewhere, has been through a similar situation before.

   When you consider what your competitors are doing, there are three routes to follow: avoid their mistakes, adapt their best community practice, and even consider working with them. The right approach will depend on your company's circumstances. While they may be your deadliest competitors, there are times when it makes sense for all companies in an industry to work together.

   For example, if several oil firms are exploring in the same country, they could collectively fund a local university engineering department to develop the technical skills needed for people to work in their industry. They share the costs, they do not lose any competitive advantage, and all benefit. Obviously when thinking about it for your company, do not go and talk to your competitors without the full support of your colleagues!

3. **Brainstorm**, thinking from a Community Involvement perspective, some possible solutions that could help the business area, based on what you have found out. This way you have at least a rough idea of how your work can make a difference before going to speak with colleagues in the area.

4. Then, and only then, **engage your colleagues from the target business** area. You may want to start with a junior contact to better understand the challenges they face or, better, speak with the senior management. You need their buy-in, so never leave engaging senior people until too late. With a mandate from "the boss," the project managers you will need to speak to will be much more accommodating. The key to success is in finding the right way to get your colleagues' attention. Maybe from your research you have found something that happened to a similar industry or competitor. This poses a perfect opportunity to approach them and ask what their plans are to avoid it happening in your company. Come prepared with some potential solutions.

5. Once you have a "license" from them to get involved, only then **start to engage and work with the business.** Take a systematic approach to develop what is needed. Besides particular community initiatives, consider what community or societal policies, standards or guidelines may be required, as well as any systems to monitor your community projects' implementation to show that it works.

6. Even if you did engage them earlier on, **secure senior management buy-in** before your initiative goes live (and even before critical development points in your project are reached). You need their support of the community work as it shows to other employees that this is an important activity for the company. The level of senior manager to engage depends on the community area you're addressing. It may be a director of a site or business area or it could be the CEO. Do not be afraid to go as high in the chain of command as necessary or beneficial.

> **Tip**
>
> Remember when working with people in a particular business area, even if they have not developed a community solution themselves, they may have some good community experience. Look out for this and try to build on it. Recognizing the positive aspects of what has been done before is better for building acceptance than ignoring or being critical of it.
>
> Other parts of this book can also help when thinking about this. Chapter 11 covers overcoming challenges and instituting change while Chapter 10, on Communications, provides tools to develop your internal communications and engagement strategy.

When and how should you try to integrate Community Involvement into a business area?

No one time is best, but a good principle is "earlier than you might think." Table 5.1 outlines useful principles to follow for the different business areas.

Building and running operations

When a company is building a new operation, how it relates to the local community is crucial in delivering a project on time, within budget, and with ongoing local support. Once an operation is up and running, maintaining good community relationships remains important because:

- It ensures the community's acceptance in keeping operations going.

- It helps in being able to recruit the right people from the local area.

- At worst, should things go wrong, there is a source of goodwill in the local community. People will be more understanding and willing to help.

Table 5.1   **When and how to integrate Community Involvement into a business area**

Business area	When to engage	How to engage – building your case
Building new sites	During the planning phase, definitely before any work has started. Work with the people developing the project to help them understand societal risks and opportunities	• Environmental assessments are usually a legal requirement but social ones are not. Do basic research yourself, then get the business to undertake some form of Social Impact Assessment (SIA) • The complexity of the SIA will depend on the type of community issues your business will face. This could range from desktop research in a low-risk country to, most complex, a Strategic Impact Assessment (for huge projects, trans-boundary with big macroeconomic as well as local community issues, e.g., BP's BTC pipeline)*
Running opera-tions	Any time once the operation is up and running	• Show how Community Involvement can help. Is there a need to motivate employees where other methods have not worked? Is there a problem with relations with the local community? • If it has been established for some time, the site manager will question why anything needs to change. Review the community activity with him or her to see how it can be improved or scaled up
Marketing	In the development phase of a marketing strategy, before any plans get proposed	• Understand your company's brand positioning, any research/insight into customers' needs and expectations, and the marketing and sales strategy • Find examples of other companies' community-related marketing and sales projects to share with colleagues as convincing best practice (e.g., Nike's community-building initiative at Nikeplus, bringing consumers with a common interest together)†
Human Resources	When they are developing their recruitment or personnel development plans. Less time-critical than when engaging Marketing, as many HR processes are ongoing, not campaign-driven	• Understand your company's HR strategy and how internal issues (e.g., employee or team skills) and external pressures (e.g., demographic changes or an industry-wide skills deficit) affect your business' needs • Look at your company's employee research or hold informal employee focus groups.‡

*   Baku–Tbilisi–Ceyhan pipeline, 1,768 km long, spanning three countries; www.bp.com/ sectiongenericarticle.do?categoryId=9006669&contentId=7015093, accessed December 2009.

†   www.nikeplus.com, accessed December 2009.

‡   A focus group is a form of qualitative research. It brings together a group of people who are asked about their attitude towards a product, service, advertisement, concept, idea, or social program. Questions are asked in an interactive group setting. Participants are free to talk with other group members.

'Developed' and 'developing' countries

While good Community Involvement has different requirements for different industries, the challenges are greater when operations are in developing rather than developed countries. If you are operating in a country with an established rule of law, which has a democratic political process, relatively high and equally distributed levels of wealth, and transparent processes between business, society, and government, inevitably it will be more straightforward to get things done. In a developing country, your company may need to contribute to the establishment of such processes and infrastructure.[4]

That said, do not assume that operations in all developed countries will be straightforward. When industrial businesses with operations in both developed and developing markets undertake risk analyses of where the societal challenges will be greatest, Italy and Australia can emerge as two countries with risks as great as those of an African country.

Why? Transparency International[5] ranks Italy 55th in its Corruption Perceptions Index, lower than you might expect for one of the G8.[6] While Australia ranks much higher in Transparency International's ratings (ninth), it has certain laws and heritage issues that bring added complexity. Protecting the rights of its indigenous people and preserving natural wonders like the Great Barrier Reef mean companies are expected to do everything possible to limit their environmental and societal impact.

The challenges also vary by industry. For example, the extractive sectors (e.g., mining, oil, and gas) have the biggest immediate impact on the environment and local communities and typically take place in parts of the world with the weakest societal infrastructure. As a result of many high-profile controversies, companies in this sector have now developed sophisticated approaches to managing societal issues.

A societal impact management system

Many leading companies have now developed a management system for societal issues consisting of societal policies, standards, guidelines, and reporting and review processes.

For companies without such a system, an excellent starting point and a common baseline are the International Finance Corporation's Environmental and Social Standards.[7] The IFC applies these standards to all the projects it finances to minimize their impact on the environment and on affected communities. These standards define the roles and responsibilities of the IFC and its client companies.

---

4 Please note we are using the term "developing countries" as a commonly used generic description for lack of a better expression to describe a country that is missing some of those elements outlined above. "So-called developing countries" may be a better, albeit longer, phrase. After all, some places can have fewer societal problems than those seen in countries typically called "developed."

5 A global civil society organization leading a fight against corruption; www.transparency.org.

6 www.transparency.org/news_room/in_focus/2008/cpi2008/cpi_2008_table, accessed December 2009.

7 www.ifc.org/ifcext/sustainability.nsf/Content/EnvSocStandards, accessed December 2009.

BG Group Social Performance Standard

The BG Group has implemented a group-wide Social Performance Standard and Management System, building on the IFC's performance standards.* The Standard is aligned to their business principles and has nine parts:

- Socio-economic Baseline Assessment
- Impact Assessment
- Consultation
- Land Acquisition and Involuntary Resettlement
- Indigenous Peoples and Vulnerable Groups
- Cultural Heritage
- Social Investment
- Social Performance Plans
- Management, Integration, and Metrics

This Standard is then supported by a number of guidelines that cover, in more detail, the "what you need to do" to meet the policy and standard.

The Standard includes a number of Social Performance metrics, covering both the process involved and the outcome. This tracks how effectively the Standard is implemented in the business and also gives guidance on what areas operations may be missing out on.

* bgara.blacksunplc.com/ara/business_review/society.html, accessed December 2009.

In particular, look at the IFC's Policy on Social and Environmental Sustainability.[8] It is an excellent starting point for developing your company's own policy. However, remember that the right (Board-approved) policy is only a first step. It is then down to the systems, processes, and training you put in place to make sure employees both understand the policy and implement it properly.

The BG Group Standard (see Box above) is relatively short, easy to use, but still comprehensive. Other companies have gone much further. Arguably the multinational mining group, Anglo American, has set the benchmark through its Socio-Economic Assessment Toolbox (SEAT) (see Box opposite). It is open to debate whether SEAT is too comprehensive to be easy to use, but Anglo American deserves praise for setting the benchmark and for making it available for use by any other company (subject to not breaching its copyright). Download a copy and decide for yourself.

Operations in developing countries

The same principles that guide good community relationships in developing countries are equally applicable, but perhaps toned down a little, to other countries. For industrial businesses in developing countries, we recommend an excellent book by Luc

8 www.ifc.org/ifcext/sustainability.nsf/Content/SustainabilityPolicy, accessed December 2009.

Anglo American's SEAT

This is a comprehensive process for managing the socio-economic impact of Anglo American's operations.*

Launched in 2003 and enhanced in 2007, SEAT is in place in 60 Anglo American sites in 16 countries. Its key steps include:

- Profiling company operations and the host community
- Identifying and engaging with key stakeholders
- Assessing the impact of operations – both positive and negative – and the community's key socio-economic development needs
- Developing a management plan to mitigate any negative aspects of the company's presence and to make the most of the benefits its operations bring
- Working with stakeholders and communities to address development challenges they would face even without the company's presence
- Producing a report with stakeholders to form the basis for ongoing engagement with and support for the community

SEAT is rolled out through an ongoing training program reaching several hundred relevant employees a year.

* www.angloamerican.co.uk/aa/development/society/engagement/seat, accessed December 2009.

Zandvliet and Mary Anderson: *Getting it Right: Making Corporate Community Relations Work.*[9] The book includes insights from almost everyone involved in or affected by the extractive industries, from companies and governments to communities and NGOs. In addition to setting up the policies and systems we outlined earlier, the authors provide practical guidance to "get it right." They outline (Chapter 1) a framework for analyzing community relations (see Figure 5.1) focused on three types of policy and practice areas: benefits distribution; company behavior; and side effects:

- **Benefits distribution**. This involves all benefits a company will bring to a community through its operations, both directly and indirectly:
  - **Directly.** Particularly important is having the right policies and systems in place to manage benefits issues, especially those covering potentially controversial areas such as hiring, compensation, and contractors.
  - **Indirectly.** For example, how can a company, through its presence, encourage positive government interventions in the community or help limit bad ones?

  A key principle, often missed by companies, is that of ensuring long-term "fairness" in a community. This is about having an equitable, not necessarily

---

9 Luc Zandvliet and Mary Anderson, *Getting it Right: Making Corporate Community Relations Work* (Sheffield, UK: Greenleaf Publishing, 2009).

Figure 5.1 **Framework for analysis of corporate–community relations**

Negative impacts	Principles for getting it wrong	Policies and practices	Principles for getting it right	Positive impacts
Communities 1. Inter- or intra-group fragmentation or division 2. Worsening quality of life (livelihood, security, disease, culture) 3. Sense of being disrespected 4. Rewarding violence or threats of violence **Government** 5. Substitution 6. Increasing likelihood of human rights abuses	**Unfair** **Non-transparent** **Disrespectful** **Uncaring** **Non-transparent** **Narrow accountability** **Non-transparent**	Benefits distribution Behavior Side effects	**Fair** **Transparent** **Respectful** **Caring** **Transparent** **Broad accountability** **Transparent**	**Communities** 1. Inter- or intra-group cohesion and cooperation 2. Improved quality of life (livelihood, security, disease, culture) 3. Sense of being respected 4. Rewarding constructive action for mutual benefit **Government** 5. Increasing the capacity of government to provide services and security 6. Reducing human rights abuses

Corporate assumptions → Corporate assumptions

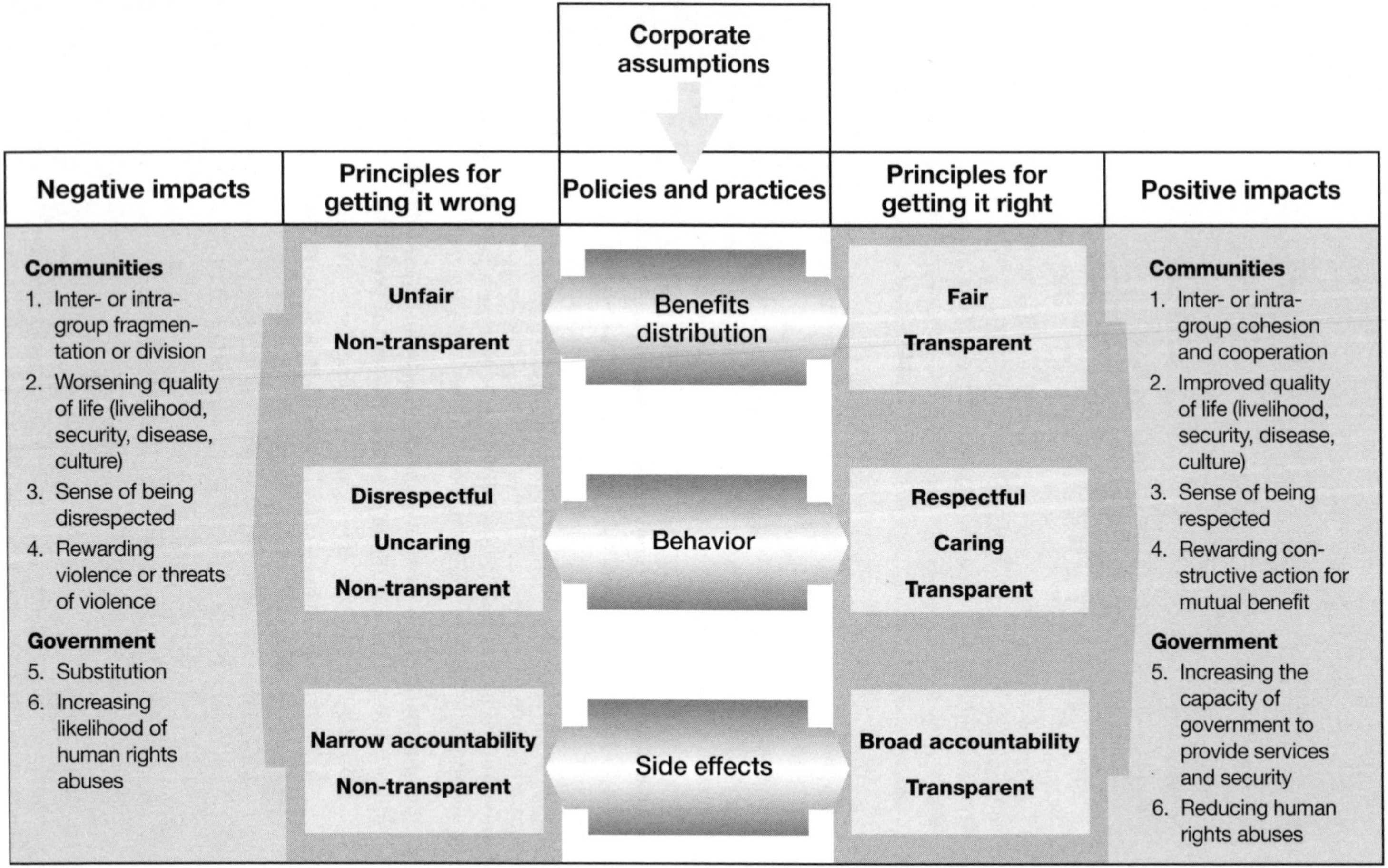

Source: Luc Zandvliet and Mary Anderson, *Getting it Right: Making Corporate Community Relations Work* (Sheffield, UK: Greenleaf Publishing, 2009): 17.

an "equal," distribution of fairness. The company needs to understand how this is defined by the community concerned. For instance, a company's preference for employing the most talented is often perceived as unfair by community members, who feel that jobs that are rightly theirs go to "outsiders." The company needs to take such actions openly, explaining its approach and, where possible, taking steps to help address long-term local employability.

- **Corporate behavior**. How a company behaves and interacts with communities on a daily basis can send implicit positive or damaging messages.

  Poor behaviors can include maintaining a distance from local people by placing an emphasis on security, or not taking the time to stop and speak to people. What has been seen to work time and again is when a company and its representatives demonstrate respect, trust, and caring in all their interactions with the local community. Such community relations behaviors can be embedded in a company's standard operating procedures and tracked with indicators: for example, a company has local support when there are low or decreasing levels of theft and damage of company property.

- **Side effects.** This is about the consequences of a company's presence in the community.

  There are many indirect changes when a company begins operation in a community – from environmental impacts to the community suddenly having more money. Companies need to plan ahead and take responsibility for these effects, working with communities to prepare for them. For example, with sudden increases in wealth, a company could offer local personal financial management sessions, so that once-poor communities know how to manage their new-found wealth.

Zandvliet and Anderson advocate three elements of engagement when undertaking community consultation and maintaining positive relationships. They are:

1. **Relationship.** Build up your relationship with local communities before getting into the detail of what it is the company wants.

2. **Procedure.** Next, once the relationship is established, develop and agree with the community and implement a transparent procedure to manage the discussions.

3. **Content.** Finally, pursue the issues the company needs to discuss and agree with the community.[10]

The elements of engagement should be followed in this order of priority. Unfortunately, because companies are results-focused, their order of importance is often reversed, so they jump into content issues first, often leading to failed relationships and long-term disagreements.

---

10 Zandvliet and Anderson, *op. cit.*: Ch. 9.

Global Business Coalition on HIV/AIDS, Tuberculosis, and Malaria

Taking the first step to build the right relationships in a community may involve working with the Global Business Coalition (GBC), a coalition of more than 220 companies united to keep the fight against HIV/AIDS, tuberculosis, and malaria a global priority. Any company working in countries heavily affected by these diseases needs to protect its workers (and operations) and contribute to community health as part of its responsibilities in supporting that society. GBC's central function is "to bring actionable knowledge to members, and bring members together to take action."*

All member companies are expected to undertake advocacy, join in partnerships with other companies and the non-corporate sector, pursue cross-sector action for prevention and treatment, and show real results. The GBC provides them with tailored support and a range of services. Its membership includes businesses in the extractive, transportation, and pharmaceutical industries, as well as manufacturers active in most affected regions.

Automotive company Daimler is a founding member of GBC. Since 2000, Daimler in South Africa has managed a workplace program that addresses the challenge posed by the disease to company employees, their families, business operations, and social and economic development. The program, which has received numerous awards, includes information, training and preventive measures, voluntary counseling and testing, and comprehensive HIV/AIDS treatment and care (including access to anti-retroviral treatment) for employees and family members.†

* www.gbcimpact.org, accessed December 2009.
† www.mercedes-benzsa.co.za/mercedes-benzsa/portal/portalsintegra/Modules_FE/Layout1/hiv.asp?ID=159&menu=2&submenu=4, accessed December 2009.

It's not just the Community Involvement Manager's job

Community Involvement, like so many parts of CR, needs to be seen as a core part of your business. It is the responsibility of many, not just one department. This is especially true in the area of building and running operations.

To do this work professionally, you need to work with people responsible for different parts of local operations. The more those who interact with the community – from the site manager to the local security guard – know the right way to behave, the more likely you are to achieve positive community relations. If you have difficulty persuading company employees to pay attention to this, get feedback from local stakeholders of how a certain department's actions are damaging the company's community relationships and make that feedback known inside the company.

As society's expectations of business increase, it is becoming more important than ever to pursue a professional approach to the operative side of Community Involvement.

Integrating Community Involvement into Marketing

Community Involvement has an important role to play in a company's interaction with its customers. Over the past decade, extensive research[11] has shown that customers want to see that the company behind a given brand has a social conscience and acts on it. From the company's perspective, there is a strong business incentive to create a powerful, emotional connection with the customer.

We will now look at how you can trigger excitement for Community Involvement in Marketing departments or, if you are from Marketing yourself, what you can do. When considering how a company can incorporate Community Involvement into its Marketing activities, two areas stand out: cause-related marketing and sponsorships.

Cause-related marketing and Community Involvement

We will touch on only the key elements of cause-related marketing (CRM) as, if you are interested in the topic in detail, it is comprehensively covered in the business bestseller *Brand Spirit*.[12]

CRM can be used for commercial benefits and as a strategic brand-positioning tool. It is never motivated by pure philanthropy. The brand is linked to a relevant social cause. For every product purchased, a certain percentage will be donated by the company, on behalf of the consumer, to the company's chosen cause.

This achieves multiple benefits. For the company, it promotes a product, while differentiating the brand and positively impacting consumer purchasing behavior. The cause itself receives attention and funding. The non-profit partner organization representing the cause receives free PR. And last, but not least, the consumers benefit in that, at no cost to themselves, they make a contribution to a cause they care about. CRM tends to work better for fast-moving consumer goods (e.g., diapers, toilet paper, water bottles) than goods that move more slowly (e.g., cars or furniture).

CRM should also create a match between the consumer's personal values and the brand's values. The research we referred to earlier has shown that consumers prefer and reward brands that support causes of which they approve. Well-known examples are McDonald's Ronald McDonald House charities, British Airways' "Change for Good" campaign, Nike's "Livestrong" campaign in support of Lance Armstrong's cancer foundation, or Volvic's "One Liter for Ten Liters" campaign.

What are the criteria for developing a solid CRM campaign? It needs to be big enough, with a significant offering, and to incorporate a simple and creative mechanism to moti-

---

11 For examples see Ipsos MORI CSR surveys from 1999 onwards, e.g., www.ipsos-mori.com/researchpublications/researcharchive/poll.aspx?oItemId=1851, accessed December 2009; Annual Edelman Trust Barometer surveys, e.g., www.edelman.com/TRUST/2008/TrustBarometer08_FINAL.pdf; GolinHarris/*Change* survey, "Doing Well by Doing Good 2005," www.volunteermatch.org/corporations/resources/docs/GH_CCS_2005.pdf, accessed December 2009; Germany: GoodBrand Survey 2006, "Ethical Consumer Behavior and Cause-Related Marketing," csr-news.net/main/2006/09/21/cause-related-marketing-good-brands-work-n-germany-too, accessed December 2009.

12 Hamish Pringle and Marjorie Thompson, *Brand Spirit* (Hoboken, NJ: Wiley, 1999).

vate consumer participation. It also requires strong communication and promotion. And, finally, it must be evaluated rigorously against set objectives.

Let's start with an example of how a Community Involvement manager could try to enhance a classic CRM campaign. Looking at two excellent cause-related marketing initiatives: Procter & Gamble's Pampers "One Pack, One Vaccine" campaign with UNICEF, where Pampers donates the cost of one tetanus vaccine for each pack bought; and the UK and US supermarkets' locally focused giving programs, mentioned in Chapter 4, where their customers are given the chance to decide who to support and with how much.

These examples use Community Involvement to engage customers, to increase loyalty and, hopefully, to sell more goods.

Where Community Involvement can play a greater role is in working with Marketing teams to make these initiatives as sophisticated, credible, and engaging for stakeholders as possible. Below are some questions to bear in mind as you develop a campaign(s).

1. What role have you identified for employees in supporting the projects? For example, can they take part in identifying possible causes and community organizations for the company to support? Can they engage their colleagues to raise additional money? And can employees volunteer in the projects supported?

2. In what other ways can the company's customers get involved in the projects? Can they get extra customer benefits from the company by doing more to support the project? Can they volunteer, maybe even together with the company's employees, in the projects? You could integrate an element into your campaign where consumers, when they buy your product, become eligible to win a trip to experience a project first-hand and volunteer on-site.

3. What societal impact does the CRM support have? Marketers typically excel at demonstrating enhanced brand positioning, better customer relationships, and increases in sales, but what about the societal impact? What difference has the initiative and investment made? The more this can be reported – quantitatively and qualitatively – the more credible the initiative is to all stakeholders.

Another example of a community initiative that grew out of a Marketing campaign comes from the skincare product manufacturer Dove. It created an award-winning, international campaign using "real" women, rather than models, to market its products. The "Campaign for Real Beauty," as it is known, has established the Dove Self-Esteem Fund, which supports self-esteem workshops for young women, among other activities. The Fund aims to reach 5 million women by the end of 2010.[13]

Taken to an extreme, a successful CRM initiative can unite the entire business. Such a campaign requires a single, powerful theme reflecting the company values and a credible link to the company's core business. This is more than just Community Involvement, requiring many parts of a company coming together; it can even act as a rallying cry to help the whole organization become more responsible.

---

13 campaignforrealbeauty.co.uk/dsef07/t5.aspx?id=8255, accessed December 2009.

Working with your Marketing colleagues, consider the following steps to integrate Community Involvement into your company's cause-related marketing.

1. Think about how incorporating societal benefits into existing Marketing plans could meet or exceed current objectives.

2. If your company already practices Community Involvement, how can you expand the concept throughout the organization, making it a rallying cry for the company?

3. Consider what level of partnership your company has with the charity/organization(s) concerned. Is it purely contractual, or is there room to develop a more sophisticated societal relationship, accruing greater benefits to both sides?

4. Look at how your company is communicating the impact of its investment (both financial and in kind). Has the impact been effectively documented (both internally and externally)? See Chapter 10 for more information.

5. Think of how further to engage customers/consumers in the project. Do you simply want their "passive" involvement in buying a product and feeling good about that, or do you want to offer them more ways to get involved?

6. Think about the same for your employees. How can they get involved – both in fundraising and in actively volunteering in the program? The more your entire business gets behind an initiative, the more successful and credible it will be.

7. Take your company's senior managers to see the program in action. For example, get your CEO to visit the developing country project being supported.

8. Review your company's approach to measurement and evaluation for its cause-related marketing initiative, in particular the societal and community benefit. See Chapter 9 for more information.

9. Obtain wider stakeholder feedback about your company's cause-related marketing. Besides what your customers think, how do other key influencers (e.g., employees, politicians, journalists, business partners) view your efforts?

Think of Coca-Cola and its unifying focus around protecting water resources.[14] This focus has strong CRM aspects, closely aligned to the company's bottled water brands. But, after the company's Chairman and CEO announced the decision to return to communities – and to nature – an amount of water equivalent to what they use in all of their beverages and production, the theme expanded beyond CRM. It is now a core part of how Coca-Cola embraces sustainability. Another example is Coca-Cola's partnership with WWF, through which the company is improving the efficiency of its water use, particularly in its agricultural supply chain.

---

14 www.thecoca-colacompany.com/citizenship/index.html, accessed December 2009.

Not just for big business

While we have used some examples that are high-profile, bringing Community Involvement into your marketing and customer relationships should be possible for any business. Even your local bakery could donate a small portion of its profits from every loaf of bread sold to support a local school-feeding program. Key points to consider are how you could undertake a societal initiative that:

- Enhances your business
- Makes your company stand out from its competitors
- Appeals to your customers

It does not need to solve the world's problems, just be relevant to your business and, from a marketing perspective, offer something that will work for your customers, appeal to their values, and support the community.

Sponsorships and Community Involvement

When people think of corporate sponsorships, typically they think of big-name, big-money activities: the world's leading sportsmen competing for glory, or major cultural events, especially concerts, "brought to you by (brand X)."

There are many Marketing activities that companies may define as sponsorship. For example, having the company's name or products associated with a monument, or even sponsoring a leading charity. This confusion continues as you try to distinguish between what is Community Involvement and what is sponsorship. We will give you our view, but expect the debate between Marketing, Communications, and CR departments to continue around the world.

Let's start with the definition of the International Chamber of Commerce (ICC)'s International Code on Sponsorship:[15]

> Sponsorship: any commercial agreement by which a sponsor, for the mutual benefit of the sponsor and sponsored party, contractually provides financing or other support in order to establish an association between the sponsor's image, brands, or products and a sponsorship property in return for rights to promote this association and/or for the granting of certain agreed direct or indirect benefits.

In defining benefits, this description is very broad. From our experience, typical sponsorship benefits for a company include:

- Brand positioning and increased brand awareness – both directly through the vehicle being sponsored and through additional activities, either by the rights holder or the company doing the sponsoring

---

15 For the full code see www.iccwbo.org/home/statements_rules/rules/2003/International%20
Code%20on%20Sponsorship.asp, accessed December 2009.

- Customer engagement, retention, and loyalty – opportunities to engage customers and other stakeholders, including offering corporate hospitality/entertainment at events and special packages or prizes for customers

- Increased sales

The ICC's definition of sponsorship covers a wide field. For the purpose of this chapter, we will focus on the two areas of sports and arts and culture, as these offer the greatest scope for Community Involvement.

In terms of money spent, in 2008 the value of global sponsorship rights was estimated at over \$43.5 billion (about €28.7 billion),[16] of which 88% involved sports rights and 2% were spent on arts and culture. The remainder covers broadcast sponsorships (2%), "naming rights" – being able to name something, usually a property (7%), and "other," unclearly defined as "environment, community, and CSR."[17] While there is a huge gap between the sums spent on sponsoring sports compared to arts and culture, the two fields offer many opportunities for the Community Involvement Manager.

It is all about activation

We'd like to emphasize that, from a Marketing perspective, Community Involvement can be a strong part of a sponsorship's "activation," and it costs comparatively little. Activation means how a company brings its sponsorship to life. It covers a host of activities – from having company-branded marketing collateral such as t-shirts and posters, through to events, corporate hospitality, and running additional projects to emphasize certain parts of the company's sponsorship, typically aligned to the company's brand positioning. This is where the possibility of running relevant community programs comes in. But, to achieve that, you have to justify why money should be invested in a community initiative rather than any other form of activation, and how it can be more effectively spent there.

How much to spend on activation is debated heavily in the sponsorship world. What is clear is that companies typically underspend and fail to bring their sponsorship to life. Sponsorship best practice strongly advocates that companies should spend at least as much on activation as they have spent on acquiring the sponsorship property.

There are two steps to integrating Community Involvement activities effectively. First, look at the sponsorship property and identify what links it could have to the local community. Consider this from the perspective of where the company's customers are, where the business is located and, of course, where the sponsorship is taking place. Put priority on whatever the company's primary motivation was behind undertaking the sponsorship in the first place.

If you have a sports sponsorship, could athletes talk to children in local schools about the "life skills" it takes to succeed, such as practice and concentration, discipline and courage, team spirit and perseverance? Could you then communicate their involvement to relevant audiences, telling the story, showing the pictures?

---

16 Source: IEG; for more information, see www.sponsorship.com.
17 TWSM, published by Sports Marketing Surveys; see www.theworldsponsorshipmonitor.com, accessed December 2009.

Second, consider what benefits could be realized by doing this. The above example will fill your sponsorship with life and give it "heart." Another benefit is for the company to be differentiated from others by having a strong Community Involvement initiative as part of its sponsorship. This is particularly useful when the property being sponsored is in a crowded sponsorship arena, such as when your company and several other companies all sponsor the same big sports events, or art exhibitions in the same city.

For art exhibitions, consider a famous artist (or artists) working with local children on creating a piece of art together, for example a public mural, which can then be shown in the presence of the artist, the children, and company stakeholders at an opening event. For example, Finnish artist Osmo Rauhala worked with high-school students in New York to produce a mural that was sponsored by Nokia.[18]

Another great example comes from the cell phone company Orange, which runs the Orange Rockcorps. Through this initiative, young people receive concert tickets in exchange for four hours of volunteer work at an Orange Rockcorps Community project in their area. To date, over 40,000 people have donated their time (e.g., repainting buildings and play areas) and benefited from free tickets to over 20 concerts.[19]

An additional reason to incorporate a Community Involvement element into a sponsorship is to add credibility to the sponsorship and to the company. Increasingly, companies cannot be seen to be sponsoring with the sole purpose of getting their logo "out there." A credible Community Involvement program can help address this while providing opportunities for raising brand awareness and for customer/stakeholder engagement.

Once you have done some thinking yourself, engage your Marketing colleagues. With their market research expertise, they should be able to decide whether a concept works for their customers and help you to build a case for Community Involvement in the sponsorship. You may also want to work with creative marketing or specialist sponsorship agencies to help develop engaging community opportunities. Then test these concepts with the sponsorship property owners.

To show how this works in practice, here are two more examples of sponsorship-driven community involvement being brought to life – one from the sports world, one from arts:

- Fast food retailer McDonald's in the UK has been the official community partner of the Football Association since 2002. Their motivation to do this came from the local presence of McDonald's restaurants, the popularity of football, and the strong likelihood that a majority of customers and their children would participate. Since 2002, the company has helped to recruit and train over 13,000 volunteer community football coaches across the country – and has widened its brand appeal to reach different parts of society. New volunteer coaches include mothers, policemen, and even priests.[20]

---

18 www.osmorauhala.net/index.php?mid=9&pid=25, accessed December 2009.
19 www.orangerockcorps.co.uk, accessed December 2009.
20 www.mcdonalds.co.uk/sports/coaching/coaches.shtml, accessed December 2009.

- International bank HSBC's "Cultural Exchange," a global arts sponsorship initiative, is active in over 20 countries. In Indonesia, the initiative supports the Imogiri Batik School, among other projects. After a 2006 earthquake destroyed the Batik painting and production center at Imogiri, HSBC helped to restore this museum and workshop, enabling 100 skilled Batik painters to return to work.[21]

The sponsorship world is still establishing its relationship to the concept of CR, and not all sponsorships integrate it yet. We know of at least one multinational sponsorship that could not offer a sponsorship package featuring any CR or Community Involvement elements, as its only business model was based on the value of broadcasting rights.

However, this is changing. Increasingly, the enlightened holders of sponsorship rights see adding Community Involvement activation as the next opportunity in effective sponsoring. Rights holders such as FIFA (International Federation of Association Football)[22] will integrate social content into their sponsorships and share the costs with the sponsors. This is the way forward for sponsors, as acknowledged by one of the leading sponsorship consultancies, brandRapport: "in doing so, [sponsorship rights holders] will be taking a long-term ethical view that realizes that if it's good for the sport or community they're working in, then ultimately it will benefit their own enterprise."[23]

Finally, you need to demonstrate – to society and the company – that the Community Involvement element of the sponsorship not only counts, but also makes a difference. We will keep coming back to measurement and evaluation as an integral part of all Community Involvement activities (see Chapter 9 for detailed information). It is especially important in the context of Marketing and Sales activity to put measurement and evaluation processes in place from the start. If a company cannot show the benefit it is bringing to society through its actions, its efforts will have been in vain and not taken seriously. Equally, showing the link between Community Involvement and brand awareness and preference, customer loyalty, or even booming sales will guarantee future, bigger community investments from the Marketing side.

A final word on having integrity and credibility when undertaking Community Involvement as part of Marketing and Sales. If your core business operations and behaviors are not run in a sustainable, responsible, ethical manner, you can undertake as many Marketing and Sales initiatives as you like, but your customers, as well as the wider society, will not take you seriously!

What it means to be seen as an ethical business varies slightly by industry, but research by GfK[24] and others has shown a fairly consistent pattern across many sectors. In addition to treating employees fairly, ethical brands are defined, largely, by the following criteria:

---

21 www.hsbcculturalexchange.com/indonesia_2.php, accessed December 2009.
22 www.fifa.com/aboutfifa/worldwideprograms/index.html, accessed December 2009.
23 Taken from "Who Pays the Bill?" by Rob Pope, brandRapport, *SportBusiness International*, July 2009.
24 One of the largest market research companies in the world (www.gfk.com).

- Avoiding harm and/or limiting their impact on the environment
- Treating producers/suppliers fairly by ensuring good working conditions and paying a fair price for local products (broadly defined as "fair trade")
- Not working with governments or investing in companies that do not uphold basic human rights
- Honesty in marketing and communications[25]

Are any of these areas problematic in your company? If so, address them first before getting Marketing and Sales to play up your company's customer-centric community commitment.

The world's ten most valuable brands in 2008, rated by BusinessWeek and Interbrand,[26] are Coca-Cola, IBM, Microsoft, GE, Nokia, Toyota, Intel, McDonald's, Disney, and Google. All excel in their overall Corporate Responsibility and Community Involvement.

Integrating Community Involvement into Human Resources

Our final category is the connection Community Involvement has to employees, typically through what is called HR or Personnel. There are three areas that good Community Involvement can have a profoundly positive impact on:

- Employee pride in and identification with the company
- Employee skills and team development
- Employee recruitment

Employee pride in and identification with the company

Pride and identification tend to be an indirect positive effect rather than one that is the primary driver for community initiatives. Having the support of senior managers – particularly those that approve the funding for your projects – is important, but even more satisfying is when employees are proud of what the company does and actively involved in its community projects. Employee enthusiasm is one of the criteria that will secure the continuation of projects from senior managers. HR will feel good that your activities are contributing to employee retention and loyalty, increasingly important for companies competing for the best employees.

There are two ways to go about gaining such support. The first is to create an initiative so good that everyone feels an almost instant affinity with it. This requires creative communications (as well as an amazing project that is well designed and evaluated). The

---

25 Taken from Chris Davis and Corinne Moy, "The Dawn of the Ethical Brand," *Admap Magazine*, June 2007.
26 bwnt.businessweek.com/interactive_reports/global_brand_2008, accessed December 2009.

second, and more typical, way is to get employees to experience the community work that you do. This can be done directly, via Employee Volunteering opportunities in your projects (see Chapter 8), or indirectly, by involving people they know. You could involve their friends or family. For instance, if you have an education program for children, why not run a family day at your offices so employees' children can take part?

Anecdotal feedback from employees about the importance of programs is one indicator of employee pride and identification and, as shown in our GlaxoSmithKline interview in Chapter 10, an effective way to secure the support of an incoming CEO.

It is important to put in place robust measurement processes to demonstrate your projects' value to employees. Try to obtain a mix of quantitative and qualitative feedback. For example, use your company's annual employee opinion survey to ask employees whether they know of and how proud they are of their company's involvement in X project. Alternatively, run mini focus groups with participants before and after their participation as volunteers to get feedback. Chapter 9 will give you further practical information.

Employee pride and identification will be shaped not only by the actions of a company in its community. If the pay, the kind of work, working conditions, and other material and intangible benefits are not right, even the most compelling community programs won't boost employee pride and identification. But, for the company that is already doing well in these areas, the right Community Involvement can make a good company great.

Community Involvement to develop employees' skills

Volunteering in Community Involvement projects can play an important role in employee and team skills development, serving as a low-cost tool to develop the following skills:

- Planning and organization
- Leadership and management
- Effective communication
- Teamworking
- Motivation and involvement of people
- Time management
- Budget management/decision-making
- Creativity/innovation
- Measurement and monitoring
- Diversity awareness

Employee Volunteering can be integrated into your company's HR learning and development systems very effectively. Table 5.2 is an example taken from part of an Employee Volunteering skills matrix used by E.ON UK in 2005 and shows how, in this case, various types of employee mentoring programs helped strengthen employees' skills in what E.ON identified as core company behaviors:

Table 5.2 **Employee Involvement skills matrix**

Volunteering task	What	Time commitment	Eligibility	Benefits	Skills
Right to Read	Literacy support for primary school (age 4–11) pupils	1 hour per month	All employees	• Networking opportunities • Time management • Communication • Coaching skills • Planning and organizing	• Analyzing and problem solving • Diversity management • Communication • Building relationships • Drive and initiative
Student Mentoring	Befriending secondary school (age 11–18) pupils. Acting as a role model	1 hour per month	All employees	• Interpersonal skills • Coaching skills • Acting as a role model • Communication • Planning and organizing	• Analyzing and problem solving • Diversity management • Communication • Building relationships • Drive and initiative

Depending on the level of support you have from HR, there are many ways to bring Employee Volunteering to life. Like E.ON, several companies have aligned the volunteering opportunities they offer with a skills matrix, so employees can be certain they are meeting their personal development needs through the type of volunteering they pursue. Think about working with your HR colleagues to do this for your company and make sure you have a process to measure the effectiveness of such employee development.

Creating excellent Employee Involvement is covered in detail in Chapter 8. It is worth considering how to use it at all levels of the organization by offering sophisticated types of volunteering. Everyone benefits, from new employees just beginning their careers to the seasoned executives with MBAs who are looking to broaden their skills. We know of a top BMW manager who worked for a few weeks as a volunteer in a drug-counseling agency. He claimed the experience changed his life, his personal insights, and his commitment to society.

Recruiting employees and developing the employees of the future

The final opportunity to integrate Employee Involvement into HR is via the recruitment process. Truly you are now in the domain of the HR department and, similar to working with Marketing colleagues, the role of the Community Involvement Manager here is about helping HR colleagues realize community-relevant opportunities rather than creating and running such projects by yourself.

Work with your HR colleagues to look at recruiting not only from the usual sources. Companies, especially big firms, have a number of standard recruitment channels, including job advertisements, recruitment agencies, headhunters, their own employees, and exhibitions. Unfortunately, everyone is chasing the same recruitment paths while the pool of "talent," especially in the Western world, is contracting. For example, Germany faces a major demographic challenge. Estimates put forward by the Institute for Employment Research (IAB) indicate that the potential labor force (labor supply) will shrink more than twice as fast as the overall population from 2010 to 2050.[27]

Would it not be better to find alternative sources of motivated employees? Can you do this while also meeting societal needs by improving the overall employability of the community? This is a route some companies are pursuing by targeting those typically seen as "unemployable." For example, how can you get the long-term unemployed back into work? What about those with disabilities? Or those recently out of prison?

These groups have great potential and, with the right support, skills, and confidence, they can become highly talented, loyal employees. Meanwhile the company gets the added benefit of improved reputation by making a major societal contribution.

Of course this is not easy. It requires changes to the typical recruitment process and the skills of the people managing it. On-the-job training for new employees will need to be revised with the right support in place inside the company to ensure such people come, contribute, and want to stay. The good news is: there is considerable support – both in expertise and financially – from governments and local agencies.

Two programs in the UK run by leading employers show this in action:

- Since 2004, retailer Marks & Spencer has run Marks & Start, a work experience program for the homeless, disabled, single parents, and the young unemployed in which the company partners with NGOs such as DisabledGo, Business Action on Homelessness, Gingerbread, and the Prince's Trust. Every year, 650 people go through the program, which involves a two- or four-week work placement, usually in Marks & Spencer stores, but occasionally also in their offices. In addition to structured training, participants have the day-to-day support of a coach and a "buddy." Travel expenses, free meals, and a reference are also part of the package. Currently, 40% of adult participants go on to get a job. Over 1,000 employees who act as buddies or coaches find Marks & Start very rewarding. It also helps the company with both recruitment and employee development.[28]

---

27 J. Fuchs and K. Dörfler, "Projektion des Erwerbspersonenpotenzials bis 2050: Annahmen und Datengrundlage," *IAB Forschungsbericht* 25 (2005).

28 corporate.marksandspencer.com/howwedobusiness/our_policies/funding/marks_start, accessed August 2009.

- National Grid, the UK and US energy infrastructure utility, has for many years run a pioneering young offenders retraining program. It works by engaging with over 20 prisons targeting both adult and young offenders. Every trainee is offered support and mentoring both pre- and post-release in order to ease the transition from prison life to the world of work. Over 1,000 offenders have participated. The societal benefits speak for themselves, with a reoffending rate of only 7%, compared with the national average of over 70%. As it costs approximately £40,000 in the UK to keep a person in prison for one year, there is a significant saving to taxpayers. In 2003, the Chancellor of the Exchequer (now the Prime Minister) in his budget statement asked National Grid's CEO to lead the program's expansion across all industries in the UK. Over 80 companies are now engaged in this program.[29]

These initiatives focus on the skills development of future employees, where a company's contribution to society can be so much more than just being a good employer paying a fair salary.

It may also be worth looking at whether the recruitment challenge your company has is just yours or one for the entire industry. If it is an industry-wide problem (e.g., the lack of engineers in Western society), there may be bigger, more long-term initiatives a company could take part in – either alone or with other companies.

For example, a company could develop education programs at schools focused on a particular industry theme. In the UK, in 2009, E.ON launched "plugin2engineering," an education program tied to the national curriculum aimed at equipping students aged 11–16 years with science skills, while promoting engineering as a career.[30] Meanwhile, in Germany, the engineering giants Bosch and Siemens have taken this concept a step further, launching an acclaimed project at the kindergarten level to embed an interest in engineering among children at a very early age.[31]

Community Involvement can play several useful roles in HR. Externally, it can demonstrate the responsible approach of your company to the societies in which it operates. Internally, your company's promotion of Employee Volunteering can show how it supports people playing a role in shaping society. Increasingly people want the opportunity to be not "just" employed but to have the sense that their work is contributing to a greater good. As all three of the Business Integration areas covered in this chapter demonstrate, the right Community Involvement initiatives can do that and much more.

---

29 www.nationalgrid.com/youngoffender/index.asp, accessed December 2009.
30 www.plugin2engineering.co.uk, accessed December 2009.
31 www.spiegel.de/wirtschaft/0,1518,560250,00.html, accessed December 2009.

Appendix 5.1. Summary of where to integrate Community Involvement into your business

Business area	Community/societal impact	What's in it for the business area?	Community actions to improve
Building new sites and running operations	Both direct and indirect. Direct quality of life impacts include: • Financial from increased employment • Environmental impacts • Health & safety Indirect effects could include: • An influx of new people into a community • Investments in community facilities	• Gaining and maintaining the "license to build" and "license to operate"	• "Process" elements: having Board-mandated societal standards, policies, and guidelines implemented and monitored, including training on how to manage these • Behavioral elements: demonstrating respect, building trust • Thinking through possible consequences/side effects of your operations • Having the right personnel with the right skills
Marketing and Sales	Can be minimal or can use marketing budget to have a positive societal impact	• Brand benefits: improved reputation, brand image, brand preference, proof points* • Improved customer relations leading to increased loyalty and/or sales	• Consider how to integrate cause-related marketing initiatives into marketing plans • Look at enhancing sponsorships by bringing in Community Involvement elements • Ensure all actions have a credible (measured) community benefit that is not just done for marketing spin
Human Resources	Already has an impact by employing people and in how a company treats its employees Potentially can combine some of its recruitment and employee development efforts with community projects to deliver a greater societal benefit	• Increased employee pride and identification with the company • Employee skills and team development • New recruitment channels	• Link Employee Involvement with personnel development • Look at how recruitment of employees can address societal issues through community programs where there is high, long-term unemployment

*   Proof points are ways of demonstrating the company's brand positioning.

6

Make it stand out

How to create and implement leading
Community Involvement programs

This chapter is the heart of the book, as it will be your flagship Community Involvement programs that will have the biggest societal impact and will win you the most stakeholder recognition.

It is no accident that this chapter is at the center of the book – a lot of what you need to create and implement for leading Community Involvement programs is covered in the chapters before and after this one (see Figure 6.1).

Figure 6.1 **Leading Community Involvement programs and related elements**

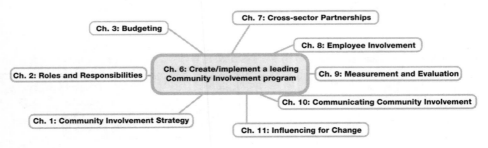

You need to do all of the following: devise a strategy (Chapter 1), budget for and staff your program (Chapters 2 and 3), partner well across sectors (Chapter 7), involve employees (Chapter 8), measure, evaluate, and report on your activities (Chapter 9), leverage results in internal and external communications (Chapter 10), and do a lot of influencing (Chapter 11). What you learn from these chapters is important, because these are the key elements you will need for your project to become the truly inspiring, industry-changing, society-shaping one you hope to create.

Done right, this project can be the core of your company's "personality" in the community, shaping the image of the organization and enhancing its reputation. If your company has a framework for overall Social Performance Management, creating and implementing a leading Community Involvement program is part of excellent social performance.

Interview with Celia Moore: Working for a smarter planet

Celia Moore is Head of Corporate Community Involvement for EMEA at IBM. Before joining IBM, Celia had extensive experience of engaging the corporate sector in social issues, and creating public–private partnerships, from various roles in the voluntary sector. She was Deputy Chief Executive and Operations Director at Action Resource Centre, a UK agency specializing in business involvement in the community. Prior to that, at Apex Trust, she worked with companies to employ white-collar ex-offenders, and engaged corporate executives to run careers advice sessions inside juvenile offender institutions and residential children's homes. From there, she went on to specialize in developing preventive services for young people at a social services policy unit and a government-funded Trust, the Intermediate Treatment Fund.

Where in the company is your function based?

CM: "Last year IBM created a new organization combining the Marketing, Communications, and Citizenship functions. The thinking behind this change is to integrate the organization's culture and brand, both of which are based on the company's values, and to build a new profession that encompasses expertise in the workplace and the marketplace. Before that, we were part of the Technology and Innovation division, reflecting the fact that we draw on IBM's technology capability to build solutions for critical community needs. At IBM, we do not have a CR or Sustainability department: all relevant sustainability areas are deeply embedded in the respective business functions."

What is your company's Community Involvement strategy?

CM: "We deploy IBM's most valuable capabilities, assets, and resources: our research and technology, our consulting and IT services, and our talent. All of these are integrated in innovative global programs we create to assist communities around the world make progress on critical social issues that are also important to our long-term business success. We prioritize our investments in line with our business growth strategy and engage our employees as a key component through volunteerism."

What are your areas of strategic involvement?

CM: "We focus on four principle areas: helping to raise the standard of performance in education; contributing to economic development, especially in developing markets; fostering learning about cultural diversity; and addressing humanitarian needs. For each of these areas we create programs that integrate core IBM capabilities and adapt the solution to the local environment. The following are some examples:

"In education, our goal is to contribute to systemic change in schools. We help teachers to transform their practice through collaborative working and integrating IT into their teaching and learning in the classroom. A global education community has been created through our programs, and we leverage that for cultural exchange. For example, we have an active community of children in kindergartens who exchange cultural insights with children from other countries by sending their favorite toys on trips abroad! This program was part of the European Union Year of Intercultural Dialogue in 2008 and had a great impact on teachers' practices and classroom innovations.

"The World Community Grid applies IBM's technical expertise to address humanitarian challenges that have a direct impact on long-term economic development. The program utilizes grid computing technology to harness the unused power of individual computers, and to apply this to complex scientific research. In five years it has grown to be one of the world's top ten supercomputers, and produced research results for disease therapies, environmental management, and food production that would not otherwise be affordable or doable in a reasonable time-frame. It's a simple process for anyone to volunteer the spare capacity of their PC or laptop.[1]

"A program that has created huge excitement and interest both internally and externally is the Corporate Service Corps. It's a great example of how we bring business needs and Community Involvement together. We send our top talent as volunteers for a one-month consulting assignment with organizations in emerging markets to help with economic and social development. They work in the country with government-supported programs and in NGOs. We typically send a team of ten people from all around the world, and they work together in smaller groups to complete their assignments. Each supported organization receives several months of pro bono IBM consulting time – and our people deliver high-quality, creative work."

How interested are employees in getting involved in this?

CM: "IBM developed the Corporate Service Corps to reflect the changing expectations of employees in the compact between employer and employees. The trend we see is that younger employees no longer expect to join a company for life. Our employees now have different expectations. They are seeking flexibility and they want to experience the world in different ways. At the same time, we want to attract employees who are keen to join IBM because they want to make a difference to the world – through the ways we apply scientific insight and technology across our business. And, to serve our global customers, we need people who can work comfortably in virtual multicultural teams.

"We started out providing 200 places a year, but immediately it was so popular we increased the program to 500 places a year. That means we are sending 50 teams to support communities in different emerging markets each year. The paybacks from the program are huge. On the one hand, the teams contribute substantive work on important projects. They also raise IBM's visibility, build relationships with influencers, and gain personal insight into doing business in growth markets. And, at the same time, they feel that they get so much back. When I ask them about their experience afterwards, a lot of them talk about having felt connection with their colleagues, having found 'a new family.' Some of them say, 'I am a different person; it has changed me.' They have learned

---

1 www.worldcommunitygrid.org

a great deal from living in a multicultural team for a month and the intense personal experiences and connection to IBM colleagues generates very high motivation."

Apart from the Corporate Service Corps, what else is there in terms of Employee Involvement?

CM: "Engaging our employees is a powerful way to extend our reach into communities and at the same time grow our understanding and capabilities in different cultural contexts. We run a global volunteering program, On Demand Community, which has a website for employees and retirees to learn about volunteering and a set of on-demand tools based on the successful technology solutions created exclusively by IBM for schools and community agencies. These tools provide volunteers with myriad choices of meaningful volunteer opportunities, resources and specific activities designed to help make them more effective volunteers. Since its inception in 2003, over 130,000 employees and retirees have registered and performed over 6 million hours of volunteer service around the world."

Can you say more about how you integrate Community Involvement with business activities?

CM: "At IBM we have always seen the interdependency of our business with the communities where we operate and the value in helping communities succeed. This has contributed to our innovation, forward thinking, and core culture. In the current context of dynamic global integration and the economic downturn, our Community Involvement strategy and our business strategy are even more convergent. From a business and societal point of view, developing solutions to global problems like energy efficiency, secure water supplies, safe food and improved healthcare is an imperative. From IBM's perspective, these challenges have created an opportunity to think and act in new ways – economically, socially, and technically. We view the possibility that comes from the pervasiveness of electronic sensors, combined with the ability to connect multiple devices via the Internet and to create new intelligence from data by applying advanced analytics, as an opportunity to make the world work better – to create a Smarter Planet. This is a strategy we are pursuing through our core business, and also developing Community Involvement programs like our partnership with the Nature Conservancy Council on Water for Tomorrow."[2]

Do you run any of your programs by yourself, or what organizations do you partner with?

CM: "*All* our programs are done in partnership. Partners bring core competency in key areas that IBM's expertise complements. For example, our partners have in-depth experience of social needs in emerging markets and play a key role in the Corporate Service Corps. For the World Community Grid, we work together with research organizations. Partners are the means to build sustainability into programs, so that IBM's initial investment creates long-term change. IBM also stays involved after the start-up

---

2 www.ibm.com/ibm/ideasfromibm/us/environment/100807/index.shtml, accessed January 2010.

stage, for example through engaging our volunteers, but it is essential to have partners who will manage programs for the longer term."

How does your company's top management support you?

CM: "Our CEO provides personal leadership, and Community Involvement is a responsibility of one of the IBM Board Committees, the Directors, and Corporate Governance Committee. In each country, the Country General Manager personally leads CSR. They're very active in our community programs, and leverage the value from our partnerships for relationship building. Our CFO is also clear about the relevance of our Community Involvement in creating value for the company."

What about implementing programs in different countries? What differences do you perceive?

CM: "Our strategy is to invest in global program solutions that meet common needs on a global basis. Major investments in education such as in our TryScience.org website enable much higher value to be delivered in each country than could be achieved by spreading the budget across multiple one-off projects. Of course, when it comes to implementing, programs are localized to meet the specific context. Our partnerships are key to this, and we select partners who are best placed to deliver high impacts. For example, in emerging markets, government has a key role in social development, and NGOs are often not so well developed to engage in partnerships at a strategic level."

How do you account for the longer-term impact of your programs?

CM: "For our major programs, like KidSmart for early education, or Reinventing Education, which works with school systems on their change agendas, we have external evaluations done at country level, often involving university departments or expert agencies. For example, Harvard University is involved with evaluating the work of our Corporate Service Corps."

How do you experience the business benefits of your involvement?

CM: "IBM participated in a recent McKinsey study, "Valuing Social Responsibility Programs."[3] This researched whether you *can* associate business value with CSR investments. The report was positive on business benefits, including increased revenue, reduced risks, and enhanced relationships. For IBM, there are many tangible benefits from our community investments. For example, through some of our programs, IBM Research helps to develop and test new applications. And the reputation we gain from our Community Involvement is huge – reflected in multiple awards and ratings as well as wide-scale media coverage. We also know that our leading position on Community Investment is important for employee attraction and retention. Through our Community Investment we develop a number of valuable relationships with external stakeholders, including high-level contacts with government."

---

3 corporatefinance.mckinsey.com/knowledge/knowledgemanagement/mof.htm, accessed January 2010.

Where do you see Corporate Community Involvement going in the future?

CM: "I see the trend clearly going towards integration with business strategy and corporate identity. Companies are becoming more aware of the value of developing programs that advance their business agenda while contributing positively to the community. For example, the financial services sector is now very engaged with helping small business and with offering micro-credits, and financial services companies are testing new products in emerging markets. Other consumer products companies are finding new markets and innovating their product range."

Finally, what would be your advice to new practitioners who would like to establish leading programs on behalf of their companies?

CM: "I would say four things. First, make sure programs are owned and led from the top, by your company's leadership. Second, make sure your programs are an expression of your business, leveraging your company's core competencies and assets. Third, involve your employees. Meet their aspirations to get involved. There are vast opportunities. Then, with leadership, engagement, and business alignment in place, work strategically with partners to combine your particular expertise with theirs to leverage programs most effectively."

From strategy to action planning

You have followed the process outlined in Chapter 1, defined the larger cause your company wants to commit to, and created an overall Corporate Community Involvement strategy.

Now you need to create a leading Community Involvement program. The classical stages of project management apply:

- Initiation
- Planning and development
- Implementation
- Monitoring and controlling
- Closing

For your specific context, the initiation and development phases will include concretely:

- Identifying your community partner organizations
- Developing your joint project
- Designing an initial project plan
- Considering which markets take priority for implementation
- Working out costs and who will pay for what
- Considering the legal framework and project governance

We will engage with each of these aspects and then with managing the project, including a program spanning several countries. Once your implementation is under way, we will remind you about involving employees, measuring and evaluating your program, and leveraging results in your communications.

We will then share with you some advice on:

- Scaling up successful programs

- Deciding whether to end a program

Initiation and development

Identifying your community partner organizations

First of all, you need one or more partner organizations competent in the subject area you want to address. How do you find your partners? Other organizations can help. Looking internationally, you can turn to the World Business Council for Sustainable Development,[4] the European Foundation Centre,[5] or the United Nations Development Programme.[6] The Boston College Center for Corporate Citizenship,[7] Business in the Community,[8] the International Business Leaders Forum,[9] or CSR Europe[10] might also be able to help you. And talk to your local government and relevant ministries, or leading academic institutions. They all have extensive networks and may be able to help "match" you with the right organizations.

When looking for a good "fit" for collaboration in your future partner organizations, during your due diligence you should look for organizations that are:

- Committed to your chosen cause

- Active in the markets in which you want to get involved in the community

- Have a good track record – both for their project management and the results they achieve and for their financial management

If you are looking to implement a national program, you will focus on government or non-profit partners in that country. If you are looking to implement a global program, you will need to assess whether you would like one global partner organization that can subcontract with local partner organizations, or whether you prefer to look for different partners in each country yourself and want to contract with each partner in each country individually. Clearly the latter will take longer and will be a more complex and demanding process.

---

4 www.wbcsd.org
5 www.efc.be
6 www.undp.org
7 www.bcccc.net
8 www.bitc.org.uk
9 www.iblf.org
10 www.csreurope.org

For example, for an international program, if you would like to get involved with children and young people and would prefer one global partner, you will probably find yourself looking at the International Youth Foundation,[11] Save the Children,[12] Plan International,[13] or SOS Children's Villages.[14] When intending to design a program supporting social entrepreneurship, you might turn to Ashoka.[15] If you are interested in an environmental educational program, you might get in contact with WWF.[16]

The benefit of working with such a global partner organization is that they usually already have a strong network of local partner organizations. They also tend to have an impressive track record not only in managing global programs, but also in working with global companies and managing such partner relationships. This is not to be underestimated – if you partner across sectors with organizations that have never partnered with a company before, inevitably you will spend more time on building the partnership than you would with an organization more experienced in cross-sector partnerships.

By assessing two or three potential partner organizations (per country or on a global level) and looking for answers to these questions, you will have ample comparable data on which you can base your final choice of partner as an informed decision.

For advice on how to develop and then successfully manage your cross-sector collaboration, turn to Chapter 7.

Here are some key questions to ask when you interview a potential partner organization as part of your due diligence

Does the prospective partner organization have:

- A sound management and governance structure?
- A record of financial stability and reliability, including solid funding from other sources?
- A convincing project track record, showing real impact in the community?
- Reasonable standing and respect within its own sector?
- Skills and competencies that complement those of your company and of other potential partners?
- Competent staff who are:
  - Experienced and reliable in the development and management of projects?
  - Good communicators and team players?
- Is there a values fit between the NGO and your company?
- Is there an image fit for the two of you to approach the public together?

11 www.iyfnet.org
12 www.savethechildren.org
13 www.plan-international.org
14 www.soschildren.org
15 www.ashoka.org
16 www.wwf.org

Developing your joint project: What can a leading program look like?

Next you will start to design and implement your community program together. Today, it is commonly accepted that a leading Community Involvement program should keep as close as possible to a company's core competencies. If the meaningful contribution of your company's core competencies is key: What can that program look like? How can you make it happen? Who do you need internally to make it happen? Involve Business Development, R&D, and any other "best minds" in the company in some creative thinking.

High-profile Community Involvement programs are about shaping the future. If you want to create a leading program, you cannot think small. You cannot do what everybody else is doing. Your aim needs to be to "change the game." TNT's and Betapharm's leading community projects have already featured in Chapter 1. Other companies that have clearly changed the game in Corporate Community Involvement are information technology companies such as Intel, IBM, and Microsoft (also featured in the interview in Chapter 1). They each took on a cause and made a *surprising* difference. There was innovation in their programs. Never before had a company done what they did.

One of the first highly praised Community Involvement programs, starting as early as 1993, was Intel Computer Clubhouses.[17] Comprising a network of over 75 Clubhouses in around 16 countries and regions worldwide, this is an after-school program set up to provide community-based technology-learning programs, enabling young people, aged 10–18, in underserved areas to acquire the tools necessary for personal and professional success. The program provides them with access to high-tech equipment, professional software, and volunteer mentors to help them develop the self-confidence and enthusiasm for learning they need to be successful in the future. The Intel Computer Clubhouse Network is a project of Intel Corporation, the Museum of Science, Boston, and the MIT Media Laboratory.

A leading program today is IBM's Reinventing Education.[18] IBM is contributing innovative education solutions using its advanced information technologies and research expertise. Through Reinventing Education, IBM is working with school partners throughout the world to develop and implement innovative technology solutions designed to solve some of education's toughest problems. To each school grant site, IBM is contributing more than just money; the company is dedicating its world-renowned researchers, educational consultants, and technology. Reinventing Education also includes an interactive web-based "Change Toolkit" based on the work of Professor Rosabeth Moss Kanter[19] of Harvard Business School. The toolkit, which is accessible to all educators, is designed to help school leaders expand and sustain their education reform efforts. It contains information on effective change strategies; diagnostic tools for organizational readiness; case studies; and tools for data-driven decision-making, quality teaching,

---

17 www.computerclubhouse.org, accessed December 2009.
18 www.ibm.com/ibm/ibmgives/grant/education/programs/reinventing, accessed December 2009.
19 One of the most influential business and change thinkers in the world and an advocate for leadership of sustainable enterprises.

and effective interventions. The program also offers a forum for online collaboration, with shared access to the skills and expertise of educators around the globe.

Here are a few more snapshots of some leading companies and their successful Community Involvement programs.

Microsoft: Partners in Learning[20]

The company engages in numerous, country-by-country, public–private partnerships for IT curriculum development, and teacher and student training. This is a global initiative designed to actively increase access to technology and improve its use in learning. The company's goal is to help schools gain better access to technology, foster innovative approaches to pedagogy and teacher professional development, and provide education leaders with the tools to envision, implement, and manage change. The vision is to have innovative schools, innovative teachers, and innovative students. The program started in 2003 and is envisioned to run at least until 2013. More than 3 million educators have been trained and more than 80 million students reached, in over 100 countries.[21]

Nokia: access to education through BridgeIt[22]

Nokia combines existing mobile technologies to deliver distance learning content to teachers/students in developing countries (e.g., science videos ordered via mobile phone and delivered via satellite). BridgeIt's goal is to significantly increase the quality of teacher instruction and achievement among primary-school girls and boys in math, science, and life skills through the innovative use of cell phone and digital technology. Programs have been delivered through multi-stakeholder platforms, including government, NGOs, and business-to-business customer companies.

Lafarge: partnerships with CARE and WWF[23]

Lafarge and CARE signed a new partnership agreement in 2009 to last three years, comprising a health program, a low-cost housing program, and a tool for assessing actions led on the ground in participating countries. Lafarge also became the WWF's leading industrial "conservation partner" in 2000. Their renewed partnership covers five key areas of commitment, including climate change, biodiversity, and sustainable construction.

Unilever: 'Water and Sanitation for the Urban Poor'[24]

Unilever has been praised for providing technologies for the provision of water, sewage, and waste-water disposal through a cross-sector partnership with Water Aid, WWF,

---

20 www.microsoft.com/education/pil/partnersinlearning.aspx, accessed December 2009.

21 www.microsoft.com/uk/education/schools/partners-in-learning/history.aspx, accessed December 2009.

22 www.nokia.com/corporate-responsibility/society/universal-access/bridgeit, accessed December 2009.

23 www.lafarge.com/wps/portal/2_1-En_direct, accessed December 2009.

24 www.unilever.com/sustainability/hygiene/partnerships, accessed December 2009.

Thames Water, Cranfield University, and the United Nations Development Programme. This program also stands out as being a real multi-sector platform for change.

Accenture: pro bono consulting and business skills training[25]

Accenture offers what they call outcomes-focused pro bono programs, providing in-kind (no fee) professional consulting services to non-profit organizations. Other professional services companies such as Ernst & Young, Deloitte, and KPMG also offer this. Employees are often given the option to take a leave of absence to volunteer their time and professional skills to consult with NGOs in both "developed" and "developing" countries. Thousands of hours of consulting time are donated to dozens of non-profit organizations in countries around the world. This is an example of replicating a model that works and taking it to scale.

Social entrepreneurship

Another possible program aspect to take into consideration is that of supporting social entrepreneurship. Social entrepreneurs are individuals who recognize a social problem and use entrepreneurial principles to organize, create, and manage a venture toward creating social change. Whereas business entrepreneurs typically measure performance in profit and return, social entrepreneurs assess their success in terms of the *impact* their programs have on society.

Social entrepreneurs need considerable help to succeed. Organizations such as Ashoka provide networks and consulting for their entrepreneurs. Ashoka, the world's first and leading association of social entrepreneurs, was founded by former McKinsey manager Bill Drayton. Ashoka works on three levels: first, identifying, electing, and supporting leading social entrepreneurs financially and professionally; second, bringing communities of entrepreneurs together to help leverage their impact, scale their ideas, and disseminate their practices; finally, helping with building the infrastructure and financial systems needed to facilitate the growth of social innovation globally. To achieve this, Ashoka builds partnerships and bridges to the business and academic sectors. Ashoka operates in 60 countries and supports 2,000 leading social entrepreneurs.[26]

A well-known social entrepreneurship model is that of microcredit, the most famous example of which is the Grameen Bank founded by Muhammad Yunus, with whom the Bank shared the Nobel Peace Prize in 2006.[27] The Grameen Bank has provided the poorest of people with minuscule loans, creating the spark of personal initiative and enterprise that would help them to break the devastating cycle of poverty and change their lives for the better – and for the long term.

Other microcredit programs, modeled on Grameen, have sprung up around the world, and the microcredit concept has now helped millions of the poorest people

---

25 www.accenture.com/Global/About_Accenture/Company_Overview/Corporate_Citizenship/ Time_and_Skills/Pro_Bono/default.htm, accessed December 2009.

26 2009 figures.

27 www.grameen-info.org, accessed December 2009.

worldwide. The Grameen "village phones" is another idea that has taken off and been replicated in many countries: women in poor villages can get a small loan to purchase a cell phone and charge villagers a small amount for using the phone for calls and text messages, earning enough for the women to buy food and clothing and to send children to school. If your company is not a bank, but you are interested in supporting a micro-credit program, consider partnering with a bank to make your company's products or services available to poor people, so they can make a living.

Be inspired by existing initiatives

All of these examples should give you and your potential partners a number of ideas for how you can get involved. You may also consider not entirely "reinventing the wheel," but seeking inspiration from an existing, successful initiative and adapting it for your company and your partnership. That way, you can bring a proven "what works" model to greater scale.

Designing an initial project concept

Once you and your partners have a good sense of what your program will be about, you will need to define it. To do this, it helps to write a concept paper together – or to ask your project partners knowledgeable in community development to write it. For such an initial concept, it can be helpful to consider the following categories:[28]

- **Type of project.** For example, curriculum development, training, replication of existing program. What difference can this project make, what makes it special, and why it is relevant? Why is your intended project approach important and worth the effort?

- **Brief background to the project.** What is the problem to be addressed and what important contextual information is needed to understand the problem? Why does society need your program? What is your and your partners' experience and capacity to enable you to carry out the project?

- **Goals and objectives of the project.** In addition to thinking about the goals and objectives, what is the theory behind your strategy to effect change? In other words, why do you think your activities will make a difference and improve a social condition?

- **Description of target groups.** Which population groups will be influenced by your project? Where are they located and what are their basic characteristics (age, gender, occupation, socio-economic status, etc.)?

- **Activities and time-frame.** In addition to considering the activities to be implemented, decide whether your program will carry out the activities directly or will subcontract them to other organizations. Identify which partner organizations will work with you on which parts of the project.

---

28 Adapted from International Youth Foundation, "Guide to Concept Paper Development" (2004).

- **Outputs.** What are the direct products of your project activities, such as training courses, events, conferences, publications? What is the approximate number of beneficiaries?

- **Outcomes.** What effect will the activities and outputs have on the target population? How will it change their lives?

- **Budget.** Provide a general budget overview. What is the breakdown between start-up costs and implementation costs?

- **Potential employee participation.** How do you anticipate the company's employees will be able to participate in the project activities as volunteers?

You also need to identify the scope of your project, so there are more questions to ask, depending on where you want to go: How big or small do you want to make it? Will it be international? Will it be one program to be replicated country by country? Or will there rather be an umbrella theme, flexible enough to be adapted and customized based on local needs? Will the program be implemented only in countries in which your company has a strong local staff presence, or can it also be implemented in the absence of company employees on the ground? Do you want to commit to a three-year project right away, or do you want to start with a one-year pilot?

Think carefully about these aspects, and take them into consideration when planning and designing your project.

Which markets should you prioritize for implementation?

If your company is global, it is important to assess which markets you should prioritize when implementing a global Community Involvement program. A good mapping process that applies specific criteria will help such an assessment.

To demonstrate the importance of this, we know of a CEO of a major multinational company a few years ago who asked his Community Involvement managers: "I will be

Criteria for country selection can be:

- The number of employees you have per country/location
- Which markets generate the biggest sales?
- In which markets does your brand tracker show that customers appreciate your company or brand(s) the least? Where are there the worst percentages for "a brand that I can trust"?
- In which countries does your Employee Opinion Survey show the lowest results for employees thinking that the company is socially responsible?
- Which countries have the greatest societal need for the issue you aim to address?
- What are your priority countries in emerging markets?

From a comprehensive assessment of these criteria, you can establish the priority markets for implementing your Community Involvement program.

meeting with President Putin in three months – can we have a Community Involvement program in Russia by then?" We also know of a senior vice president responsible for Business Development in Africa saying: "Kenya and Nigeria are two of our fastest-growing markets. How quickly can we have a Community Involvement program in each?" While this raises the stakes, it provides a great opportunity to get something developed fast.

Cost considerations

How much your company will need to invest really depends on the kind of program you are looking at. Anywhere between a few hundred thousand and several million euros or dollars per country per year is likely for a leading Community Involvement program. When planning for these kinds of program from a head office perspective, take into consideration macro indicators such as the local comparative purchasing power against the US dollar or the euro. From one country to another, the program implementation cost may vary greatly, given the differences in local purchasing power. A program in the US, the UK, or Germany might cost much more than a program in Romania or Peru – or, to put it differently, with the budget you can put in, each euro or dollar spent might have comparatively more impact in low-cost countries.

Again, when planning for these kinds of program from a head office perspective, if the funding for local program implementation is coming from head office over, for example, a three- to five-year period, once you have settled on a level of funding per country, consider the potential volatility of each country's local currency exchange rate against the currency in which you are budgeting, and how this may impact intended local program delivery. You may want to budget for some currency exchange fluctuation – or agree on concrete funding levels in each respective local currency – rather than endangering local program delivery because of a sudden lack of funds in local currency.

Then consider start-up versus ongoing program cost – if you need to design curriculum or training content, you may need to spend more money in the beginning. Think about language and especially cultural diversity and possible translation and content adaptation costs for program materials. For an ongoing program with an established structure and materials, additional cost is more likely to be for scaling up of the activities.

Cost considerations are also dependent on program typology and intended delivery: Is your program a curriculum-based, skill-building program? Does it involve providing technological equipment? Is it a volunteer-based program? Your chosen typology and delivery will also determine what kind of budget will be needed.

Chapter 3 gives you overall guidance on budgeting details.

Legal considerations and governance structure

This is a complex area and we suggest you work with your legal department on it.

In terms of **legal considerations**, consider that for each country you may need to start with a Memorandum of Understanding between you and your partner organization before working toward a full contract.

If you have a global framework contract with one international partner organization, each local country agreement could be an appendix to that contract. This could make it easier for your country businesses to get involved.

In your contract, you should cover program objectives, terms and conditions, and financial commitments. If you jointly create a name for your program, consider trademark rights and who owns them. For any materials developed, define intellectual property rights and copyright ownership.

What is the length of the term of this contract? What do you want to include about mutual conduct? What needs to be included to cover confidentiality?

You will need to set terms and conditions for reporting processes as well as for regular audits and reviews. How do you want to communicate to the public – jointly or individually? This aspect will need to be covered as well. Who is legally accountable for what? Do you and your partner(s) want to agree mutual exclusion of liability? You will also need to decide how you agree between you to undertake dispute resolution, and you need to cover rights to termination and notice periods. As you can see, your legal department will definitely be of valuable help with all this.

Governance is about defining the various decisions and steps needed for effective program development, management, and growth. Who will be in charge of these? It is helpful to establish that clearly. Don't just think about this as a formality for the contract! Good governance needs to be lived and it is critical for a successful program. Agree on governance principles, and then ask your legal advisors to help you turn your agreement into legally recognizable terms. The next chapter looks in depth at how you build up your partnership and apply that good governance.

Implementing and managing the project

Once you have established your legal framework and your budgeting, it is time to start implementing and managing your project. To do this, it will be helpful to create a concrete project plan or action plan, with clearly defined deliverables, roles, and responsibilities assigned, and milestones for achievement listed in a timetable. Also define operating guidelines as well as measures for success.

Figure 6.2 shows a basic action-planning template to follow.

Figure 6.2 **Basic template for an action plan**

Key steps	Responsible	Timeline	Status

The outline for a more sophisticated project management plan is provided in Appendix 6.1 on page 145. If you need a template for a project timeline, there are many available for free download on the Internet.[29]

---

29 We like to use "Vertex 42: The Guide to Excel in Everything"; www.vertex42.com/ExcelTemplates/timeline.html, accessed December 2009.

You will then put activities into place that will create project outputs and outcomes. This will involve coordinating people and resources, as well as implementing the activities of the project in accordance with your project management plan. See to it that you and your partner(s) manage implementation processes well together, sticking to timelines and agreed deliverables.

You might consider starting implementation with a pilot project in one country or one region, to see how it develops and what you can learn from it, and only then take it to more sites or more countries.

If you notice that things aren't going as planned, you need to identify problems as soon as possible so that corrective action can be taken – you want to get on track again quickly. For high-quality process management and effective joint problem solving, make sure you have regular mutual feedback processes built in and attended to.

To make sure all of these processes are covered effectively, you can also look at the checklist of key management, framework, and process aspects provided in Appendix 7.1 on pages 166f.

Managing several country programs

When you manage a global program, you will be busy for much of the time with internal negotiations: for example, explaining the Business Case for Community Involvement to a country's managing director (you will find the arguments in Chapter 1), identifying and training a local manager to take on Community Involvement (get advice on this in Chapter 2), or assessing local non-profit organizations for suitability for partnership, using the criteria outlined earlier in this chapter.

If you are a global Community Involvement manager or director overseeing local country programs, it is important to maintain a good relationship with your colleagues on the ground (as well as with their superiors). Be in touch regularly (e.g., quarterly) to receive their updates and offer your support.

If you can, visit each country program once a year. Your personal presence "on the ground" will make all the difference: you gain a much better understanding of programs and their development from experiencing them directly, you can problem-solve in person rather than trying to do it remotely, and you can offer personal praise and encouragement for work well done. You will also come back with plenty of stories that you can use for internal and external communication of your program.

The relationships between your local colleagues and the local cross-sector partners may require attention from time to time as well: Are they working well together? Are they achieving their objectives with each other? If there are challenges, how can you help them handle them? Do they need training in joint partnering? If you have one international partner organization, you should oversee and support these issues together.

Program elements

Whether you run a global or single-country program, as part of your program management it will be important to include the following three program elements:

Engage employees

To make your program complete, engage your company's employees as volunteers. See detailed advice on this in Chapter 8.

Measure and evaluate

To make sure your program delivers and can be continuously improved, make sure you plan for a sound measurement and evaluation process. Chapter 9 tells you how. IBM, for example, can take pride that "rigorous, independent evaluations from the Center for Children & Technology and the Harvard Business School have told us that our significant investment of technology and know-how is having a positive, measurable impact on our school partners."[30]

Communicate

This is about having credible, exciting information you can communicate. Make sure you leverage your program's results in effective communication to all relevant stakeholder groups, so you can earn recognition for your good work. Chapter 10 suggests the most effective ways of doing this, together with your partners.

Scaling up a successful program

If your Community Involvement program is successful and making a real difference to society, you and your partners may want to explore whether it merits scaling up and expanding beyond your original plans – to other geographical areas, or to more institutions reaching more beneficiaries.

One way of funding this is for your company to pay for it. Another opportunity is to create a (corporate) platform and get other companies/organizations on board. You could involve your supply chain: are there companies that would like to become partners in your program, perhaps to tighten their business relationship with your company and also to upgrade their own Community Involvement?

Or are there other companies, typically not competitors, but from complementary industries, that would be interested in joining such a platform? For example, Nokia for many years ran an innovative work-skills training for young Black university graduates aged 20–28 in South Africa who had been unemployed for at least one year, with the aim of developing these young people's professional skills by bridging the gap between tertiary education and the world of work. Aspects of the course included understanding the professional world, attitude to work, how to look for and retain employment, financial management, and computer and entrepreneurial skills. At the same time, the program emphasized interpersonal and teamwork skills, self-confidence, conflict resolution and problem-solving skills, and the motivation to succeed and be responsible to one's community.

---

30 www.ibm.com/ibm/ibmgives/grant/education/programs/reinventing, accessed December 2009.

The program drew such interest because of its success (70% placement rate in employment upon completion of the training) that companies from several industries as diverse as mining and banking (Lonmin, Anglo Platinum, People's Bank, BMW) and organizations such as the Embassy of Finland Local Cooperation Fund joined the program. USAID and Lions Clubs International then took the program to Mozambique, Malawi, and Rwanda. All companies and organizations contributed jointly, co-managed elements of the program, and communicated jointly to the public; and all benefited from high local and regional recognition – and also from selecting a few qualified graduates as new employees.

As this example illustrates, in emerging markets, very often international development agencies, your home country's ministry for international development, USAID, or the local ministry of education may be interested in contributing funding and expertise, and jointly taking a program to scale. While not without their own challenges, these can be dynamic, multi-sector alliances, which for some years have been considered the "second generation" of Corporate Community Involvement[31] because they go beyond single-company involvement. This kind of commitment becomes increasingly important for impactful programs to reach meaningful scale.

Co-creating a good ending

You may have made a contract for your program for a fixed period of time. The business environment is dynamic and things change. Your program will require regular revision (see Chapter 9 on measurement and evaluation), and during the last year, before it ends, you will need to decide: Do you want to continue? Do you want to expand or scale down? Do you prefer to discontinue?

If you decide to discontinue your program, for example in favor of a new, more promising initiative or simply because your company's involvement in that program has reached the end of its natural life, it is important to plan your "exit" well. There should be a gradual phasing-out of your company's involvement and support. Communicate your reasons for discontinuing to your partner organizations clearly and in a sensitive and appreciative way (also see advice on this in the "Moving on" section in Chapter 7, pages 164f.). Explore with your partners what a wind-down phase could look like, during which you gradually phase out financial support. This gives them an opportunity to look for other sources of funding if they intend to continue the program. Look at and document your joint achievements and your learning together, and celebrate them. This will help ensure you end the relationship as friends, proud of what you have achieved together.

---

31 Expression coined by Simon Zadek of AccountAbility, in a presentation at The Conference Board, February 2002.

Where is the trend going?

The field is continuously developing, and there is a call to action for companies to take their Community Involvement to the next level. That call is coming from informed stakeholders such as Corporation 20/20,[32] CSR Europe,[33] and the European Commission. They are asking companies to avoid isolation or fragmentation by each running their individual programs. Underlining the importance of cooperation between all players in society in joint efforts, the call to business is to form new alliances to take effective societal solutions to scale together – and be recognized for it.

As we mentioned in Chapter 1, education, health, jobs, and the environment are the key issues on people's minds. Challenging global pressures such as climate change, increasing scarcity of natural resources, technology acceleration, demographic change, and deepening social divides have also become ever more pressing, making us fundamentally question our established ways of living, consuming, and sharing resources.

New solutions will need to be found, and these challenges can only be addressed through close cooperation both across and within sectors, and by taking shared responsibility.

The right ideas at the right time can be contagious and lead to systemic change. As a company, your task is to contribute to global sustainable development – no less. This is your company's opportunity to contribute to a better society, a better world even, and to stand out for that contribution. Whether your company is a big multinational with 100,000 employees and products sold in 140 markets, or your company has 2,000 employees in one market – if you come up with solutions that work, then they will be universally relevant. Other companies, organizations, and government will notice, and your solutions will be replicated. Any company can become such an agent for change and improvement. The business benefit is for your company to be seen as a true leader, enhancing your business in the process. By following the advice in these chapters, combined with some innovative thinking from the best minds in your company, you too can get there.

---

32 www.corporation2020.org, accessed December 2009.
33 www.csreurope.org, accessed December 2009.

Appendix 6.1. Sample outline for a project management plan[34]

1. Overview
    1.1. Project Purpose, Objectives, and Success Criteria
    1.2. Project Deliverables
    1.3. Assumptions, Dependencies, and Constraints
    1.4. References
    1.5. Definitions and Acronyms
    1.6. Evolution of the Plan

2. Project Organization
    2.1. External Interfaces
    2.2. Internal Structure
    2.3. Roles and Responsibilities

3. Managerial Process Plans
    3.1. Start-Up Plans
        3.1.1 Estimation Plan
        3.1.2 Staffing Plan
        3.1.3 Staff Training Plan
        3.1.4 Resource Acquisition Plan
        3.1.5 Project Commitments
    3.2. Work Plan
    3.3. Control Plan
        3.3.1 Data Control Plan
        3.3.2 Requirements Control Plan
        3.3.3 Schedule Control Plan
        3.3.4 Budget Control Plan
        3.3.5 Communication, Tracking, and Reporting Plan
        3.3.6 Metrics Collection Plan
    3.4. Risk Management Plan
    3.5. Issue Resolution Plan
    3.6. Project Close-Out Plan

4. Technical Process Plans
    4.1. Process Model
    4.2. Methods, Tools, and Techniques
    4.3. Configuration Management Plan
    4.4. Quality Assurance Plan
    4.5. Documentation Plan
    4.6. Process Improvement Plan

---

34 This template is from shareware downloaded from www.projectinitiation.com, October 2009.

7

How to manage cross-sector collaboration

This chapter will help you to work well with community partners including non-governmental organizations (NGOs), government, international agencies, and academic institutions. The aim is to make partnerships stronger, more effective, and more sustainable. Towards that goal, this chapter covers a number of concepts, definitions, and checklists that you can work with in practice to make sure your partnership is successful and achieves what you hope for and expect. Much of the material for this chapter is drawn from The Partnering Initiative,[1] the specialist global program of the International Business Leaders Forum (IBLF),[2] with a well-established international reputation for promoting excellence in sustainable development partnerships. The chapter features an interview with Ros Tennyson, Founding Director of The Partnering Initiative, and then offers detailed insights into developing partnering relationships, structuring and reviewing the partnering process, and also addressing potential partnering challenges.

Interview with Ros Tennyson: Developing the art and science of cross-sector partnership

Since 1992, Ros Tennyson has led the IBLF's work in cross-sector partnering. Over the years, this has involved partnership promotion and partnership-building activities in more than 30 countries as well as the development and delivery of tailored training programs for corporations, NGOs, the World Bank, and UN agencies. Since 2001, Ros has been Co-director of a Post-Graduate Certificate in Cross-Sector Partnerships, an initiative run as a collaboration between IBLF and the University of Cambridge Programme for Industry. Since 2007, she has been Director of the Partnership Brokers Accreditation Scheme that was developed in 2003 as

---

1 www.ThePartneringInitiative.org; Veronica Scheubel, co-author of this publication, is an Associate of The Partnering Initiative.
2 www.iblf.org.

a collaboration between IBLF and the UK's Overseas Development Institute. She is the author of many papers and toolbooks on the subject, notably *The Partnering Toolbook*,[3] now available in 18 languages, and *The Brokering Guidebook*.[4]

How did you get into your work on cross-sector collaboration? What is your background?

RT: "I have quite an eclectic background, a very diverse career path – which, to me, almost seems to be a prerequisite for this kind of work. I have a theater background and training, and I bring certain skills from my drama training: for example, I find it comparatively easy to 'get inside the skin of other people' and understand perspectives that are different from my own. The training also involved developing sensory perception, observation, listening, and intuitive skills. All this serves me well in empathizing with the context and circumstances in any given partnering constellation and situation. I don't go in with too many preconceptions, and I am open to learning what is needed.

"I do encourage my colleagues to operate that way. In my view, a good partnering expert is not someone who tells other people what to do – but someone who will ask the right questions to bring relevant issues to the surface and enable understanding, collaboration, and appropriate action.

"After my early work in theater, I worked in the field of social development. I grew up in a Quaker household, so that shaped my understanding of the world. My parents had deep commitment to social issues, and they instilled that values-based philosophy in me. With a strong focus on injustice, I worked with refugee resettlement, disabled people, with the housing association movement, and more – always trying to be creative and looking for approaches and solutions outside of mainstream thinking and practice. Before I came to IBLF, I was the CEO of a holistic health charity, and I undertook some training in action research and participative research[5] at the time."

What brought you to IBLF?

RT: "I was invited to join IBLF by the then President, HRH The Prince of Wales, and the CEO, Robert Davies. In 1992, the partnership work required quite a pioneering spirit! I started with a big question about what 'partnership' really meant. I guess my starting point was that the planet as we know it will simply not survive unless we learn to collaborate. To me, cross-sector collaboration is a fundamental approach to strong and well-regulated societies, with profound implications at a much wider level.

"For nearly 20 years I have been working on the issue of cross-sector partnerships to understand, interpret, support, and build capacity of both individuals and organizations. To me, partnership is a process of empowerment through collaborative leadership."

---

3 R. Tennyson, *The Partnering Toolbook* (London: International Business Leaders Forum, 2004, repr. 2006).

4 R. Tennyson, *The Brokering Guidebook* (London: International Business Leaders Forum, 2005).

5 Action research challenges traditional approaches to social research. It is not research *on* people, conducted by "outside experts," but participative research *with* people, where the researcher participates in a community that jointly co-creates the inquiry, and works with participants through cycles of joint action and reflection.

So what's your message to CEOs and companies?

RT: "My message is: Companies don't operate in a vacuum, separate from society. The best companies know that they genuinely need to engage and that meaningful engagement requires changes in practice – partnership is not about quick fixes. The best companies are creating sustainable business models, all the while maintaining a willingness to keep learning and improving as they go along. And, in that context, partnership is not an add-on, but fundamental to good business practice. Partnership is the connecting thread between sectors to develop a common agenda."

Can you name some companies whose approach you commend?

RT: "The kinds of partnership with which we are primarily concerned operate as voluntary collaborations between organizations that have found single-sector solutions to be inadequate. They are dedicated to finding sustainable and innovative approaches to intractable problems that benefit from a pooling of resources and competencies. We have had the fantastic opportunity to work with some outstanding companies.

"They've been really open to experimental approaches, which has been a remarkable privilege for us. To name just a few of the many, Rio Tinto, Nike, Shell, and Standard Chartered Bank have been really willing to explore their partnering questions with us, supporting our inquiry, drawing their own learning from our work together and internalizing that learning within the company. Most impressive has been their willingness to share their learning through our publications.

"On our website, we have taken an 'open source' approach, making a wealth of information and learning available to everyone interested, entirely for free. This would not have been possible without the support of those companies and others."

You also offer a training program for "partnership brokers." What made you create that?

RT: "We first looked into offering a specialist training for partnership brokers in 1992. At the time, we were working with partnerships on a case-by-case basis, and we realized a need for coherent and practice-based theory to be articulated. It is important to have an intellectual underpinning as well as skills and competencies. We first took a strategic decision to align with a university for academic credibility, and we found our academic counterpart in the University of Cambridge Programme for Industry (now the Programme for Sustainability Leadership). This was a partnership case study in itself! Together, we created a compelling academic paradigm, and students joined from every sector, including UN agencies and governments.

"Then in 2003, by popular demand, we partnered with the Overseas Development Institute, the UK's leading independent think-tank on international development, to co-create the Partnership Brokers Accreditation Scheme (PBAS), which offers a professional training based on skills development and application. Today, we are proud to say that more than 300 people from 40 countries have completed the first level of PBAS, carrying their learning into their organizations, their cross-sector partnerships and their national contexts. They are operating essentially as change makers or – my latest favorite concept – 'invisible leaders.' "

How do you see the future of partnering and of The Partnering Initiative?

RT: "I have seen the word 'partnership' so loosely used in so many contexts. Nowadays, to avoid misunderstanding, I prefer to use the term 'multi-stakeholder' or 'cross-sector collaboration.' Some years ago, I began to feel finally that the tide was turning, that the idea of cross-sector collaboration was taking hold as a serious response to societal challenges. Slowly people are becoming more rigorous and more competent in their partnership work.

"Cross-sector collaboration is far more widely recognized, and while each collaboration or partnership is entirely unique – conditioned as it always is by its specific context, culture, and capacity – the process of partnering is genuinely universal: based, as it is, on human nature, communication skills, and some common insights into social organization.

"This understanding continues to underpin all our work and informs our publications, case studies, training programs, advisory services, and tools. We continue to be a hub for innovative thinking, to offer ongoing learning for practitioners, to promote rigorous good practice, and to support cross-sector partnerships. At the same time, while working under the umbrella and on behalf of an organization, the IBLF, the leading-edge nature of the work requires us to operate essentially as social entrepreneurs and change agents."

When you look at organizations, how do you think they can get "ready" for cross-sector collaboration?

RT: "My key question to any organization interested in cross-sector collaboration is whether *the organization as a whole* is ready to change its practice – even to give up something, as all good partners should be prepared to do in return for other benefits. To be a 'partnership-ready' organization (from all sectors, not just business), you are likely to operate in some kind of an open-system approach, in active relationship with and responding to the world around you. We intend to soon publish a new toolbook that is directed at organizations rather than individuals and which will propose how any organization can become 'partnership-ready.' There are, in our experience, quite a large number of organizations who need some serious help with this!"

And when an organization is "ready," what kind of people does it need for good cross-sector collaboration?

RT: "From the beginning it was clear to me that the individual is crucial in building and maintaining collaborative approaches to development. We need new, facilitative models of leadership, but this is a case of building on, not dispensing with, individuality. Good partnerships are always underpinned by confident and creative personalities who have learned how to work together to maximize the benefits from their individual talents."

The importance of partnerships in delivering strategic Community Involvement

Partnering is an important approach in any strategy to address societal and community issues, since it can improve any program's effectiveness and sustainability.

> The decision to partner is taken when there is a serious expectation that significant results will be achieved more effectively together than could have been achieved through other single sector solutions or ways of working.[6]

The measure of success of any partnership is the degree to which activities have led to sustainable outcomes that benefit society beyond the lifetime of the partnership itself.

The success of your Corporate Community Involvement activities may critically depend on how well you partner with organizations from different sectors, so it is essential that you understand and monitor the quality of such partnerships and other forms of collaborative relationships with your community and other partners. Your partner organizations may have needs, goals, and expectations quite different from your own, and, in order to work well together, it will be helpful to understand those differences and to learn how to value diversity. How well partners understand each other impacts on how well they are able to work together, which in turn influences their ability to achieve project goals.

What is partnership?

The Ashridge Centre for Business and Sustainability defines partnership as:

> Three [we would modify this to two] or more organizations . . . acting together by contributing their diverse resources to pursue a common vision with clearly defined goals and objectives. The objective of a partnership should be to deliver more than the sum of the individual parts.

The term "partnership" can be used to describe many types of relationship but, essentially, partnerships are a collaborative mechanism to support the successful delivery of concrete projects.

Partnerships are numerous and diverse in character. They can include: business-to-business partnerships; tri-sector partnerships between business, government, and civil society; business–NGO partnerships; and public–private partnerships between government or intergovernmental organizations and companies. Partnership to address global and local issues is a proven practice that is promoted and applied by recognized institutions such as the United Nations and the World Business Council for Sustainable Development.

---

6   E. Halper, *Moving On: Effective Management for Partnerships Transitions, Transformations and Exits* (London: International Business Leaders Forum. 2009): 3.

Why partner?

Our working hypothesis is that improving societal conditions around the world will not be achieved by any one sector alone. This is in itself a major reason to partner, but there are also significant benefits and potentially greater impact to be gained from systematic collaboration between different organizations whether at global, regional, or national levels. By being effective at partnership management, companies can increase the scale and pace of their Community Involvement work. They can co-create solutions and share risks.

The value of partnering

The value of a multi-stakeholder partnership is that organizations bring specific sets of competencies, experience, values, priorities, resources, and styles of operation that can be harnessed to work together around a common vision in order to achieve a common goal. Any partnership is influenced by the particular mix of partners in a specific cultural, economic, and geographic context. No partnership will be like any other, though all partnerships benefit from the diversity of perspectives, contributions, and cultures. It is within the richness of the partnership "mix" that there lies the potential for innovation.

Key criteria for skillful and successful partnering

What follows is some concrete advice for practical partnership development and implementation, starting with the earliest phase of establishing a good working relationship and the many phases of collaborating to develop and implement projects to an eventual parting of the ways on project completion – or a decision to continue your partnership into a new phase.

Forging good partner relationships

Do your two (or more) organizations fit together?

As partnerships serve different purposes, each partnership may be structured differently, with a diverse range of partners and differing levels of engagement and roles. Inevitably, partnerships will also be influenced by the characteristics of and the personalities from the partner organizations and the operating environment.

Partnering takes time. Our advice is to devote just as much to it as to project management. If you think you have identified your partner organization(s), take time out to get to know each other, more than just one two-hour meeting. Devote a series of meetings to it, even a couple of two-day workshops. It is worth the investment – it can avoid more time-consuming and costly problems and challenges, even the breaking apart of the partnership, in the future.

Be curious about each other; don't be afraid to ask (and answer) lots of questions, and also test your assumptions about each other. As partners, you may sometimes feel as if you come from different "worlds," even if your buildings are just around the corner from each other – simply because your organizational cultures appear to be so different. "Clashing" values, views, approaches, and ways of working can quickly solidify into barriers to mutual understanding and respect.

Explore your mutual histories and cultures – tell each other your organizations' stories. What seems similar? Where do you see fundamental differences? What are your mutual vision, mission, and values? Do those "match"? How does each of you define success, and what strategies do you use to achieve it? What do you look for in each other that will add value to the partnership and its project?

Also talk about your mutual ways of working. What are your expectations of each other, e.g., for communications processes and for decision-making? What are your mutual needs?

Touch on the topic of how you each define time and speed: often, things move very quickly in the corporate world, with managers facing the pressure of three-month targets. In the NGO world, time sometimes seems to pass more slowly – social change, especially with vulnerable groups in society, cannot be pushed so that results meet deadlines! In government, laws and regulations need to be passed, and that requires time as well.

Last but not least, look at whether you use language differently. It will be important not to assume that your partners will understand your words and behaviors – quite the contrary, what you say and do might be misinterpreted and misunderstood. We have often witnessed how NGOs changed their language to "corporate speak" so they could be understood by their corporate partners! It can take time to develop your "common" language with each other. Because of that, check with each other. Say, for example: "Thank you for explaining your needs. Allow me just to paraphrase what I heard to make sure I have understood you."

Out of these explorations you will be better equipped to start working together.

Building the relationship

Once you have started to get to know each other, the key to effective cross-sector partnering lies in cultivating a positive working relationship. Good relationships tend to be based on familiarity and trust, and both may not be present at the beginning – they need to be developed, and trust is earned over time. Establishing the relationship is part of your contracting – it is the informal part of it. Relationship building takes more time and effort than just getting to know each other.

Some partnerships take longer than others to build. Be aware that you may need to spend the first few months of your partnership building the relationship. This can feel tough – there will be deadlines to hit, and you'll want to focus on the project. Taking suf-

If you take sufficient time to build your joint *values-based leadership* together, you can then build *fact-based project management* on that solid foundation.

ficient time for relationship building and listening to each other's needs is important and worthwhile. It ensures that both (or all) sides can then feel comfortable enough to focus on operational project management. This also facilitates discussions on important issues, joint problem solving, and resolving areas of divergent opinions.

Respect your partners for what they bring to the partnership

In the process of getting to know each other and building your relationship, also understand that you and your partners may be working from uninformed underlying assumptions and prejudices. The following are commonly occurring prejudices that can impact unhelpfully on partner relationships unless they are addressed:

- Other sectors sometimes tend to view **the public sector** as: bureaucratic, dogmatic, election-focused, rigidly structured, lacking motivation, slow.

- Other sectors sometimes tend to view **business** as: time constrained, short-termist, hard-nosed, shareholder-focused, profit-driven, image-obsessed, having hidden motives.

- Other sectors sometimes tend to view **civil society organizations** as: lacking professionalism, narrowly focused, unrealistic, insufficiently informed, lacking accountability.

Getting beneath these assumptions and prejudices begins to allow a better understanding and analysis of what each sector stands for and what they are able to contribute to a partnership; for example:

- **The public sector** stands for law and regulations, physical and social infrastructure, safety nets, peace, and protection. It brings to the partnership connectivity with the wider policy landscape and provides access to relevant existing initiatives as well as physical resources such as facilities or funding.

- **Business** stands for trade, provision of goods and services, employment, HR development, a supply chain, standards setting, and social investment. It contributes dynamic work practices, management know-how, and access to latest thinking on efficiency and effectiveness as well as funding.

- **Civil society organizations** stand for social cohesion, education, stakeholder legitimization, a service-delivery culture, and individual development and self-expression. They bring connectivity to the situation on the ground and the actual needs of beneficiaries as well as their expertise in social development.

Developing a successful cross-sector partnership involves more than simply contracting an organization to deliver a service. It is important to respect your partners for what they bring to the partnership. The knowledge of development, the project experience, and the social network that an NGO can bring are just as valuable as the funding and management know-how that a company can contribute.

Accordingly, if there is a good balance of power in a partnership, partners will find they value each other for the contribution each organization makes, understanding that each party is needed for the partnership to achieve its objectives. There will be a sense of mutual respect, despite potential divergences in terms of size, resources, or the influence each partner brings to the table. If it's working, the balance of power does not feel uncomfortable. This is also called "partner equity." Note that equity is *not* the same as equality: "Equity implies an equal right to be at the table and a validation of those contributions that are not measurable simply in terms of cash value or public profile."[7]

Write a partnering agreement

A partnering agreement is a memorandum of understanding or an "agreement to collaborate." It may precede or be made in addition to a formal, legal contract (which may only be completed later). Ideally, such an agreement will cover a statement of intent for your partnership and will list the partners involved and the resources they contribute. It will state partners' expectations and objectives and will outline structures, procedures, roles and responsibilities, and "ground rules" for cooperation. It may refer to planned project activities as detailed in a separate legal contract and will also outline partnership review processes.

Write your partnering agreement together as part of your partnership-building process, as it should help you to understand where all partners are coming from, to find out what they're hoping to achieve and to get hopes and fears aired early on.

The partnering cycle

The Partnering Initiative uses a partnering cycle framework to illustrate the phases that need to be understood and managed in any partnership (see Figure 7.1). Note that the partnering cycle is different from a project cycle.

The 12 phases of the partnering cycle shown in Figure 7.1 are explained below:

Scoping and building

1. **Scoping.** Understanding the challenge; gathering information; consulting with stakeholders and with potential external resource providers; building a vision of/for the partnership

2. **Identifying.** Identifying potential partners and – if suitable – securing their involvement; motivating them and encouraging them to work together

3. **Building.** Partners build their working relationships through agreeing the goals, objectives and core principles that will underpin their partnership. This is where contracting comes in, both formally and informally.

4. **Planning.** Partners plan a program of activities and begin to outline a coherent project.

---

7 R. Tennyson, *The Partnering Toolbook* (London: International Business Leaders Forum, 2004, repr. 2006).

Figure 7.1 **The partnering cycle**

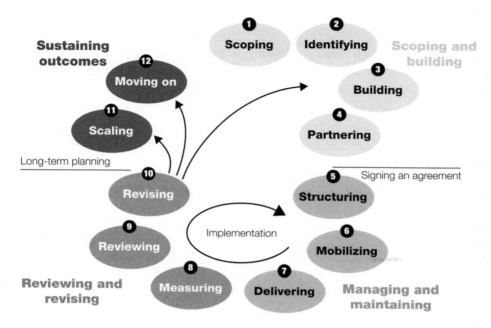

© The Partnering Initiative

Managing and maintaining

5. **Structuring.** Partners explore structure and begin to manage their partnership.

6. **Mobilizing.** Partners (and other supporters) identify and mobilize cash and non-cash resources.

7. **Delivering.** Once resources are in place and project details agreed, the project implementation process starts – working to pre-agreed timetable and (ideally) to specific deliverables.

Reviewing and revising

8. **Measuring.** Measuring and reporting on impact and effectiveness – outputs and outcomes. Is the partnership achieving its goals?

9. **Reviewing.** Reviewing the partnership. What is the impact of the partnership on partner organizations? Is it time for some partners to leave and/or new partners to join?

10. **Revising.** Revising the partnership, program(s), or project(s) in the light of experience

11. **Scaling.** Building appropriate structures and mechanisms for the partnership to ensure longer-term commitment and continuity (if necessary)

12. **Moving on.** Sustaining or terminating. Building sustainability or agreeing an appropriate conclusion

Partnering – both an art and a science

As you may have gathered from the cycle, there is both a "relational" and a "rational" side to partnering. These are sometimes referred to as the "art" and the "science" of partnering.

While it may be obvious that the quality of partner relationships will have an impact on the partnership's effectiveness, and that enthusiasm, a collaborative attitude, ideas, and inspiration are needed, a good relationship is not itself sufficient for the good functioning of a partnership. Partnering processes also need to be well managed, with principles, frameworks, processes, and tools, and this is easier if the partnership is well set up and has good procedures governing its operations. That's the "science" bit.

Effective management of partnerships

We have engaged with the relational side of partnering. We now turn to management frameworks and processes.

Good partnerships are an effective mechanism for working together in terms of innovation, effectiveness, and sustainability. But, as we said before, they take effort. In making that effort, partners are taking both a strategic and a practical approach to jointly affecting societal change.

While the types of partnership are limitless, there are some universal management, framework, and process aspects, and it is helpful to pay attention to these in order to sustain the success of a partnership from a "science" perspective. They are:[8]

- Appropriate representation

- Sufficient resources

- The right distribution of roles and responsibilities

- Sound decision-making

- Sound leadership

- Effective meeting processes

- Effective work processes

---

8 These key aspects have been distilled by the IBLF from observing partnering practice across the world over a period of more than 18 years.

- Good and transparent communication

- Trust and teamwork

- Commitment

Partners should define together how to achieve these aspects. Do some thinking together: what does each of these aspects mean to you and to your partners? Once you have all agreed on your understanding of them, how can you make sure your own partnership is achieving them?

A checklist including a brief definition of each aspect is provided in Appendix 7.1 on pages 166f. You and your partners can work through it together step by step to make sure you have everything covered.

The art and science of partnering

Partnering as an "art" requires:

- Insight, imagination and feeling
- A vision of the future
- People skills
- Active listening
- Good engagement skills

Partnering as a "science" requires:

- Good knowledge, analysis, and thinking
- Management skills
- Precise and transparent communication
- Efficient processes
- Well-developed tools and frameworks
- Professional detachment

Adapted from R. Tennyson, *The Brokering Guidebook* (London: International Business Leaders Forum, 2005).

Transparency – and how it leads to *trust* in partnerships

Transparency does not mean that partners need to share "warts and all." It does mean being open and clear with your partners about your values, constraints, and any organizational processes that may affect how you work in partnership. Transparency helps each partner understand the perspective of the other. It is particularly important in terms of:

- Shared goals and drivers for the partnership (revealing underlying interests)
- Resource mapping (managing the expectations and constraints of each partner regarding contributions, both financial and in kind)
- Monitoring and evaluating the partnership

Partnering roles and responsibilities

Partnering is a complex activity requiring partners to take on different roles at different stages. You need to make sure that there is good leadership and decision-making, and to assign roles and responsibilities so that all relevant tasks are carried out and all relevant processes managed. You need people who make sure that communication flows well between partners and that information and reports are being disseminated. Often it is also helpful to have a partnership facilitator – a "partnership broker." The concept of a partnership broker has been developed by the IBLF over ten years. It is increasingly used to describe individuals – either internal or external to the partnership – who manage the partnering process.

The "go-between": the role of the partnership broker

A partnership broker is an intermediary between different partners, operating in an active rather than passive way. They essentially perform a service on behalf of the whole partnership by supporting and promoting a systematic partnering process and, as a result, a more effective and productive partnership.

Partnership brokers are the "facilitators" of the partnership – a very critical role.

A broker – either through formal or informal appointment – helps the partners navigate the partnering process. Whoever takes on this role must be accepted by all partners as supporting all partners – working for the sake of the partnership, even if he or she come from one "side" or partner. (If they are not trusted in that way, it can be the broker who becomes a problem.)

This is especially important for a company to consider. It will have invested sometimes substantial sums in a partnership, but reassurance that the project is going to work will not be given by having a company employee as the broker to try and "steer" the partnership, even with the best of intentions.

Besides facilitation, a broker must have skills in these areas:

- Negotiation – building consensus from diverse underlying interests (good listening skills needed)
- Coaching and empowering team members
- Monitoring – ensuring good governance and genuinely "value-adding" activity
- Mediation, both in the pre-partnership phase and if conflict arises

Drawn from R. Tennyson and L. Wilde, *The Guiding Hand* (London: International Business Leaders Forum/UN Staff College, 1998).

Reviewing your collaboration

You have established a working relationship. You have put management frameworks and processes in place and assigned roles and responsibilities. You have worked quite far through the partnering cycle, and your joint project is up and running. As partners, you will have reached first milestones together. It's time to turn your thoughts to monitoring and review.

As well as reviewing the project itself, why do you also need to collect feedback from each other on the state of your partnership? Because, as your partnership progresses, you will want to make sure that:

1. The partnership is effective in achieving its aims.

2. The partners are all benefiting from their involvement.

3. Partnering is the best way to achieve the mutual goal.

Very simply, your project's performance will be shaped by all the partners' satisfaction (or dissatisfaction) with the partnership. The project's success depends on a number of different players working as a team made up of individuals from different organizations. To help the team deliver effectively on the partnership's goals and provide benefit to all, participants need to regularly reflect on and learn from what is working well and what is not.

This information enables the partnership to make the necessary changes to improve effectiveness. Collecting such feedback is an important element in promoting good partnership management and is considered good practice. If it is done well, it can result in a more fruitful collaboration to support the successful delivery of your project.

Feedback process – different from evaluation

Evaluation is undertaken, often at the *end* of a project, to assess the degree of impact of the partnership's program of work. It may look at the "how" as well, but usually the "what" is the priority.

The difference with partnership feedback is that it is best understood as an *ongoing process* – supporting the partner relationships on which the partnership is based and the effective functioning of the partnership.

Both a good relationship and well-managed partnering procedures governing a partnership's operations are important for the success of a partnership. Periodic feedback on both ensures that partners will be able to identify, understand, and then actively address some of their potential challenges. This will prevent unresolved problems from jeopardizing the successful achievement of the goals of the partnership and the partners and the partnership's sustainability.

A partnership feedback process can be conducted at any point in the lifespan of a partnership – and it should also be undertaken regularly. We recommend a joint assessment at least once a year, ideally every six months.

With all the feedback partners can provide about their partnership, as well as feedback on the project, the information collected provides a rich picture of the partnership's relationships and working dynamics. It is important for partners to get access to all the feedback to see where it has been doing well and where there might be room for improvement. Interviews or questionnaires to individual partners could form part of this. The feedback collection process can then be followed by a feedback session where partners work collaboratively and commit to take action where needed.

Running partnership feedback sessions

Partners need to encourage each other in feedback sessions in a respectful and open manner – both to appreciate what they have done well together and to talk through any aspects of partnership that may need addressing.

Good feedback sessions can be lively and vigorous. They can involve both acknowledgment and celebration of success *as well as* exploration of disagreements or challenging issues. The latter parts of feedback sessions may sometimes feel difficult, but they can be the more rewarding, since they are more likely to lead to constructive changes and, ultimately, stronger partnerships.

Mutual learning and personal and professional development opportunities more often come from facing up to challenges than from an easily achieved consensus. The underlying basis of a cross-organizational partnership is, after all, to benefit from diversity of perspectives and contributions.

During the feedback sessions it is a good idea, more than ever, to remember the key aspects of partnering and stay true to any ground rules partners may have agreed in the early days of their working relationship.

For partnership feedback sessions to be effective, we recommend following this six-step model:[9]

1. Talk jointly through each partnering aspect and the positive experiences or challenges partners may have around it.

2. Aim to fully understand each other's organizational perspectives or other sources of difference.

3. Talk through how a specific aspect of partnering could be either further enhanced or meaningfully improved to the satisfaction of all partners.

4. Determine what actions should be undertaken, continued, prioritized, or even stopped.

5. Agree when you will regroup to review progress on actions following the session.

6. Commit to a date for your next partnership feedback process, perhaps in six months' time.

The feedback results can also be used as a benchmark, so partners can compare at the next feedback session and ask: "How/where have we changed/improved year on year?"

---

9 Adapted from a seven-step model developed by The Partnering Initiative for the Global Alliance for Improved Nutrition in 2008 (www.gainhealth.org).

What to do about partnering challenges

At any one time, partners may have to grapple with a range of challenges in the partnership. Once again, please note that problems in the partnership are different from problems in the project. Problems in the partnership tend to arise from:

- Individuals involved in the partnership
- Partner diversity
- The partnering process

If you have worked in partnership, some of the issues in Table 7.1 may look familiar to you.

Table 7.1 **Partnership problems**

Area of challenge	Causes
Some typical challenges arising around individuals	• There may be competitiveness between strong personalities • Key people may change jobs and leave the partnership • New people may come in, with different priorities, personalities, and approaches • There may be a lack of appropriate leadership (e.g., too weak or too dominating a lead figure) • There may be a lack of appropriate skills and competencies. Unfortunately this may also include a lack of awareness of personal limitations
Some typical challenges around partner diversity	• Partner organizations may have different drivers and motivations • They may make (often inaccurate) assumptions about each other • There may be an unwillingness to accept each other's different priorities • There may be an over-emphasis on money (as opposed to other types of resource contribution) • There may be "hidden agendas" • There may be an absence of a genuinely shared mission • There may be cross-sector or cross-cultural intolerance • There may be power imbalances – whether real or perceived
Some typical challenges around the partnering process	• Difficulties can arise in breaking away from existing hierarchical structures or systems • There may be overly lengthy (or not lengthy enough) consultation procedures • A loss of focus for the partnership may arise • There may be a failure of individuals or organizations to complete agreed tasks • There may be a general sense of low levels of commitment from some partners • There may be over-reliance on some partner organizations or specific individuals

Source: Adapted from R. Tennyson, *The Brokering Guidebook* (London: International Business Leaders Forum, 2005).

When challenges arise, it's important to resolve problems together, e.g., immediately through effective discussion, through pre-agreed annual partner review processes, or through dialogue facilitated by a competent external facilitator or mediator. Often these challenges lead to new breakthrough and so they should not be avoided.

Conflict is a situation to be understood rather than a problem to be solved. A safe setting for dialogue, competently facilitated by an independent third party, can help you achieve resolution to dilemmas and paradoxes and get to sustainable outcomes.

Sometimes partners also feel their partnership would benefit from partnership skills training or some other form of competence building. The Partnering Initiative provides such training.

'What? You're leaving?'

During the life-cycle of a partnership, there are likely to be many comings and goings of individual members of the partnership. Arrivals and departures need to be managed well. When someone leaves, make sure you:

- Celebrate achievements and contributions (however big or small).

- Spend sufficient time debriefing to capture institutional knowledge.

- Give thanks and say goodbye appropriately.

When new people join the partnership, it is a big risk to just continue with "business as usual," focusing on the project operations. With every new person joining, you need to start all over with building the relationship. Turn to the beginning of this chapter to look at the "art" of partnering.

This may sound daunting but, no, we are not joking. Very often, the importance of this is overlooked, or people assume they do not have time for it. A lot of the challenges we listed in Table 7.2 arise from new arrivals being expected to "just fit in" – but it does not work as easily as that. After all, the person leaving has not been replaced by their clone!

When new people join the partnership, in particular:

- Take time to welcome and introduce newcomers.

- Ask newcomers about themselves, their previous organizations, and what they want to know/find out about the partnership and the project.

- Ensure that partners are comfortable with newcomers and that they share any personal, team, and operational information early on.

- Transfer information as concisely and vividly as possible, and create opportunities for learning from direct experience and observation.

- Invite newcomers to make requests or suggestions as well as share their own experience or new ideas.

- Use their arrival as an opportunity for the partners to take stock of the current state of the partnership.

Sustaining, renegotiating, or exiting a partnership[10]

If a partnership is sustainable, this might be based on partners feeling that both the partnership *and* the joint project have been implemented well. Ideally, partners have met both overall partnership goals and their individual organization's goals:

Added value of partnering – to the project and to society

If all partners recognize that their partnership provides added value to the project and to society, they find that they are achieving together what none of them could have done alone. They experience their partnership as having a real, long-term impact on the community, multiple stakeholders, society, and often even public policy.

Added value of partnering – to participating organizations (mutual benefit)

All participating parties in a partnership gain value for their own organization and see their individual organizational goals fulfilled. Partners experience a clear organizational benefit from participating in the partnership.

Experiencing this combined added value often leads to a willingness to continue working together and to continue contributing resources to the partnership for as long as the partnership is necessary to develop or deliver a community project.

When you have collectively reviewed your partnership, you can make decisions about its future. You may decide to sustain the partnership, integrating anything useful you have learned from your feedback and review process. In some cases, you may realize that the partnership would benefit from returning to the scoping and building phase in the partnering cycle.

> ## The most successful partnerships produce *multiple benefits for all partners*, such as:
>
> - Access – to institutional learning, cross-sector resources and support, network relationships
> - Efficiency – through shared costs and better delivery systems
> - Innovation – through developing new ways to address issues and complex challenges
> - Effectiveness – by creating more appropriate products and services
> - Mitigated risk – by sharing risk and responsibility
> - Enhanced reputation and credibility – through project and partnering success

---

10 Much of the content of this section was informed by E. Halper, *Moving On: Effective Management for Partnerships Transitions, Transformations, and Exits* (London: International Business Leaders Forum, 2009).

Moving on

In other cases, a partnership may have reached its "natural" ending, e.g., because a project is completed and its goals have been achieved. Partnerships should not be sustained for their own sake, but only as long as they are needed for project delivery. Once this objective has been reached, partners can consider whether another institution can take over the project, or whether such an institution should be created.

Then again, not all marriages are made in heaven, and, if a partnership is not working, it can be best to part ways. It should never be a goal of a partnership to last forever. In that sense, moving on eventually should be seen as inevitable. However, this does not mean that it is easy. In the best scenarios, partners keep in touch and remain connected well after their initial program of work is completed – sometimes even developing new initiatives together. In the worst scenarios, things break apart, and previous project success is compromised. To quote Ros Tennyson, "messy endings virtually guarantee that the value of what has gone on before, however good, is seriously undermined and marginalized."[11] Moving on is not straightforward, and you need to navigate your own approach.

In that context, we want to emphasize that every aspect of the partnering cycle is important, yet often in practice the later stages are given less care and attention than the formative ones. As a result, effective and systematic partnership-building processes have become more commonplace, but the moving-on aspects of partnerships are misunderstood and undervalued in many instances.

A partnership is a voluntary collective activity, and especially for corporations, moving on is a natural part of doing business. Reasons for moving on may include: project completion; a failed project; a reduction in or a withdrawal of resources; changing partner priorities; seeing new partnering potential with different organizations; or a changing political, social, or economic context. It is crucial to manage the expectations of your partners about the duration of the partnership from the beginning. You will need to balance, on the one hand, providing security and demonstrating an interest in sustainable outcomes while, on the other, transparency about the finite nature of your company's involvement with the project.

The different role of each organization in the partnership (e.g., as funder, implementer, or even beneficiary) will affect how that organization views moving on. Each partner will be affected by this differently, and all kinds of psychological factors can come into play. Sometimes partners prefer to keep a partnership intact and unchanged rather than to address the moving-on issue and a potential sense of loss.

It will be important to have a "moving-on conversation" together, covering many aspects:

- What are the most important elements of the partnership, and how can they be protected?

- What are we most proud of in the partnership's achievements, and how can those aspects inform our moving-on decisions?

---

11 Halper, *op. cit.*

- What are the potential moving-on options? How can we explore each of these to arrive at the best one for all concerned?

Navigating moving-on conversations requires as much tact and sensitivity as was needed in the early relationship-building phase of the partnership – perhaps even more. This includes being genuinely interested in the perspectives of others, really listening to their thoughts and concerns, and being prepared to rethink your own views. Here the designated partnership broker or an external facilitator or mediator can take on a helpful role, to assist partners in sailing through any "stormy waters."

Whichever reason prompts a decision to move on, it is important to recognize the outcomes from the partnership – there can be achievements even in a "failed" partnership. And a departure and an ending also always leave an open space for something new to arrive.

Communicating a moving-on decision externally

In communicating a moving-on decision externally, e.g., to beneficiaries, the community, local government, or the wider public, make sure you are sufficiently transparent to stakeholders while respecting individual partners' needs for confidentiality. Perhaps you can provide a report of project activities and community impact, including some success stories. Contact personally those stakeholders that might prefer a face-to-face approach to receiving written communication.

Finally, why is partnering worth the effort?

Multi-sector partnerships rarely offer quick, comfortable, or easy solutions. Rather, they require hard work and perseverance. When such partnerships are founded on mutual values, are innovative and well managed, mutually empowering, and leading to sustainable outcomes, they are capable of achieving far more than one sector could by working alone.

Appendix 7.1. Your partnership: checklist of key management, framework, and process aspects

You can use the third column of this checklist to assess for your own partnership(s) whether – and how well – each aspect is covered. Use checkmarks or a score; or write "okay" or "needs attention"; or cross out the aspects that you think are well covered and circle or highlight the ones that need addressing. For those areas that you think could be improved or need addressing, try to bring the issue to a partnership meeting or feedback session.

Aspect	Description	Your partner-ship status
Appropriate representation	• Each partner is actively present and participating • Each person has sufficient authority to represent and make decisions for her/his organization *and* also have the appropriate competencies (knowledge, skills, experience) to engage in active discussion • Representatives have regular enough contact to allow relationships to be built (The role of representative can be shared by more than one individual from each partner organization)	
Sufficient resources	• The partnership is well equipped with staff, funding, equipment, etc. to address the tasks at hand and implement the work that has been agreed on	
Roles and responsibilities are clearly defined and well distributed	• The partnership is making optimal use of each partner's unique skills, perspectives, and resources • The partners understand and accept the rationale for the division of labor between them and deliver accordingly	
Decision-making	• There is a sound, transparent decision-making process established through: – Inclusiveness of the decision-making process for areas of strategic importance: all voices will have been heard before decisions are taken – Decisions based as often as possible on the consent of (at least) the majority of all partners (but partners can be empowered to make decisions within their assigned areas of responsibility) – Decisions taken that result in a collective sense of positive momentum and progress	
Leadership	• One or several individuals can clearly articulate the partnership's goal, providing strategic guidance, motivating and inspiring all participating parties towards good partnering and high achievement, and empowering and enabling all participating parties towards full involvement and effective delivery • Leaders encourage sufficient dialogue and manage differences of opinion well	

→

Aspect	Description	Your partner-ship status
Good meeting processes	• Partners give input to agendas and meeting logistics; meetings are timely and effective, with a well-prepared agenda and a sense of structure and pace • Partnership meetings are chaired to encourage participation from all partners and reinforce a sense of equity	
Work processes	• There is a clear, mutual understanding of deliverables, accountabilities, and time-frames, timely contributions from all relevant parties, and effective joint documentation and delivery • Working together, partners regularly review them and their potential further optimization	
Good and transparent communication in the partnership	• All participants understand what they are doing and why, they have timely access to all important and relevant information, communication is documented, and records are circulated to all • Partners feel comfortable having open conversations about all aspects and issues concerning both the partnership *and* the project they are working on • Partners feel able to talk to each other about their individual and shared partnership goals and the quality of their collaboration	
Trust and teamwork	• Partners have confidence in each other being able to deliver on their jobs. They can rely on each other to complete mutually assigned tasks well and on time, and they know they can call on each other to help each other out as and when needed • There is a sense of sufficient responsiveness, flexibility, and support • Partners can talk to each other openly when problems arise over difficult issues • There is a sense that partners have a consideration for each other's interests and will be willing to change what they do, if necessary, to help meet each other's individual goals	
Commitment	• There is a sense of full commitment, experienced through a contribution of good resources, a regular and active presence at meetings, and tasks finished well and on time, even early • There is an attitude of caring – about both the project *and* the partnership – and of wanting to do everything possible to contribute to the success of both	

Source: Adapted from the Partnership Enhancement Tool developed by The Partnering Initiative for The Global Alliance for Improved Nutrition in 2008.

Appendix 7.2. Literature by The Partnering Initiative referenced in this chapter

Halper, E. (2009) *Moving On: Effective Management for Partnerships Transitions, Trans-formations and Exits* (London: International Business Leaders Forum).

—— and V. Scheubel (2005) *Engaging with Our Partners: A Guide to Partnering Literacy* (London: International Business Leaders Forum/Nokia).

Tennyson, R. (1998) *Managing Partnerships* (London: International Business Leaders Forum, out of print).

—— (2004) *The Partnering Toolbook* (London: International Business Leaders Forum, repr. 2006).

—— (2005) *The Brokering Guidebook* (London: International Business Leaders Forum).

—— and L. Wilde (1998) *The Guiding Hand* (London: International Business Leaders Forum/UN Staff College).

8

The power of Employee Involvement

Employee Involvement is an integral part of your Community Involvement strategy. It is the personal involvement of employees in the communities where they work and live that will make your Community Involvement come to life.

Employee Involvement is a "triple win" for employees, communities, and the company. It provides communities with much-needed help, motivates employees in their day-to-day work, and increases corporate image and reputation. It can also be activated as a strategic HR tool.

The chapter starts with a best-practice interview with a leading practitioner and then helps you understand better what Employee Involvement is and how you can make the Business Case for it. A practical five-step process with detailed checklists will then help you pursue a structured approach to designing your own Employee Involvement initiative.

Getting management and employees on your side

For many companies, especially in the US and the UK, volunteering is part of the national culture. For them, the value of Employee Involvement is self-evident.

In cultures less familiar with Employee Involvement, you may need to argue your case to get Employee Involvement started in your company. Senior management may question whether employees will be interested, or how much it will cost the company to give employees paid time off for volunteering.

Experience shows that the interest from employees is always there, in every country where a company operates. Even if your company has just five employees in a given country, they will appreciate the opportunity to contribute to their community on behalf of the company. Even skeptical managers have found that employees want and support volunteering with great enthusiasm and commitment.

Interview with Thomas Baumeister: Generating real commitment

Thomas Baumeister is Head of Volunteering, Region Germany, within Deutsche Bank's Corporate Citizenship unit. Thomas has been with Deutsche Bank, one of the world's leading financial service providers, for more than a decade, working in Corporate Responsibility since 2005. With a Master's degree in psychology, an MBA, and a strong background in Human Resources, management development, leadership training, organization consulting, coaching, and conflict moderation, he is an experienced change facilitator. In this interview, he offers a glimpse of his approach.

What worked well and what didn't work in getting Employee Involvement started at Deutsche Bank?

TB: "In the beginning, we saw that Employee Involvement worked really well in the US and the UK, and realized that models applied there could be replicated throughout the company. Later, the decisive factor for 'upgrading' Corporate Volunteering was that we took a more strategic approach to it. Corporate Volunteering is now firmly positioned as one of the cornerstones of our 'Building social capital' agenda and adds credibility to our 'Passion to Perform' claim. Needless to say, management commitment is essential in securing resources. In terms of motivating our volunteers, we noticed that 'mass communication', i.e., intensive internal communications efforts reaching out to employees via mails, the Intranet, and the employee magazine, were able to set the scene, but were not sufficient to motivate colleagues to actually get involved. Talking to people individually and targeted one-on-one communication was much more successful in the early stages. Mobilizing volunteers is a 'relational' business. Now that Corporate Volunteering has gained more awareness, the formal communication channels work better, simply because we have so many colleagues who have become ambassadors for the cause."

How did you put that "relational" business into practice?

TB: "It is important to have access to people throughout the company, being able to speak to everybody without getting caught up in the hierarchies. To mobilize the grassroots, I make use of informal networks. However, I would warn against a 'one size fits all' approach for communication. Motivations differ considerably, especially in a company that is as diverse as Deutsche Bank. You need to think about target group-specific communication; you need to think about what makes people's eyes shine."

How did you then get employees to turn out in large numbers to volunteer?

TB: "Well, to cut a long story short, goodwill is initially most important. And, in order to gain employees' goodwill, you need to offer a playing field of different activities that you just let run for the first two years. We also noticed that, although in the beginning we had to 'advertise' activities and talk about them a lot, the snowball effect then kicked in: things seemed to gain momentum and became increasingly self-organizing. Participation figures reflect an 'S'-shaped curve of growth in every region: a slow start, a steep rise, and then flattening out again at a higher level."

So, did you and your team manage all those activities yourself, and were they all successful?

TB: "It turned out that our initial efforts to manage volunteering projects for various employee target groups just centrally was not the most effective way to go. We learned early on that the bank needed capable non-profit partners that would assume project management responsibility. We also learned that some projects simply didn't fly – and that trying to keep them alive was futile. My advice is: dare to exit if it doesn't work – even if you have to disappoint some partners. A pioneer phase is about trial and error. You need to be willing to learn from mistakes, and then you continue with those projects that turn out to be popular and thus successful. Employees will vote with their feet! A recent highlight for Deutsche Bank was the city of Munich's 850th anniversary in 2008: 400 employees contributed more than 850 days of volunteering as a 'birthday gift,' as they felt strongly about it."

How do you let employees know about what's on offer for them?

TB: "Since 2006, our support for employee-driven activities has been posted online, and this led to a sudden growth in uptake. We wanted to capitalize on that. We are now thinking about offering interactive functions on our Intranet. Volunteers can then post their own projects and invite others to join them. Once again, the site is intended to improve self-organization."

What are employees' preferred volunteer activities, and what are yours?

TB: "Interestingly, our colleagues don't seem to go in so much for activities that require their specific professional expertise, but prefer teamwork projects with very hands-on tasks. My hunch is that employees prefer to do something different from their day-to-day work, and they like to experience themselves and their colleagues in new contexts. At the same time, our focus has shifted from quantitative to qualitative growth. What counts for us is societal impact. In terms of such impactful activities, mentoring, for example, works quite well and offers employees flexibility in the time they contribute. People get personal, relational benefits from mentoring, as they connect well with their mentees. These are often youngsters with a migrant background, sometimes even head teachers of schools interested in getting a different perspective on leadership and management.

"We want to expand on projects that build on the professional competencies of our people. That means we want to extend our scope of volunteer consultancy services, building stable, long-term relationships with organizations that will allow an outgoing group of volunteers to hand over projects to the next incoming group."

Can you give us a few numbers about how volunteering has developed at Deutsche Bank?

TB: "Happily! In 2008, Deutsche Bank's Employee Volunteering at the global level was at 14%, and Germany saw the biggest increase: 17% (+3%) of employees made use of our offers of financial support, paid leave or organizational support. Employees contributed a total of almost 36,000 days in 2008, an impressive figure in light of the fact that almost 80% of the time invested is in fact employees' leisure time. Our intention is to drive volunteering levels within Deutsche Bank on a global scale up to 20% within the next few years. We are also considering introducing a Global Community Challenge to further motivate our colleagues across regions to commit themselves in their local community.

"In terms of paid time off for Employee Volunteering, currently, Deutsche Bank employees in Germany, and soon the US, can take one day per year, and employees in the UK, Australia, and New Zealand can take two. Young graduates get several days of paid leave for volunteering in specifically assigned projects, as part of their training. And, of course, our Corporate Community Partnership program offers longer-term professional assignments with microfinance institutions and social entrepreneurs."

What about budget? How much does the company make available for this?

TB: "Even in the current challenging times, Deutsche Bank dedicated an expanded budget of about €6 million [about $9 million] for 2008. This included Matched Giving funds of about €4 million. Part of volunteering project budgets is spent on Bank-driven programs, which are regionally organized by the Corporate Citizenship function. A larger part is currently spent on employee-driven projects; that means volunteers can apply for these funds to support the projects they propose."

How do you work with the various functions throughout the company who support you in getting volunteering to work?

TB: "We work on two levels. On the more formal side, the commitment of Deutsche Bank's senior management smooths the access to regional and divisional management. In presentations and one-on-one meetings we explain our portfolio and the central support we offer. Some regions and businesses are very interested, others less interested, so we focus on the ones who are ready to commit themselves and rely on the 'infectious' effect of positive examples. At the other end of the scale, we stay close to the informal networks of corporate volunteers who will take an active role in organizing their peers."

What advice would you give your peers in other companies who are just starting out with their Employee Involvement?

TB: "For Deutsche Bank, what worked well was first of all to provide a range of volunteering offers that people could easily subscribe to. Second, it was important to maintain the spirit. It takes passionate people to start things off and drive them forward. Then, in the process, it is essential to keep a self-evaluating attitude to continuously improve the offer to employees."

What about the business benefits from Employee Involvement?

TB: "Our brand experts emphasize that Employee Involvement helps build our reputation in a local community in a very tangible way, since external stakeholders usually take notice of both the employees who volunteer and the company behind them.

"Internally, Corporate Volunteering has done its share to strengthen Deutsche Bank's profile as a 'responsible corporate citizen': more than 80% of our global staff strongly agree with the statement 'I feel proud that Deutsche Bank supports employee volunteer work.'

"Business benefits often materialize indirectly, and sometimes even in paradoxical ways. The mechanism is well expressed in a famous quotation from Brecht's *Threepenny Opera*: 'For all chase after happiness, it eludes them everywhere.' It may thus not be helpful to start with the question 'How can we achieve the best business results?' Instead, it may be better to start with the question 'How can we make an impact on society and meet the needs of our staff?' If this goal is adequately achieved, one should not get too anxious about expecting immediate business results."

What is Employee Involvement?

Employee Involvement is about your company's employees making a contribution to the communities where they work and live, on behalf of and in the name of your company.

When it comes to practical implementation, Employee Involvement is easy. In fact, it's the easiest part of Community Involvement to get started on. Why? Because people actually like to get involved. All you need to do is offer opportunities and enable them.

Who's doing it? And what are they doing?

All major multinational companies provide Employee Involvement opportunities, as well as many small and medium-sized companies. Some companies have "social days," volunteering for any good cause; other companies strive to be more focused and contribute their core competencies to community causes. Many companies aim to offer employees a good mix of activities.

The case for skill-based volunteering and secondments

Accenture Development Partnerships puts pro bono consulting in the service of international development organizations. PricewaterhouseCoopers sends young consultants on secondments with NGOs and finds that this not only supports communities but also helps the company develop its people. TNT sends employees with specialized skills to all parts of the world to help its community partner, the United Nations World Food Programme (WFP), build its internal capacity. TNT also has an employee Emergency Response Team on standby to help WFP in any emergency situation. Cisco's Leadership Fellows Program places high-potential employees at non-profit organizations for 6–12 months with the task of ensuring a specific project is successful. McGraw-Hill's "Writers to the Rescue" program matches individual employees to non-profit organizations to serve as volunteer writers, editors, and communications specialists. UPS's 40-year-old Community Internship Program immerses senior-level executives in a variety of social and economic challenges.[1]

A best-practice example for mentoring is IBM's MentorPlace. As the company explains on its website:[2]

---

1 Points of Light Foundation, *The Promise Employee Skill-Based Volunteering Holds for Employee Skills and Nonprofit Partner Effectiveness* (Washington, DC: Points of Light Foundation, 2007).
2 ibm.mentorplace.epals.org/WhatIs.htm, accessed December 2009.

MentorPlace is a volunteer program that brings adult professionals and students together in online relationships focused on academics. Employee-volunteers are charged with providing students with academic assistance and career counseling, while letting them know that adults do care about their issues and concerns.

In leading companies, Employee Involvement consists of three core elements:

1. Employee Volunteering
2. Matched Time
3. Matched Funding

1. Employee Volunteering

The International Business Leaders Forum defines Employee Volunteering as "The mobilization by businesses of the time, talent, energies, and resources of their people to contribute to the community."[3]

Employees volunteer as individuals or as teams, with paid time off (e.g., two days' paid leave per year).

A time-off policy allows employees to volunteer in the community during regular working hours. Generally, time-off policies are an effective way of encouraging and recognizing the contribution employees make to the community.

As we hear from our peers in business, on average internationally, companies (e.g., IBM, Ford Motor Company, Accenture, PricewaterhouseCoopers, Nike, E.ON, Nokia, Pfizer, TNT) give employees two days' paid time off for volunteering per year. KPMG gives employees three and a half days a year, while Timberland gives employees up to 40 hours per year, and three weeks' paid leave if employees want to help out with disaster relief. If you are just starting out with Employee Volunteering, the best approach is to give guidance, make sure a time-off policy is encouraged, and then allow the employees and their line managers to get the balance right. Even if you don't start out with a time-off policy (and many companies still don't have them), you will still find that a lot of employees are interested in volunteering in their own time. If you then find there is a good uptake of volunteering by employees, your company (the Executive Board or the Board member in charge of HR) can formalize your company's time-off policy later on. This can then serve as a reward and recognition for employees' volunteer efforts, and can motivate more employees to become active.

Volunteering for retirees, families, customers, and business partners

It is increasingly popular to also coordinate volunteering activities for the company's retirees, and to count their hours volunteered towards the company's time contributed to the community. This recognizes the potential of the company's retirees to make a difference and activates an ambassador group for the company. Both General Mills and

---

3 As defined in ENGAGE launch presentation, 2002. For more information on ENGAGE, see www.iblf.org/docs/engage/engageflyer.pdf, accessed December 2009.

Hewlett Packard have created formal retiree volunteering programs. HP says about its retiree volunteers: "Imagine the impact 40,000 experienced and highly skilled volunteers could make by focusing their energies on social and environmental issues around the world."[4]

It is becoming just as popular to invite customers, business partners, or employees' families to join in a company's volunteer efforts. In China, it has long been an established practice to plant trees with customers and business partners. Toshiba, Hitachi, Hewlett Packard, and ConocoPhillips do this regularly. Companies find that this joint outreach to the community actually improves customer and business relationships. For volunteering events on weekends, employees often like to bring family members along.

Companies also like giving names to their Employee Volunteering programs, e.g., IBM's On Demand Community, Timberland's Path of Service, Disney's VoluntEARS, or Nokia's Helping Hands. Many companies use the program name on t-shirts for volunteering activities to create a sense of team and corporate identity.

2. Matched Time

Many employees volunteer for charitable causes during their own free time. Matched Time is about recognizing and celebrating those who are truly making a difference to their community.

Here's how it works. Based on the number of hours volunteered per employee (say 50, 75, or 100), the company contributes a certain amount per hour volunteered to the charity supported (up to a limit). For example, for every 50 hours volunteered, the company gives €X.

Any kind of charitable organization supported by employees is eligible for Matched Time, provided it meets the criteria in your company's Corporate Giving guidelines (see Chapter 4). Claims for Matched Time should be formally confirmed by both the employee and the charitable organization supported, and the company should always donate the money to the supported organization directly.

3. Matched Funding

Through a mechanism known as Matched Funding, employees raise funds for charitable causes of their choice and their employer matches the amount raised up to a certain amount annually per employee. It's important to note that Matched Funding is designed for employees who *raise* funds for charity. It requires the active involvement of the employee. It is not designed to be claimed by any employee who has simply *donated* money to charity. The only exception to this is where a business-wide initiative is supported (e.g., employees collectively contributing money to the United Way in the US or collecting money to contribute to a disaster relief organization). Any kind of charitable organization supported by employees through their fundraising is eligible for Matched Funding. As with Matched Time, it must meet the criteria in your company's Corporate Giving guidelines (see Chapter 4), and the company should always donate the money to the supported organization directly.

---

4 www.hp.com/retiree/volunteering.html, accessed December 2009.

Tax implications for Matched Funding and Payroll Giving

In some countries, tax questions may be raised by HR. For example, is the matching of funds a taxable benefit to employees? Please note that, in tax terms, you can easily argue that the company's matching of employee donations is not a taxable benefit to employees. It is a charitable contribution by the company to organizations in the community. Through their own choices of charitable organizations, the employees simply give the company pointers on how to allocate corporate donations.

What is Payroll Giving, and how can it be linked to Matched Funding?

Another mechanism for triggering Matched Funding is Payroll Giving. Payments that employees make to charities through a Payroll Giving scheme are deducted from their pay before tax. This means that employees are given tax relief on their donation immediately and at their highest rate of tax.

Payroll Giving is also the most cost-effective way for charities to raise money. In many countries there are Payroll Giving agencies that help companies administer their Payroll Giving scheme. In the UK, for example, we counted seven registered agencies. Companies tend to add a certain percentage to employees' Payroll Giving as part of a Matched Funding scheme and pay all administration costs, so employees can be sure that 100% of their donation goes to their chosen charity.

How many employees can get involved?

The good news is: as many employees as want to can get involved. However, it takes time to successfully engage employees, including time to shift your approach if it is not working so well right away. The current international benchmark for Employee Involvement is 30% of employees actively involved in the community, through Matched Funding, Matched Time, or Employee Volunteering.

Three champions in the field are: General Mills, with 82% of employees volunteering;[5] Disney, with its VoluntEARS dedicating 569,000 hours of volunteer service in 2009 alone, and, since the program's inception in 1983, VoluntEARS in over 42 countries having donated more than 5 million hours of service;[6] and IBM, with over 130,000 employees and retirees having registered and performed more than 8 million hours of volunteer service through its On Demand Community Employee Volunteering initiative, launched in 2003.[7]

---

5 www.generalmills.com/corporate/media_center/news_release_detail.aspx?itemID=37911& catID=227, accessed December 2009.

6 corporate.disney.go.com/responsibility/community.html, accessed December 2009.

7 www.ibm.com/ibm/ibmgives/index.shtml, accessed December 2009.

How much does it cost?

Employee Involvement is a low-cost activity. It does require resources to make it happen, especially motivated employees, but the actual cost – in terms of employees and money – is low. While costs will vary by country, below is a summary based on the three types of Employee Involvement.

Employee Volunteering

You will need time to organize it and funding to pay for materials (e.g., paint for building renovations, trees for planting). There may be other logistical costs such as hiring a bus to transport a team to a given location. Sometimes costs are incurred by the charitable organization for arranging the activities. All details should be discussed between your company and the non-profit organization in the pre-activity planning meetings. You may also want to provide company-branded t-shirts or packed lunches. Finally, it may be worthwhile from time to time to hire a photographer for PR purposes. Much will depend on the scale of your volunteering. For a team of ten, the time and funding needed won't be much; for a team of one hundred, you will need more equipment and a lot more planning to ensure it will be a fantastic day for all.

Matched Time

Since this involves giving money to the charitable organizations supported by employees, there's more of a cost, but it won't be much. First, there are unlikely to be a great many employees who are active with a charity for 50 or more hours annually, and the number diminishes the higher you set the threshold. Just don't set it at an unattainable level: 50 or 75 hours per year is sufficient. Second, the amount of money you agree to donate can be fixed at one amount, or offered at a flexible level, say between €250 and €2,000 (about $375 and $3,000). You may want to have a company-internal panel decide how much to give, based on the impact the money will make to the organization concerned. Proportionality is key here. The right amount will vary by country, e.g., €500 (about $750) will go a lot further in Slovakia than Italy.

Matched Funding

This is the only part of Employee Involvement where costs can spiral upward, and you will need to budget for this in your Corporate Giving. Set clear parameters (e.g., the maximum amount per employee your company will match).

In addition, allocate some funds for internal Communications activities around Employee Involvement. (For more information on this, see Chapter 10.)

Personnel requirements

The size of your company, the number of countries where you operate, and the size of those operations, will all affect your personnel needs. In a smaller company, one part-time employee per country spending about 30% of their time organizing Employee Involvement may be enough. In a bigger company with larger operations, you may find you need an Employee Involvement manager to lead the programs, supported by additional personnel (e.g., Employee Involvement coordinators and administrative support) as necessary. Job descriptions for Employee Involvement managers and coordinators can be found at the end of Chapter 2.

Insurance

Before your employees go out to volunteer in the community, discuss any insurance requirements with your HR colleagues. Regulations vary from country to country. Generally, if employees volunteer on company time, they should be covered by insurance.

The Business Case for Employee Involvement

If you strive for successful Community Involvement, you cannot achieve it without having some form of Employee Involvement: stakeholders would simply not consider your involvement complete.

Nowadays, with increased stakeholder expectations, strategically managed Employee Involvement can help strengthen a company's image by:

- Involving employees, customers, and business partners in community activities

- Contributing real value to the communities where employees work and live

- Winnings hearts and minds – internally and externally

From a company perspective, Employee Involvement benefits communities, employees, and the company in a "triple win." Communities get valuable help, as well as access to a range of skills and resources from the private sector. Employees get personal satisfaction from contributing to society, experience themselves and others in different roles (e.g., suddenly a personal assistant is in charge), and gain new skills and experience.

Benefits of Employee Involvement to the company

While it's all well and good that its communities and employees benefit, usually your business will want a little more. Your senior management will probably start to get interested in Employee Involvement when you tell them how it contributes to long-term value-generation for your company externally by:

- Having a positive impact on the communities in which the company sells or operates

- Positively influencing stakeholder opinion, including brand preference, customer retention, and loyalty

- Enhancing corporate reputation and helping reputation risk management by building goodwill in the community

- Contributing to the social brand dimension and the desired image of "human and trusted"

- Fostering a positive image in Investor Relations, as a relevant aspect of Socially Responsible Investment

Having heard about reputation benefits, senior managers may become even more interested when you explain the use of Employee Involvement as a strategic HR tool, with benefits such as:

- Promoting team-building and strengthening team spirit

- Generating a sense of accomplishment and pride among employees

- Contributing to the quality of internal leadership: giving employees an opportunity to experience themselves in different roles and responsibilities

- Increasing motivation

- Improving working climate, retention, and loyalty

- Having a positive impact on corporate culture: with the right program, you can start to bring corporate and personal values together

The competition for qualified and motivated talent in an increasingly globalized world is widely recognized – and more and more prospective employees want to know about their future employer's Corporate Responsibility record. In a study conducted at top universities in the US in 2001, high-potential graduates named the following three top criteria for selecting their future employer:

- What will my job be about?

- How much will I be paid?

- What is the company's Corporate Responsibility record, and does it include Employee Volunteering?

According to the Universum Pan European Student Survey 2008,[8] when choosing their future employer, the best business and engineering graduates from top institutions in 11 countries now look for companies having a high standard of ethics and strong commitment to Corporate Responsibility.

Employees are proud to work for a company that is socially involved and feel a higher degree of identification with the company. In Germany, 80% of job seekers prefer to work for companies that are involved socially and environmentally, while 40% would accept less pay for the opportunity to volunteer during work time.[9] This is why increasingly companies are leveraging their Corporate Responsibility profile in their recruitment. Employee Involvement helps address this area, although obviously your company has a

---

8 www.universumglobal.com/IDEAL-Companies-Rankings/The-Pan-European-Graduate-Survey, accessed December 2009.

9 M. Blumberg and V. Scheubel, *Hand in Hand: Corporate Volunteering als Instrument der Organisationsentwicklung in Deutschland* (Bremen, Germany: brands & values GmbH, 2007).

number of other Corporate Responsibility areas to address. The benefit here is that you can describe activities in which employees can get directly involved, regardless of their future role with you.

Companies that offer strategic Employee Involvement are perceived as attractive employers and benefit from improved employee attraction and retention. Strategic Employee Involvement has a direct impact on a Company's workplace image. Companies that leverage Employee Involvement as a strategic HR tool often position it as a means of promoting better work–life balance and as part of the company's Employee Value Proposition.

> When Nokia's Moscow office was fairly new and had just recruited 40 employees, country management and HR took all employees to an orphanage on the outskirts of the city for a volunteering and team-building day. The employees painted and renovated a building, played and ate with the children, and brought clothes and toys for them. After a long and fulfilling day, one young employee sank into his seat on the bus, saying, "Now I really understand the Nokia values."

Selling it to your Board

So what if your Board asks about the cost of giving employees two days of paid leave a year for volunteering. Wouldn't this be an amount that goes into millions? What is your answer?

First, you will need to build up Employee Volunteering. You can be proud if you actually reach a target of 30% of staff volunteering. Second, you can count and attach a monetary value to all the hours contributed by employees on company time – and report that monetary value in your Corporate Responsibility report as a contribution to the community. Third, this represents low-cost personal development for many employees who would otherwise not benefit from this type of development. Last, but not least, the Board may like to hear how much money can be saved on other team-building activities that involve travel and hotels, possibly event agencies, outdoor activities, and dinners plus drinks.

Experience demonstrates that employees get more out of volunteering than out of event-style team-building, and they can still have their barbecue and a few drinks together in the evening. HR departments find that employees come back from volunteer days feeling fulfilled and more connected to the company's values. They find that Employee

Tip for getting your Board on board

When you go about convincing your Board, consider inviting them to take part, individually or together, in their own volunteering experience. Seeing is believing, after all! Senior managers or Board members who have participated in volunteering activities are often the best advocates for your program, helping with internal marketing and external visibility.

Volunteering, apart from benefiting both communities and employees, actually saves the company money that would otherwise be spent on potentially less meaningful team events.

Figure 8.1 will help you to make the Business Case for Employee Involvement. Participation can reach remarkable levels when informal networks receive the formal support of their management.

Figure 8.1 **The Business Case for Employee Involvement offers a triple win**

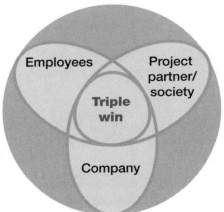

- Imparting new ideas, experiences, skills, and social competency
- Facilitating team-building
- Conveying experience of creating impact
- Improving personal satisfaction

- Getting started through help from enough committed individuals
- Accountable on-site benefit
- Professional-ization of project partners
- Stabilization of local infrastructure

- Credibility and reputation gain as good Corporate Citizen – employees as company ambassadors
- Development of networks in society
- Strengthening the "one-company culture," supporting brand values
- Increasing employees' identification with the company, and more employees get engaged in the following year

Source: adapted from a graph by Deutsche Bank

Getting started: the five-step process

You will need personnel and some funding to get started. Ask your business for the modest support you will need. Once you have appropriate resources in place, you can follow a simple **five-step process** (see Figure 8.2).[10]

Figure 8.2 **A five-step process for designing your Employee Involvement initiative**

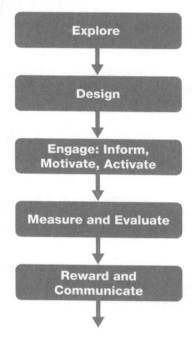

We will now expand on the five steps outlined in Figure 8.2 with checklists for each step.

---

10 Developed by M. Blumberg and V. Scheubel for M. Blumberg and V. Scheubel, *Hand in Hand: Corporate Volunteering als Instrument der Organisationsentwicklung in Deutschland* (Bremen, Germany: brands & values GmbH, 2007).

Step 1: Explore

Within the community

Checklist 1. Ask community organizations the right questions:

✓ What key issues is your organization currently facing?

✓ What experience do you have of working in partnership with companies?

✓ How do you currently use volunteers within your organization?

✓ What kinds of roles do they or might they play?

✓ In which areas of our work could your employees bring the most benefit, in terms of skills, practical help, financial advice, project management, strategic management, and research and development?

✓ Do you have a project manager/coordinator who would be our main contact?

✓ Could you help us with evaluating our contributions?

Within the company

Checklist 2. Find out from different departments, e.g., HR, Internal Communications, senior management

✓ Is there buy-in from senior management? Is someone prominent (e.g., a Board member) willing to champion the cause of Employee Involvement?

✓ Is there HR understanding of the strategic value of Employee Involvement?

✓ What social issues could employees impact the most? Which of those are most relevant to your company?

✓ What kind of help could employees provide in the community?

- Sharing company-relevant expertise?
- Using employees' general business expertise?
- Providing "extra pairs of hands"?

✓ How much operating budget will you need to start Employee Involvement activities?

✓ How much staff support will be needed?

✓ Will Internal Communications support you, and how can you work together?

→

✓ Does the company need/want to provide training for volunteers? How can this be done? Through the company's learning and development department? Through NGOs requiring the help of volunteers?

✓ What do you need to arrange in order to offer Matched Time or Matched Funding?

✓ Who needs to agree on a policy regarding paid time off for volunteering?

✓ Will insurance or health and safety issues need to be clarified before the first employees go out volunteering on company time?

✓ What practical support will be needed for volunteer projects (e.g., transportation, equipment, food/snacks)?

With employees

It is important that the activities offered match employees' interests and abilities.

Checklist 3. Ask employees the right questions:

✓ What kind of volunteer activities would you be interested in?

✓ How much time would you be willing to spend volunteering?

✓ How often would you like to volunteer?

✓ What talents or skills could you/would you like to contribute to the community?

✓ Have you volunteered before? What experience could you offer? (It can help to remind employees that caring for an elderly relative or coaching at the local football club counts as volunteering.)

You can find out informally through conversations or create a short questionnaire that you circulate among your colleagues. Communicate clearly and consider offering a prize draw in which all returned questionnaires will be entered, or offer to donate a small amount of money per questionnaire returned to a charity of the employees' choice – a good way to ensure a higher return.

Remember to think about the different needs of office workers and remote or home-based workers; nine-to-five and shift workers; or white- and blue-collar employees. They won't all have the same requirements or expectations related to volunteering, and what may be a great concept for one group could be wholly inappropriate for another. Teams on production lines, especially, may find volunteering difficult. Their line managers will often argue that they can't just close down a whole line for a day. A little flexibility is needed here, and creativity to find solutions; for example, having unemployed community members come to the factory for work shadowing or interview practice.

Depending on the country where you are developing Employee Involvement, don't forget about the role of Employee Unions and involve them early on. Since Employee Involvement benefits employees, unions are generally supportive. It's always easier to be an advocate if you have been involved in an initiative's creation.

Step 2: Design

Designing an effective program requires that you invest enough time, effort, and attention to detail at the outset.

Checklist 4. Design a comprehensive program:

✓ Contact relevant community organizations, build relationships, and agree on cooperation: how to work together, what type of activities would meet both parties needs, etc. (e.g., through a Memorandum of Understanding).

✓ Design an Employee Involvement action plan, also considering relevant volunteering activities (more on types of activities later).

✓ Set clear goals for what you want to achieve (e.g., get the engagement of 10% of employees in the first year).

✓ Design a matching mechanism for Matched Time/Matched Funding including:
  - How to apply and report funds raised/money and/or hours contributed
  - How to direct money to recipient organizations

✓ Design an Employee Involvement Intranet site with information, FAQs, activities, contact details:
  - Outline the employee experience of what it is like to volunteer, what's involved, and what people get out of it
  - Feature employees' volunteering stories

✓ Design an Internal Communications initiative to raise awareness among and motivate employees.

Scale or skill?

Employee Volunteering on a large scale works best if you offer various activities, differentiated according to the level of time and competencies committed. This won't happen overnight but will build up over time. Some activities will work well; others won't.

If you want to get lots of employees involved quickly and count plenty of hours, you may want to organize Social Days or Team Days. A lot of companies also find that, for volunteering, an 80:20 rule applies: 80% of volunteer hours tend to be clocked in through easy, done-in-a-day activities such as tree-planting; cleaning up parks, forests, or beaches; or painting a school. For many companies, skill-based volunteering (e.g., providing accounting or communications assistance) appeals to a smaller number of employees and generally needs to take place on a regular basis.

Of course, there are notable exceptions. IBM claims that all of its Employee Volunteering in 67 countries is skill-based. Their On Demand Community employee volunteering initiative equips employee and retiree volunteers with a set of 150 on-demand tools based on the technology solutions created exclusively by IBM for schools and community agencies. These web-based tools provide employee volunteers with choices of meaningful opportunities, along with training, resources, and specific activities designed to help make them more effective volunteers. The tools also offer valuable assistance to schools and not-for-profit organizations.

It will be important for you to think about strategic weighting of activities. What matters most to your company? Getting in the big numbers of volunteer hours contributed? Contributing your employees' core competencies? A solid mix of both? Different activities bring different benefits to the company, so an Employee Volunteering program can be designed strategically, based on your specific goals and objectives.

Figure 8.3 **Employee Volunteering framework**

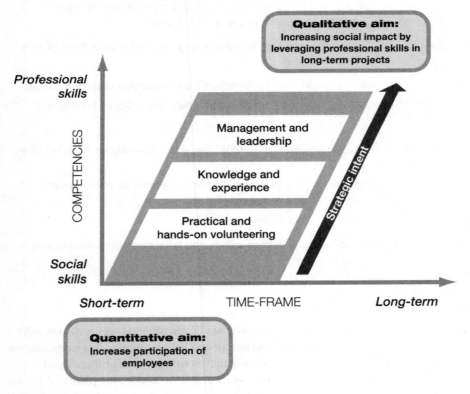

Source: Deutsche Bank

Types of Employee Volunteering activities

As mentioned above, Employee Volunteering can happen in a number of different ways. It is useful to consider the range of possible activities in order to ensure that every activ-

Different types of Employee Volunteering activities

- **Done-in-a-day projects** (e.g., "one-offs," grassroots activities, any good cause). Local activities/events designed to involve all or part of the workforce. Often used for team-building and increasing motivation, these work best when used to kick-start longer-term projects, or as a "global service day."
- **Team development assignments.** Projects created by the community organization in cooperation with the company, designed both to benefit the community and to meet the company's own team-building/personnel development goals.
- **Regular volunteering.** An employee takes on an agreed regular volunteering role, e.g., a coaching or mentoring role for an individual (in school, youth, or adult) who would benefit from such a relationship. Make sure the employee is comfortable and understands the skills required to do this effectively. Ensure appropriate guidance is provided.
- **Skill-based volunteering.** Employees contribute their professional knowledge and skills (e.g., strategy consulting, financial advice, project management, marketing, communications, HR know-how) pro bono to community organizations.
- **Non-executive roles.** There are a number of non-executive roles that employees can take on in a voluntary capacity, such as serving as a trustee, governor, committee chair, or treasurer at a community organization.
- **Secondments.** The employee (or retiree) works full-time as a staff member of a community organization, with salary and expenses covered by the company.

ity is appropriately tailored to the needs of the community, employees, and the company.

Step 3: Engage: Inform, Motivate, Activate

To actively engage employees, you will need to collaborate with colleagues responsible for Internal Communications (some companies additionally have HR Communications).

Step 4: Measure and Evaluate

See also Chapter 9.

Measure output

This is most easily achieved through an Online Reporting Tool posted on your company Intranet. You can buy one off the Internet or ask your IT Support to help you create one. Measuring outputs is essential for CR Reporting, with such data commonly requested by ratings agencies such as the Dow Jones Sustainability Index.

Checklist 5. You can inform employees and motivate them to become active in Employee Involvement through:

✓ A lively Employee Involvement Intranet site full of information, opportunities, and stories, as well as articles in employee magazines, brochures, and flyers

✓ A "road show," carried out at a series of venues such as company cafeterias (see Employee Involvement Road Show)

✓ Announcements/presentations at monthly or quarterly employee meetings

✓ The active involvement of senior managers who not only champion Employee Involvement in speeches/emails, but also volunteer alongside employees

✓ An Employee Involvement guide booklet

✓ Promotional materials such as banners, posters, and give-aways

✓ Recognition and rewards

Employee Involvement Road Show

This can be an effective approach to informing and motivating employees. A series of road shows are easy to organize, if you follow the simple steps below:

- Choose appropriate locations (e.g., company cafeterias)
- Decorate the location (e.g., with banners and posters)
- Set up information tables with brochures, PCs showcasing the Employee Involvement Intranet site, and sign-up lists for activities
- Engage colleagues from HR and Internal Communications to conduct employee outreach
- Develop a slide show/video about Employee Involvement and broadcast on a big screen
- Invite representatives of your chosen community partner organizations to introduce their organizations and volunteering activities at information booths
- Invite community beneficiaries to tell employees about how their lives have been affected by volunteer activities
- Invite employees who have already volunteered to talk about their personal experiences and the value they got from them
- Engage a senior manager to talk about/champion Employee Involvement, formally or informally
- Distribute to employees low-cost giveaways (e.g., baseball caps, key rings, coffee mugs, and t-shirts) that showcase your company's Employee Involvement logo or otherwise tell the story of your Employee Involvement initiative

Checklist 6. Key output elements to capture are:

✓   Matched Funding – amount raised by employees, amount contributed by company, number of employees supported

✓   Matched Time – amount of time given by employees; amount of money donated by company number of employees supported

✓   Number of employees volunteering, and as a percentage of total staff volunteering

✓   Total number of hours volunteered by employees

✓   Monetary value (in-kind) of hours volunteered (e.g., $20.25 per hour was the international standard for 2008)[*]

To professionally manage your Employee Involvement work, you may want to also track:

✓   Number of organizations helped

✓   Number of beneficiaries (individuals assisted) in communities

✓   Number of employees having received volunteer training

✓   Number of employees volunteering regularly (versus just once a year)

[*]   www.independentsector.org/programs/research/volunteer_time.html, accessed December 2009.

Measure outcomes and impact

See Checklist 7.

Please note: you can measure many of these as part of your company's annual HR survey, but you may also want to follow up directly with the volunteers for more detailed, qualitative feedback.

It is also helpful to speak to the community partner organization after, for example, a team volunteering activity for a debriefing to evaluate how it went, what was helpful, and how to do it even better next time.

Tip: start small. Walk before you run

To get employees started on various types of activities, consider launching a few volunteer pilots led by individuals who have demonstrated their commitment to your goals. That way, you can test, learn from the experience, and then refine your approach. Those who participate early on can become ambassadors for future activities, spreading the word about their experience and recruiting more colleagues.

Checklist 7. To capture the outcome of your efforts, answer the following questions:

✓ What were the outcomes for the community and beneficiaries?

✓ What is the impact on employee motivation and satisfaction? Conduct a qualitative assessment of how employees feel about volunteering, e.g., are they feeling

- More connected to local communities?
- A sense of personal growth and development?
- A sense of reward?

✓ Do volunteer feedback forms provide good material for reporting and storytelling?

✓ What is the impact of your Employee Involvement efforts on staff retention and loyalty? What about on corporate reputation?

✓ Because of Employee Involvement, are employees:

- Identifying more with the company?
- Experiencing a match between corporate values and their personal values?
- Perceiving the company as socially responsible?

Online Employee Involvement tracking tools

As their Employee Involvement gets more sophisticated and takes place in more countries, many companies find it is easier and more reliable to set up an internal online reporting tool. An example is the GIFTS tool used by organizations such as Barclays,[11] which implemented GIFTS in October 2000. Before GIFTS, the company's grants management system, which consisted of another software program and Excel spreadsheets maintained by different staff in numerous locations, was very time-consuming. Someone would have to type in all the voucher data by hand and community managers could not access it. With offices in 63 countries around the world, one of the challenges Barclays faced was how to record community activity across the world. Barclays wanted their data to be live and accessible in real time.

An online reporting tool is useful for managing Matched Time and Matched Funding. It is also good for tracking volunteer activities, but outcomes and impacts may require community or HR experts to analyze the information. You could ask your IT colleagues to build your company's own online reporting tool.

---

11 See www.microedge.com/products/casestudies/barclays.asp, accessed October 2009

Use measuring and evaluation as a management tool

Use the results from your evaluation to set targets for next year and decide on future activities and improvements to your engagement, activation, and recognition processes.

Setting up a new Employee Involvement program is a steep learning curve. It is also good practice to get into the habit of regularly assessing how the management of the program could be improved both internally and with community partners. This will help your program become more efficient and help you extract learning for effective future activities.

Step 5: Recognize, Reward, and Communicate

It is important to recognize employees for their contributions to their communities. Regardless of the country or organizational culture in which employees live and work, recognizing, rewarding, and communicating their efforts will contribute to maintaining and increasing their motivation, and spreading the Employee Involvement spirit throughout your organization.

Make sure you let both employees and top management know how many colleagues volunteered and how many hours they contributed. Also, take the time needed to capture and communicate success stories. If you have impressive numbers and stories to show, get them into your CR and Annual Report.

External communication of Employee Involvement

Reputation gain is a major benefit of Employee Involvement. You can help achieve this through having employees talk about their activities on behalf of the company to their families, friends, and acquaintances – and also customers and business partners. Do not underestimate the value of word-of-mouth publicity! You can also work with your NGO partners to get the word out to local and regional media. Your NGO partner can invite

Checklist 8. Ways to recognize and reward Employee Involvement efforts:

✓ An acknowledgment email automatically generated in response to employees reporting their monetary contributions and/or volunteering hours through an online reporting tool

✓ Storytelling on the Intranet and in employee magazines – collect quotations from volunteer feedback forms to provide good material

✓ Outreach to local/regional media, especially when your activities coincide with national/international events (e.g., International Volunteer Day, Earth Day)

✓ Annual awards or celebration events (e.g., recognition by the CEO, a festive dinner with the Board, a volunteer summer party, a prize for the most outstanding volunteer team to dedicate to a charity of their choice)

a local reporter to your activity, or place a photo and an article in a local or regional newspaper. Keep your colleagues in the Communications department informed about your activities. Every once in a while, they may be able to spotlight your efforts as part of a wider initiative, e.g., the aforementioned Earth Day on April 22 or International Volunteer Day on December 5. (See Chapter 10 for further information on how to communicate Community Involvement activity internally and externally.)

Employee Involvement success factors: A summary

You have now worked through a number of checklists. Here's one last checklist to help make sure you succeed:

Checklist 9. Summary of success factors for Employee Involvement

✓ Check out good practice from other companies. Join networks and/or talk to peers in charge of Employee Involvement activities at other companies.

✓ Get buy-in and, wherever possible, enlist the active participation of senior management. Engage a senior-level champion for your Employee Involvement initiatives.

✓ Appoint a coordinator to make it happen and make sure the work is in his or her objectives.

✓ Create a clear action plan for delivering against agreed objectives.

✓ Work with community organizations that know what they are doing and that are prepared to address your company's needs and expectations, as well as their own.

✓ Pick community projects that really need help and make a difference.

✓ Anticipate and address any health, safety, and liability issues.

✓ Engage the hearts and minds of employees.

✓ Prepare employees beforehand: make sure they have all the information and potential training they require in good time.

✓ Agree at an early stage about how Employee Involvement activities will be measured.

✓ Recognize and reward employees' efforts and contributions.

Appendix 8.1. Further assistance

Helpful tools include:

- Checklists of competencies and skills related to specific volunteer opportunities

- Briefing notes to prepare employees prior to meeting with community organizations

- An online reporting and feedback tool to record employees' contributions

Volunteer centers

In many countries, national, regional, or local volunteer centers can help your company get started.

Idealist.org offers a comprehensive list of volunteer centers and associations internationally and by country, including the US and Canada, Western and Eastern Europe, Asia, Africa, and South America, at www.idealist.org/volunteer/vol_sites.html, accessed December 2009.

If you want to get started on your own and contact NGOs in your country directly, easy starting points tend to be:

- International Federation of Red Cross1 and Red Crescent Societies (www.ifrc.org)

- UNICEF (www.unicef.org)

- Plan International (plan-international.org)

They are experienced in working together with companies and will be prepared to work with your company's volunteers.

You can also join ENGAGE, an international program that brings together businesses and community organizations around the globe to increase the quality and amount of Employee Involvement in their local communities (www.engageyouremployees.org).

9

'You can't manage what you don't measure'
How to measure, evaluate, and report Community Involvement

Evaluation is not done for its own sake. It provides you with much-needed management information: you can review your program, compare results, and make informed decisions about what to do next and how to improve on what has come before.

In this chapter, we will look first at the measurement and evaluation (M&E) of Community Involvement, and then at how you report your results. We want to help you feel comfortable with M&E as a planning and management tool. Using a simple, easy-to-follow eight-stage process, M&E can (and should) be fully embedded as a standard part of your Community Involvement program management.

The eight-stage approach to M&E[1]

Stage 1: Make a commitment to evaluate

First, you and your colleagues need to be committed to evaluation. Often, M&E gets attention only as an afterthought, when a project is already well established and has been running for some time. Doing it this way, you run the risk of doing exactly what you want to avoid: evaluating for the sake of evaluating.

Historically, M&E has not addressed the results of charitable giving, seeing it as inherently "good." However, measuring expenditure in isolation is not an indicator of good Corporate Responsibility and societal impact.

---

1 Adapted from Boston College Center for Corporate Citizenship's Seven Steps, and 'Evaluation in Ten Stages' developed by Catherine Shaw, National Children's Bureau, London.

M&E in eight stages

Stage 1: Make a commitment to evaluate
Stage 2: Clarify the purpose of your evaluation
Stage 3: Frame evaluation questions and identify data you need to answer those questions
Stage 4: Evaluation design and selection of methods
Stage 5: Planning, practicalities, resources
Stage 6: Data collection
Stage 7: Analysis and interpretation, reflection and action
Stage 8: Reporting and dissemination

External stakeholder audiences have become more demanding and want to know what *difference* a company's funding made. Accordingly, companies have become increasingly dedicated to and sophisticated about measuring program results and impact. They now apply the same rigor of continuous improvement to their Community Involvement as they do to their core business.

Your project management will not be complete without sound M&E. Fundamentally, we believe you can't manage what you don't measure. M&E is a planning and management tool to both *prove* and *improve* outcomes and impact of overall Community Involvement and specific programs, in terms of both societal results and business benefits.

Stage 2: Clarify your purpose and objectives

Already in your project planning phase, think carefully, together with your NGO partner(s), about what program and business outcomes you would like to see.

Examples of social and business objectives for a Community Involvement program could be:

- **Social objective.** "Change attitudes and behavior around access to education among teachers, children, and parents"

- **Business objective – external.** "Positively affect the opinions of key stakeholders about the company"

- **Business objective – internal.** "Increase employee motivation and retention through employee volunteering"

Plan carefully in order to reach these objectives and consider what metrics will help you know if you are making progress along the way.

Stage 3: Frame evaluation questions

Based on the objectives you define, next work out what questions you want to answer about your program activities.

The key questions are: What is the model of change you want to implement, and what do you need for that? How much change do you want to see? How much are you prepared to pay for that?

Other often-asked questions include: Is our program needed in society? Is it worth undertaking, and do we have a reason to continue? What would convince us of that? Are we making a difference? What can we improve? How can we have a bigger societal impact?

And from a business perspective: Is the program good value for money, both for society and for the company? Is it cost-effective? How much "effect" do you get for your money, for society and for the business? For example, your program might make a big change to the learning of teachers and children, but it might reach too few teachers and children overall, being too costly on a per teacher/per child basis.

It can be helpful to start thinking first of the qualitative, long-term outcomes you would like to achieve, and then work backwards, considering what that would mean in terms of numeric output, and – last, but not least – in terms of the input contributions your company would have to make.

It is easy to get confused by such notions. Figure 9.1 should help to explain.

Figure 9.1 **The LBG model**

	Inputs			Outputs		
	Cash	Time	In-kind	Leverage	Community benefits	Business benefits
Community activity	Total cash contributed	Value of the time contributed by employees during company time	The "at-cost" value of in-kind contributions	Additional contributions to the activity from other sources	Quantified details of how the activity has benefited society, e.g., number of people helped	Quantified details of how the activity has benefited the company, e.g., value of positive press coverage

Community and business impacts
Assessment of the long-term achievements of the activity, i.e., how is the world a better place as a result?

Source: LBG: www.lbg-online.net

The LBG model is used by companies around the world to assess and report on the value and achievements of their corporate community investment.

Input is about your company's contribution, e.g., program funding, employee volunteer hours, or management support. This tends to be quantitative/numerical information: How much money and how many hours have you contributed?

You then undertake **activities** to implement your program and achieve objectives. This leads to both outputs and outcomes.

Output is about *quantitative* measurement: it is about resulting numbers/statistics, e.g., how many teachers and children participated in your program? How many hours did they spend in class using your program's educational materials?

Outcomes are about the difference your program made, and you usually have to make a *qualitative* assessment of that. Many people, such as LBG in their model, also speak about **impact**: the potential *longer-term* effects for beneficiaries and in society overall.

You can see that evaluating outcomes is more difficult and more demanding than simply counting numbers.

When monitoring output and assessing outcomes, it can also be useful to distinguish between direct and indirect beneficiaries of your programs:

- Direct beneficiaries are usually those who participate directly in your program.

- Indirect beneficiaries tend to be those who, although not participating directly in your program, will still benefit from it in some way (e.g., families or communities).

Defining and selecting Key Performance Indicators

Key Performance Indicators (KPIs) are financial and non-financial metrics used to help an organization define and measure progress toward predefined organizational goals. They are the basis for collecting **evidence**. Based on specific KPIs, you can set the output and outcomes targets you want to reach year on year, manage your program accordingly, and then measure and evaluate to prove the tangible societal and business results of your Community Involvement.

In Appendix 9.1 on pages 209f., we offer you a list of sample output and outcomes KPIs for a corporate-funded youth education program in schools. These examples might trigger your thinking about KPIs for your own programs.

Stage 4: Evaluation design and selection of methods

In designing your evaluation, you should also be guided by the right kind of questions from the start: How do you prove that your Community Involvement project has made a real difference to society? How do you prove that from creating societal impact, your business has also benefited in its reputation, brand image, customer purchase intentions, or overall stakeholder relations? Your personal hunches and anecdotal experience are not sufficient proof – you will need solid data.

Design your evaluation so it is "fit for purpose." Think about what evidence you need. What data would be credible and convincing for each relevant internal and external stakeholder group?

How will you collect that evidence? Your overall approach will probably comprise a combination of methods. You will probably monitor quantitative data, asking: How much? How many? This is about collecting a record of inputs and outputs.

Qualitative data will usually occur in the form of words, spoken or written. Qualitative methods assess outcomes and impact, asking: Did we make a difference? To gather qualitative data, you can ask people to describe their experiences. If a project is a success, express your findings in the language of positive change, showing what has improved for beneficiaries; a "before and after" model can be helpful. Assessing that often includes the use of questionnaires or interviews with participants, getting together focus groups for a discussion of their experiences, or observing participants in a program. You may also consider other more creative routes, such as taking photographs or making videos.

Where it comes to assessing business results, there is also a combination of approaches available: To assess employee awareness and opinion, work with HR to use your company's annual HR survey as well as your own questionnaires to employees or employee focus groups. For external stakeholder opinion, make sure stakeholder attitudes to your Community Involvement are included in ongoing stakeholder research in the company, or commission some qualitative stakeholder and opinion leader research yourself. To gauge overall public awareness, can your Communications colleagues monitor your media coverage for you? Your Marketing colleagues might want to assess in their quarterly consumer studies whether customers are aware of your Community Involvement activities, and how that impacts on their opinion of the brand and the company. Do they think yours is a brand they can "trust"? Do they feel more loyal to your company or brand?

Participative approaches to Measurement and Evaluation

Participative approaches are about doing research not only *on* people, but also *with* people, involving beneficiaries in designing and understanding the research. User involvement in research certainly takes more time and effort, but it will get you richer results. It may also help you get more accurate assessments: you may have designed questions for beneficiaries, but they may not cover the very experiences that were most important to them and that they really want to talk about.

Using innovative and creative approaches for a qualitative assessment, increasingly researchers invite program participants to keep diaries or make scrapbooks, or to take pictures themselves. This approach also gives you the much-needed human-interest stories that will bring to life the numbers you report.

Distinguish between project and process evaluation

While you should be measuring and evaluating input, output, and outcomes of your projects and programs, you should also evaluate your own and your partners' management processes: Are they efficient? Are they effective?

Process evaluation is about asking the question "How well did we do it?" It is about the quality of delivery. Accordingly, you will usually look to collect qualitative information.

Consider the quality, efficiency, and effectiveness of your cooperation with government or NGO partners. Your criteria might be the quality of your trust in each other, the quality of your combined teamwork, the effectiveness of leadership and decision-making, or the efficiency of communication and transparency between you, including your mutual reporting processes. You might also want to look at whether meeting and work processes are efficient and effective, or whether they cause frustration and you encounter stumbling blocks.

The quality, efficiency, and effectiveness of NGO partners' cooperation with community beneficiary organizations are also relevant. What about the communication between them? Is that flowing smoothly? Is training delivered well? Is your NGO partner supporting and supervising beneficiary organizations (grantees) appropriately? Is the financial distribution to all implementing parties running smoothly, correctly, and as planned? Is the reporting from the beneficiary organizations/grantees to your partner timely, and does it cover all relevant data?

You may also want to look at the process in the quality of program delivery, e.g., asking, "How are teacher's lessons being delivered in class? Does that work well for the students? (How) could that be improved?"

Internally, what about HR processes for promoting and enabling volunteering? Are those effective? Could they be improved?

How about the capacity building your company is contributing toward your NGO partner(s)? For example, have employees helped an NGO with its Communications strategy or Marketing plan, or with upgrading its IT? Have top managers helped an NGO with its strategy? All of this counts and is worth capturing.

Stage 5: Planning and practicalities – costs, time, and expertise

Make sure that you budget sufficient for Measurement and Evaluation: about 5–10% of your overall Community Involvement program budget is reasonable. The more you invest in a community initiative, the more you need to be able to thoroughly evaluate it. On the other hand, don't overspend on M&E. It needs to be affordable, and it needs to be relevant.

Remember that the M&E process takes time. Plan for M&E phases when you design your project timelines. Be realistic: e.g., don't measure too early, but when your NGO partner will have its first results to show. In any social program, the first year might be entirely about putting things in place, so there might not be much to measure yet. Participation numbers can then be monitored on an ongoing basis.

Where it comes to outcomes, the more vulnerable the beneficiaries' group supported, the more sensitive you may need to be about how long it may take to see meaningful change. You probably can't expect to see results after only six months, but it may make sense to undertake some outcomes assessments once a year, starting at least at the end of year two. At the end of your program, for example if it was designed to last three or five years, take a retrospective full review.

Having gained a key understanding of M&E, you do not necessarily have to carry it out yourself – you can commission and oversee it. Aspects to take into account are:

- What data is already being collected, and who has data and can contribute it?

- What new types of data do you need to collect?

- Do you need to do that yourself, or who can help you with it?

Some data may come from your NGO partners: they may already have developed an M&E framework that could be applied or modified for your program. For sound M&E, you may also want to consider external assurance and accreditation, using third-party evaluators for robust and credible assessment of your program outcomes that you can report on. Involve a university research department or a professional research company. To give some examples:

Nike worked with the International Center for Research on Women to develop and implement a framework that measures the impact of initiatives aimed at developing self-confidence, decision-making, and other life skills among young girls.[2]

Nokia with their NGO partner the International Youth Foundation worked with the Center for Youth Development at Brandeis University to assess the improvement in life skills among 2,500 young people in ten countries that participated in their joint Make a Connection program.[3]

Adobe worked with the Education Development Center to put an impact measurement framework in place for its Adobe Youth Voices program, which focuses on life skills and technology skills for underserved youth of middle- and high-school age.[4]

One final methodology to consider for tracking the business benefits of Community Involvement programs is to use the marketing technique of econometric modeling. This is a forecasting and analysis technique employing mathematical equations used in this case by companies to look at the individual effects of various possible drivers of sales. For example, what contribution do various marketing techniques such as advertising or direct marketing make to the sales being made? It is possible to link this to community programs; however, to identify a Community Involvement program through the customer data requires it to stand out from all the other company marketing and communications "noise" being made. This will only be possible with very high-profile, customer-oriented initiatives that truly stand out. For example, community initiatives by UK retailers Sainsbury's (Active Kids)[5] and Tesco (Tesco for Schools and Clubs)[6] are distinctive enough to be analyzed in this way.

Stage 6: Data collection

This is the time when you and your colleagues, partners, or contractors go "out there" to collect the evidence you are looking for, applying the design you have made and the methods you have chosen.

Stage 7: Analysis and interpretation, reflection and action

On an annual basis, use insights from the evaluation of implemented activities to review whether desired outcomes have been achieved.

A simple model you can use was developed by the Boston College Center for Corporate Citizenship (Figure 9.2). Where would you plot your community programs in relation to value to the community and benefit to the company? Do they have "star" quality?

---

2 www.nikefoundation.org/files/The_Girl_Effect_News_Release.pdf, accessed December 2009.

3 my.brandeis.edu/news/item?news_item_id=103791&show_release_date=1, accessed December 2009.

4 www.edc.org/projects/adobe_youth_voices_program_evaluation, accessed December 2009.

5 www2.sainsburys.co.uk/ACTIVEKIDS/Default.aspx, accessed December 2009.

6 www.tescoforschoolsandclubs.co.uk/how-it-works.php, accessed December 2009.

Figure 9.2 **'Star' programs deliver both value to communities and benefit to the company**

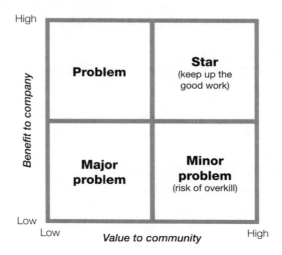

Figure 9.3 **Planning, implementation, and evaluation cycle**

If they don't, what can you improve? Or what do you need to discontinue? If you find it is worth continuing your program activities, use evaluation insights as a management tool to improve current activities and plan future program activities accordingly. Assess whether your programs are replicable and scalable, and whether you'd like to make them bigger.

As you go through your planning cycle, you may want to also re-evaluate whether your KPIs are still appropriate: have you learned something new that makes you want to readjust them, going into the next year of your program?

Improving Community Involvement program activities based on evaluation of program outcomes will lead you to further planning. In summary, see Figure 9.3 for an illustration of that cyclical management process.

Stage 8: Reporting and dissemination

To give you a comprehensive overview of requirements for reporting, Stage 8 forms the second part of this chapter.

Reporting on Community Involvement activities as part of Corporate Responsibility and Sustainability

Reporting on Corporate Community Involvement activities is part of overall Corporate Responsibility and Sustainability reporting. It would not make sense to look at Community Involvement reporting in isolation. This is why we will first give you a brief understanding of Corporate Responsibility and Sustainability reporting in general, before engaging with the kind of reporting content you can contribute from a Corporate Community Involvement perspective.

Understanding Corporate Responsibility and Sustainability reporting

Corporate Responsibility (CR) reporting is directed at communicating proven results and impact to all interested stakeholder groups (refer back to Chapter 1 for a detailed understanding of stakeholder groups). One core purpose of CR and Sustainability reporting is to build corporate reputation among stakeholders, to inform stakeholder dialogue, and to gain and maintain stakeholder trust. The data your company collects provides it with the means to satisfy the diversity of information requests of external stakeholder groups, such as international rating agencies, politicians, communities, environmental organizations, and your customers. This information helps stakeholders understand the company's current state and potential risks and how the company is addressing them, and the company's future opportunities for sustainable business and innovation.

The first and foremost external stakeholder reporting tools are your company's global and local websites and the company's annual CR report. CR reports are usually featured in full online, and many companies choose to print only abbreviated versions or brochures that feature summaries or highlights, or to showcase specific flagship initiatives.

Socially Responsible Investment (SRI)

The financial community is a key driver for enhanced transparency and more effective CR reporting by companies. An increasing number of investors — both private and institutional — are demanding more accurate information on companies' environmental and social performance to guide their investment decisions, as they believe that good performance in these areas can affect the company's overall performance.

SRI combines investors' financial objectives with their concerns about social, environmental, and ethical issues. Green, social, faith-based, and ethical funds are mutual funds using such screens for their portfolio selection. An increasing number of pension funds invest part of their money according to socially responsible criteria, and there is growing evidence of such interest groups effectively influencing business strategy: for example, by lobbying at shareholder meetings.

This has led to the development of a number of sustainability indices, and many other stakeholder groups also rely on the ratings provided by them.

Global sustainability indices include:

- Dow Jones Sustainability Index (www.sustainability-indexes.com)

- FTSE4Good (www.ftse.com/Indices/FTSE4Good_Index_Series/index.jsp)

Companies also receive reporting requests from, among others: AccountAbility, Carbon Disclosure Project, EIRIS (Ethical Investment Research Service), IIGCC (Institutional Investors Group on Climate Change), InnoVest, Insight Investments, IÖW (Institute for Ecological Economy Research), KLD, oekom research, Société Générale, and Vigeo.

With so many ratings and rankings now in existence, companies have to prioritize and make an informed choice about which indices are most important for their company to be included in. These decisions tend to be taken by the CR department together with Investor Relations.

A second purpose of CR and Sustainability reporting is to engage in extended stakeholder dialogue based on the reporting delivered. The most advanced companies are interested in how their stakeholders respond to their CR reporting information.

The Global Reporting Initiative

In many companies, CR and Sustainability reporting is guided by the requirements of the Global Reporting Initiative (GRI). GRI is a multi-stakeholder initiative. Its mission is to develop and disseminate a global framework of sustainability reporting guidelines for voluntary use by organizations and encompassing the economic, environmental, and social dimensions of their activities, products, and services. The GRI framework for reporting includes reporting principles and specific content indicators to guide the preparation of organization-level sustainability reports (www.globalreporting.org).

A third intention of reporting is to improve future internal management of CR and Sustainability activities, by looking at reported results as well as stakeholder feedback and interpreting collective data toward opportunities for further improvement.

What Community Involvement data to report

Most CR reporting focuses on governance and environmental issues, but societal impact does count and does affect overall company performance in rankings. However, given the challenge behind measuring community and societal issues effectively, many rating agencies ask only the most basic questions. Unless your company is involved in some highly controversial community issues, your objective for CR reporting will most likely be to summarize the breadth of your company's activity in a short space.

But also make sure you are collecting the data for more reasons than just filling in an external rating form. Reporting for reporting's sake is as bad as measuring without an objective. Usually it is easy to find a good reason for reporting, as companies often have no other process that takes this "helicopter view" on what a company does in its communities.

When collecting community data, try to be as comprehensive as possible. The purpose is to capture all areas in which your company runs or funds programs, projects, and activities that affect your communities. Very simply, start from the perspective: What does your business do that has a positive impact on your communities?

To summarize what may be a diverse range of activities with a community impact from different parts of your company, we recommend that you report all Community Involvement-related activity in one of four categories:

1. Community Involvement projects

2. Corporate Giving

3. Employee Involvement

4. Mandatory expenditure

1. Community Involvement projects

As we have discussed in previous chapters, Community Involvement projects are your company's community activities that involve more than just giving money. These projects are likely to involve a more structured initiative or approach that your company leads or participates in – for example, engaging in community partnerships with local non-profit organizations.

This is the area of your most extensive reporting and Table 9.1 gives you a list of aspects you should be thinking about reporting on.

Table 9.1 **Aspects to report on**

Main aspects to look at	What to report on
Project overview	Provide a short description of each project: What is it? How long will it last? The higher the budget, the more detail you may want to provide
Target group	Who is the initiative aimed at? What stakeholders is the company trying to address or target by engaging in this project?
External partners	Name any NGOs, business partners, government (national or regional) partners involved
Budget	How much money is the company investing on an annual basis in supporting the project? If your company's investment is only one part of a larger project partnership, include information about other project partners and the total budget of the project
Overall budget	If the project lasts for several years, what is the total amount to be spent by your company?
Outputs	How many beneficiaries participated in the program? How many hours did they spend in the program?
Outcomes	What happened? E.g., children improved their grades and shared their learning with their families/communities; teachers improved their teaching; schools decided to implement regular training for the future or to offer it to more children/more age groups; other companies asked to join in your initiative; government adopted your initiative as a new policy
Employee Involvement	Did the community project include an element of Employee Involvement? If so, provide any information you have on activity, charity partner supported, number of employee volunteers involved, and hours contributed (e.g., an education program at local schools, 20 employees involved, 180 hours contributed)
Process improvements	How was the delivery of program activities improved?
Business benefits	What were the benefits to the company and how were they evaluated? This is to identify what evaluation of corporate benefits from community activities took place. Provide here, e.g., stakeholder feedback, press coverage, awards received; improved brand tonality; visibility through events. Provide any evaluation figures and qualitative information available to you

2. Corporate Giving

Break down information into two further areas:

- Financial donations
- In-kind contributions

(See Chapter 4 for detailed information.)

3. Employee Involvement projects

As we saw in previous chapters, Employee Involvement has three core areas:

Employee Volunteering

Report here the number of employees participating and the percentage out of all employees who have participated, the total number of hours volunteered by them, and the monetary value of hours volunteered (US$20.25 per hour for 2008[7]).

To give you an easy example of the numbers you can report:

- Your company has 50,000 employees
- 15,000 employees have volunteered
- That equals 30% of the workforce
- The total number of hours volunteered was 225,000
- The monetary value of hours volunteered was $4.5 million (about €3 million)

Matched Time

Report on the amount of funds and number of employees supported, as well as the hours volunteered by employees that were matched.

Matched Funding

Report on the number of employees supported and the matched amount donated by the company.

4. Mandatory expenditure

This is any money that you are legally obliged (usually by the government of your country) to invest in your communities, as part of maintaining your license to operate. For example, in Slovakia, companies are required to invest a small percentage of their profits in societal programs. How they do this is up to them. Although your company may be obliged to spend this money, it is still important to capture and report to stakeholders all the ways in which the company is contributing to its communities.

---

7   www.independentsector.org/programs/research/volunteer_time.html, accessed December 2009.

Presenting your data

Make sure you present your data in the language of your audience. That means avoiding jargon and presenting it in clear and understandable forms. In addition to text, use a mix of data tables, bar charts, pie charts, maps, and pictures as appropriate.

Very importantly, do not overstate findings or draw conclusions not supported by the data. It is often difficult to "prove" a causal relationship between positive changes to participants or communities and your program. Was it really (only) your program that effected a particular change? Being transparent about this is better than overreaching. Your company's critical stakeholders could use it against you – undermining otherwise sincere work.

Share human-interest stories

Beyond figures, your colleagues and external stakeholders will also be interested in a few short but emotionally powerful human-interest stories that illustrate your program activities in a lively way. Has a top manager been personally involved in a program? Briefly share that story. Has a program beneficiary, because of one of your programs, had an opportunity to meaningfully change her or his life?

Here are a few short examples of the kind of stories you might like to share (all these events have actually taken place as part of Community Involvement):

- **Endorsement from dignitaries.** Nelson Mandela attending the opening of a school that your company helped build in South Africa; or the President of the Philippines attending the launch of your company's nationwide education partnership program in that country; or the Queen of Jordan visiting your company's youth development program in Mexico when on a state visit

- **Surprising long-term impact.** A young program beneficiary completing your company's program and, with all the confidence and skills acquired through your program, running for mayor in the local community, or starting her or his own charitable foundation and winning public funding for it

- **Improved future prospects.** Young beneficiaries from your work skills training program not only finding gainful employment, but also being promoted to higher positions in their new jobs in a matter of months

- **Your employees' contribution.** Your employees having done outstanding volunteer work in the community, such as renovating a school, building a playground, cleaning up a beach after an oil spill, or acting as mentors to disadvantaged children. At Nokia in Southeast Asia Pacific, the different countries even went into a competition with each other for who had the best volunteer team. Thailand won, with employees having done their own fundraising for a school, traveling for many hours on a bus and spending a long weekend renovating that school. This was once again a great opportunity to communicate to the media.

Communicate fully what you now know

While your colleagues will feature such information in your company's annual CR report, make sure you also provide those data and stories on the Community Involvement pages of your global and all relevant local company websites. You may have common content to feature globally, with examples of activity from particular markets. On local websites, make sure you communicate common global themes, but then focus on presenting local activities.

Some of your reporting data may also be useful for ongoing communications activities. Get your colleagues from the Communications department to integrate your information into the regular updates of your company's internal media briefing notes. This way all your senior management authorized to speak to the media will be aware of that information and can refer to it when the opportunity offers itself in the interviews they give.

This is just a start, and the next chapter is all about how you maximize awareness of your Community Involvement activity.

Why is it worth undertaking all this?

Sound measurement and evaluation of both the process and the results puts you in a position to keep improving what you and your partners do in the community. A comprehensive reporting process can reach many stakeholders and positively influence their opinion of your company's performance. In terms of proving business benefit for the company, your job will only be done when, through getting feedback from reported results, you can in turn prove that corporate and brand image have been influenced positively and stakeholder opinion has improved.

Appendix 9.1. Examples of inputs, outputs, and outcomes

Inputs

Funded by company:

- Program budget: €xx k
- M&E budget: €xx k
- PR budget: €xx k

Personnel support from company:

- Number of full-time employees working on project in CI function
- Number of employee volunteers contributing to the project
- Number of employee volunteer hours contributed to the project

Additional expertise from company – what and how much time?

Example of Key Performance Indicators, outputs, and outcomes for corporate-funded youth education program in schools

Community Involvement area of activity	Sample Key Performance Indicators
Community Involvement program results	*Output:* • Number of schools participating • Number of teaching resources distributed • Number of teachers trained • Number of days/hours teachers spent reading materials and preparing lessons • Number of hours teachers devoted to the topic in classroom activity • Number of children experiencing the lessons • Number of families aware of the program • Number of employees volunteering, also as percentage of total staff • Number of employees volunteering regularly (versus just once a year) • Number of employees having received volunteer training • Total number of hours volunteered by employees • Monetary value (in-kind) of hours volunteered (e.g., US$20.25/h for 2008* as current international standard)

→

* www.independentsector.org/programs/research/volunteer_time.html, accessed December 2009.

Community Involvement area of activity	Sample Key Performance Indicators
Community Involvement program results *(continued)*	*Outcomes:* • How did the teachers' own learning affect their teaching style? Has it become more effective/interactive? • Did children's grades improve? • How were children impacted long-term, e.g., in terms of choosing future focus areas for their studies or their work? Do they perceive opportunities for meaningful career choices? • Did children take what they learned into their families, and did that affect the whole family's behavior?

Business results	*Output:*
	• Degree of internal awareness among employees about Corporate Community Involvement activities
	• External Communications reach, effectiveness, value:
	  – Media coverage (volume and tone)
	  – Online visitor numbers (unique visits and repeat visitors)
	• Sales of products improved/markets expanded
	
	Outcomes:
	• Impact of awareness on employee opinion, motivation, and satisfaction
	• Qualitative assessment of how employees feel about volunteering, e.g.:
	  – Feeling more connected to local communities
	  – Feeling a sense of personal growth and development
	  – Feeling more motivated in day-to-day work due to the volunteering experience
	• Impact on external corporate reputation: "This company is a socially responsible company"
	• Brand tonalities, e.g., "This is a brand I can trust"
	• New or improved business opportunities, increase in sales, etc.

Appendix 9.2. Guidance sheet for planning your Community Involvement projects

When you now plan your program activities, ask yourself the questions on this checklist.

(Program)	(Description)	

Indicators		Targets
Outcomes	What would indicate we have achieved our desired outcome?	• What targets would we set? • What indicators would prove that we have reached our targets? • How do we measure against the indicators – what methods do we need to choose?
Outputs	What needs to be done for us to achieve the outcomes?	
Inputs	What resources and activities are needed?	

Here is a simple tool you can use for your target setting, based on a three-year project plan:

	Three-year target	Indica-tors	Col-lection method and fre-quency	Respon-sible	Target level reached Year 1	Target level reached Year 2	Target level reached Year 3
Outcomes							
Outputs							
Inputs							

10

'But why haven't we heard about this before?'
Communicating your Community Involvement effectively

The following best practice advice and recommendations will help you communicate the positive results of your Corporate Community Involvement and get the most out of it for the benefit of your company's reputation and the motivation of your employees. We will cover this in two parts:

- External communications
- Internal communications

As initial inspiration, a best-practice interview will highlight a successful approach at GlaxoSmithKline.

Interview with Justine Frain: It's important to be authentic

A science PhD, Justine Frain had a long career working in Corporate Communications for Glaxo Wellcome, one of two companies (the other being SmithKline Beecham) that formed GlaxoSmithKline (GSK) in late 2000. With around 100,000 employees in over 100 countries and a turnover of £24 billion ($39 billion), GSK is one of the world's biggest research-based pharmaceutical companies, supplying one-quarter of the world's vaccines.

Appointed to the role of Vice President, Global Community Partnerships, at the formation of GSK, in 2009, Justine also took on responsibility for GSK's Corporate Responsibility (CR). She reports to the Senior Vice President, Corporate Communications & Community Partnerships, a member of GSK's Executive Team. GSK's community strategy is focused on health and education and involves a mix of long-term, global programs addressing specific diseases such as lymphatic filariasis (LF) and HIV/AIDS plus others more regionally focused.

How did this role evolve at GSK?

JF: "In some ways this company is only nine years old, in others, it is a lot older. Our two heritage companies had many ongoing, long-term community commitments. The first CEO of GSK, J. P. Garnier, wanted to bring all the elements together in creating the new company. This function really came to life under him. GSK is a 21st-century company and so taking a more strategic, global approach to our community programs was a logical step."

How important is communications to your role?

JF:" I have a team of 20 in Global Community Partnerships, based half in the UK and half in the US. One of my direct reports is Communications Director for this area, focused on supporting our work. From the start, I saw this as a key role, and I still believe it's very important to have clear communications support.

"The challenge with our work with communities is how to guarantee a communications focus on it. In a very large company, there is always so much going on. We came out of a massive merger and, right from the start, we were in a position where we had great global programs, but at least half the company did not know about them!"

So this made internal audiences a focus for your communications?

JF: "Yes. The balance has evolved over time, but it will always be a major focus. We are fortunate that our Intranet site, 'my GSK,' is a really powerful tool. To give you a sense of scale, we average at least one story on our community activities a week, so that's around 50 stories a year with global reach."

What about other internal communications channels?

JF: "Increasingly, we are using video diaries to capture work in the community. We're also a part of the induction program for new employees, which provides an opportunity to position our work.

"We try to be quite diverse in what we use – for example, 'Town Hall' meetings for our employees with business leaders. Naturally we can't be at every Town Hall, so we've put together a short video showing global programs and relevant regional programs. We also have a number of plasma screens around the company.

"Online is still something we need to do more of. The company has a few blogs, and the graduate placements have their own Facebook. But, as for blogging publicly, it's still early days. Understandably, in the pharma industry, our lawyers are very cautious about what could happen, so we're taking it slowly."

What internal communications don't work so well?

JF: "Well, we used to have printed factsheets. At first, this was very important, but we ended up becoming a mini distribution center and, as the company is increasingly electronic in its communications, we don't print anymore. However, as you'll see on the website, we have PDFs of our programs for both internal and external use, which people can download and our local businesses can print if they want to. That's much more effective."

And for the future?

JF: "We'll definitely use more films. We're not quite at the 'flip video' stage yet, but not far off. I've just [July 2009] been looking at some footage shot in high definition in Africa with our CEO last week when he visited some of our projects accompanied by a journalist from the *Guardian* [a UK national newspaper]. It's being edited and will go internally and externally on the GSK site when the feature's published in the paper.

"We also have a section, called 'Your story,' where employees write on something they feel passionate about. It's a good way to get more emotion and less corporate speak.

"The point is it's important to be authentic. Of course it's a big plus that our CEO, Andrew Witty, gets what we're doing, and, while the issues and programs can be complex, he is able to communicate simply."

How did you achieve that with the CEO?

JF: "It's always been key, and we've been very lucky in having the CEO's support. First with JP then, when Andrew took over last year, he had a period 'in waiting' when he held a series of focus groups around the business throughout the world. He asked people what needed to change and what was the one thing they thought should continue. What surprised him most was the clear message he received that people said 'please don't change our community programs, the way we get involved, our generosity.'

"Obviously that was a big help, and he's shown great commitment in supporting what we do. This doesn't happen overnight – it has built up over time."

What about with other senior managers?

JF: "A key point of engagement is the regionally based governance model that agrees what we fund. Our philosophy is that it's difficult to be in London and decide how money is spent in the US or Africa. So, we have a number of regional committees with cross-business representation, each chaired by an Executive Team member. We have four committees covering the UK, US, Europe, and the rest of the world. This gets senior managers involved and gives us an inroad when they're talking with their employees.

"It all boils down to senior manager buy-in. It's very important, as it helps us to be authentic in what we do."

What other aspects are key for any types of communication?

JF: "We built the word 'partnership' into our function and our communications. Health challenges are complex problems and we just can't go it alone and think we can fix it. The very nature of what we do is about working on the ground as a partner with non-profit organizations. We try to bring that into all our communications and I hope the message is also very clear."

We've talked a lot about internal communications. What about external?

JF: "We made a decision as the corporate function to focus on a limited number of things – our global, developing-world programs and selective regional programs. For example, we run an awards program in the US and UK where the target media is local press. We do focused communications around the GSK IMPACT Awards and use an agency to do this.

"Where we do get support from the corporate team is in the developing-world programs. It's an opportunity to differentiate us from other companies. It helps as well that some of these programs are very big. Our lymphatic program is a 20-year commitment, and it's massive, almost part of the 'DNA' of the company.

"The other challenge with external is that it's hard to get media coverage for doing good. As one of my former communications directors used to say: 'We do a lot of worthy stuff; it's just not all newsworthy.' It's the nature of the media, which is not normally looking for a 'good news' story. So you've got to be different, got to have an angle, but it's tough."

You're a head office function: how do you support your local companies in communicating what they do?

JF: "Interestingly, our local companies may do more, and there are certain activities where we try and help what they do. Like most companies, we have Employee Involvement programs where we try and get people volunteering across the group. Ours is called 'Orange Day.' We put tools on the Intranet to help the local companies, including checklists, risk management guidance, etc. There are template press releases, but it's up to them what they do.

"For example, our Portuguese company is doing some amazing things with their community work, way bigger than you'd expect for the size of their business. They've decided that they want to be recognized for it and so they put the effort into communications."

How much is your communications budget?

JF: "We don't work on a fixed percentage, and I feel the same way about communications that I do about monitoring and evaluation. It is important – you need to do it – but there's no way you should spend 50% of a program budget on M&E. The money needs to go on the purpose, not the communication. So it's about doing something proportionate. On communications, I would say you should aim for no more than 5% of a program budget. In fact, ours is less, but I do make sure we have some communications budget in there."

What about measuring your communications?

JF: "We do this in two parts. First, we occasionally do a dip check: 'Where are we? What do people want?' For example, we've used SurveyMonkey [www.surveymonkey.com] internally to get feedback. Second, periodically we take a more comprehensive approach. Usually this is part of a bigger review. Recently we did this as part of an overall review of the Corporate Communications and Community Partnerships function. This has been very illuminating and, going forward, we will be much more methodical about measurement. It's common sense, really. If you produce things that are not used locally or applied consistently, then you have to question it."

What have been your experiences using communications agencies?

JF: "That depends on the program. My key advice would be to define your budget very clearly and don't end up paying for them to learn the sector. We've worked with some great ones over the years, but sometimes, by year three or four, they can lose momentum. Review the account – even if you still decide to keep them, you're putting them on their toes."

And how best do you work with your in-house communications colleagues?

JF: "My Communications Director acts as our Account Manager with the broader communications team. It's important to be really clear about what we want them to do. It's also helpful to have a calendar of forthcoming events. It's a large department, and this way everyone knows what's coming up.

"By taking the long-term perspective, we don't end up bouncing something on them. It also works well the other way round, as they've come to know we're a good source of stories. GSK has an employee magazine, so, if a business article gets postponed, that team knows we have something in our back pocket and can turn it round fast.

"I've always been very clear we're spending our shareholders' money, so we need to make communications work. Having a CEO who picks up things makes a big difference. Andrew has made 'building trust' one of his key platforms. Clearly this goes beyond community, but we have a big role to play in that going forward."

Maximizing your Community Involvement communications

Successfully communicating Community Involvement is all about how much you want to make it happen. Communications people are professionals, always happy to help, especially where good news is involved. But they will have many other issues, usually crises, to deal with. This means, if you really want your project to get great PR or have your employees love it, you'll need to support as well as challenge them – constructively, of course.

For those of you with no experience in this area, this chapter will toughen up your skills and give you some core tools and processes to use. If you have communications experience already, there may be some welcome reminders and, hopefully, a few new tools for you to use.

This chapter looks at external and internal communications separately, but there are strong connections between the two. Always make sure you think of them together and align your plans.

Working within your organization

Rarely in work is everything in your full control; usually you will need to engage other colleagues around your business. For communications, this is typically the Communications Department. Often responsible for media relations management globally, they will mainly be worried about where the next crisis might hit. However, they will also see the benefits of Community Involvement and, especially if there's good news, be more than willing to help.

There are ways to make their life easier and for you to get the most from their support. If you understand what they are trying to do and their motivation, you can tailor your plans so their involvement in communicating your project meets their wider agenda.

Always brief your media (and any other) spokespeople so they can speak about your Community Involvement projects. When they give interviews or brief politicians, make sure you have given them key messages about your Community Involvement activities. Even when not directly connected to the subject at hand, they can often talk about your Corporate Community Involvement activities as an add-on. Always keep them up to date about what you are doing.

Communications agencies

If you're in the lucky position of having agency support, that is a big help, as they're paid to focus on your project. They will be good at creating and selling stories, but they won't necessarily know your business well. Sometimes this is a blessing, as they don't have to think about office politics and can be a voice of sanity, giving the external view.

If it's a public relations agency, you'll find they're usually very media-driven. You may need to challenge them on keeping in mind your wider objectives and reaching other key audiences (see later). Always be very clear about what your objectives are and agree them (and the budget) upfront. Make sure you're aligned and that they're managing your expectations. Accept it if they tell you it's not front-page news – they're right.

External Community Involvement communications

With increasing attention paid to what companies do in the community, there are more opportunities to build your company's reputation as a responsible member of society. On the other hand, trust in business is also getting worse: while good community projects will improve trust, bad projects or even bad communication can run risks.

Your community programs have positive stories to tell, so use them properly and do it right. There are a number of steps you can follow so that you approach your communications strategically. Simply, this involves building up and then executing a communications plan. A full list of the contents of an outline communications plan can be found in Appendix 10.1 on page 228. The key elements are:

1. Communications objectives

2. Target audiences

3. Key messages

4. Communications strategies and tactics

5. Budget

6. Measurement and evaluation

7. Reporting

Setting up your plan doesn't have to be a complex exercise. You can do this on one piece of paper or on 20. What's important is that you have gone through the process and are clear on what you want to achieve and how you will do it.

1. Communications objectives

Be clear about your objective for wanting to communicate your Community Involvement. It may be one or any of these:

- To position your business as a leader in global and local Community Involvement

- To position your flagship Community Involvement programs as leading global/local Community Involvement programs, and to set a benchmark/best practice for other companies

- To establish good international/in-country relations with your external stakeholders, informing them about your company's activities in the community. External stakeholders include the media and politicians as well as customers and NGOs.

- To raise awareness of and involvement in your Community Involvement program

- To make your employees feel proud of their company, even inspire them to want to take part in your projects

- Or just to make your team, your department, or even yourself look good!

2. Target audiences

Identify your external audiences that you want to reach. This may include all or any of:

- Consumers

- Communities – local stakeholders

- Business-to-business customers

- Business partners

- Suppliers

- Investors

- Government and regulators

- Opinion leaders

- NGOs

3. Create your Community Involvement key messages

Together with your Communications colleagues (and your NGO partners), develop three or four key messages about your Community Involvement. These key messages can be used repeatedly in various contexts. This gives your project focus and, like an elevator pitch, is the important part you want people to remember if they forget everything else.

Your key messages may be a mix of big-picture and local, project-specific messages, or just very locally focused on the project. As you'll have seen from Chapter 1, the projects you do will be designed to position your organization in a certain way. How does your communication feature those overall positioning messages?

Most importantly, keep it simple; keep it relevant. What do you remember when you read a news article? Usually a general sense of what it is about and, maybe, a couple of facts. What do you want people to remember about the project?

4 Communications strategies and tactics

The essence of all good PR is for someone else to speak positively of you/your company. Think of yourself as a recipient of other people's news: the best and most credible communication tends to come from someone you trust recommending something to you.

This leads to our first tip for developing your communications strategy.

Communicate with and through your NGO partner

Journalists rarely want to promote companies through their articles. With this in mind, it may be more appropriate for your NGO partner to engage journalists, and for your company to support your partner in their approach. If your NGO partner is unfamiliar with dealing with the media, you or your Corporate Communications colleagues might offer them some capacity building in this area or generally offer assistance, e.g., developing messages, identifying key media, training spokespeople, or writing a press release together.

For press announcements or press conferences, it is also appropriate for your NGO partner to introduce your joint program and position your company as the supporting partner. Your company does not have to be in charge to get the credit.

Note that press conferences are not the right approach for every country. You may get 25 journalists to a press conference in Budapest or even 45 to one in Moscow – but nothing is worse than having your CEO or Board member turn up to a launch in, say, South Africa to discover all but one of the journalists who confirmed they'd show up have been called away to cover other breaking news. One-to-one interviews with journalists or telephone briefings can be equally effective and less stressful for community experts and press officers as well as the CEO!

If you do not have one of the following, check whether a press conference is the right approach:

- Is it "big news" (and why)?

- Are you announcing a multimillion-dollar initiative?

- Is it something that will reach lots of people?

- Are there any high-profile speakers involved: politicians, celebrities?

- What's new, original, interesting, unique?

If you can't answer "yes" to most of the above, think of an alternative tactic to a formal launch.

Avoid 'going public' too early – preferably have first results to show

We advise against running media events that are mere statements of intent – for example, announcing program activities that are only at the planning stage. Ideally, hold a media event when you can be very clear what you are doing. This may require running a program pilot that would enable you to demonstrate initial results and announce a widening of program activities, or talk about a comprehensive rollout plan. There may be other factors forcing you to communicate your work earlier than you'd like, but the more you control the communications agenda, the better messages and outcome you will have.

Reach your priority audiences

Reach your priority audiences by ensuring your communications are:

- Accessible to them

- Responsive to issues that concern them

- Engaging

Boring communication is never read or published. Find creative ways to identify core themes and larger issues in society to which you can relate your topics.

Research your target market well. What topics/issues matter to them? What makes sense to communicate? What special-interest publications can you target, related to the issues and themes you are supporting? (e.g., magazines on parenting, teachers' magazines, environmental magazines, airline magazines).

Remember media relations is not the only route

It is easy to focus exclusively on achieving press coverage. It can be just as important, sometimes even more so for your company, if you set up stakeholder briefings to communicate with politicians and other third parties. When planning any external communication, always think about how best to reach all your audiences. While key messages must be consistent, tactics will vary.

Using exhibitions, trade fairs, and conferences

As with more traditional forms of marketing, exhibitions may come in handy to promote your project to key audiences: for example, taking your schools project to a teachers' exhibition. Conferences are often better for building credibility – positioning you, your project, and your company as a leader. See what opportunities there are: giving a presentation is obvious; maybe you can also create some materials for delegates.

Online

This medium is increasingly important, for targeting both online versions of traditional media such as CNN.com and, especially, project-relevant forums or channels, for example, a teachers' site. These may not help mass awareness but will be very relevant for reaching your project's key target groups. Often forums for such groups will also be much more open to developing low-cost media partnerships. Online discussion forums are also great for getting informal feedback, although you should be aware that this might be biased.

Work with online and new media experts in your business to develop the right approach for your project.

Make your communications stand out from the myriad of other news

You can do this through:

Accessible case studies and best-practice examples
"Show and tell" works well: present lively case studies; balance "big" numbers with personal stories, interesting photographs, or short films. Have program beneficiaries available to tell their story.

What is the societal problem in question? And how is your program successful in addressing it? Try to find the story angle that makes your cooperation and your program success look unique. It is also helpful if you can position your program as a best practice for other NGO–corporate partnerships.

Famous spokespeople
Third-person testimony about your program activities works strongly in your favor. If a respected government representative or reputable celebrity supports your program, it lends your activities additional credibility. But, remember, celebrities are famous for a reason. Conduct due diligence on their reputation (e.g., verify that they haven't been involved in any scandals), and make sure they have actually visited and experienced the program before speaking about it to the media.

Have award-winning projects
Not every community project can be award-winning. But an innovative partnership, with exciting initiatives, creatively communicated and with measured, society-changing activity, will stand a good chance.

Winning awards for your community projects is a great way of getting both internal and external stakeholder attention and will help to spread the word about your company's great community efforts. Almost every market has award schemes for community projects, from the UK's Business in the Community Awards to Mexico's Empresa Socialmente Responsable (Socially Responsible Corporation). Just look around.

Summary of communications tactics

Examples of communications opportunities are:

- A program launch press conference/press announcement once a successful program pilot has taken place, e.g., after six months
- Regular (e.g., annual) follow-up press announcements, conferences, or stakeholder events for ongoing sharing of program highlights and successes
- One-on-one interviews for journalists or briefings for other stakeholders, e.g., jointly with the head of your partner NGO and a senior company representative
- TV and radio appearances for program participants, NGO, and company representatives (e.g., talk shows or special features around relevant topics)
- Stakeholder, including media, visits to program activities. Note: Make sure your stakeholders and media will mix well if you're bringing them together.
- High-level stakeholder communication to media on behalf of your company (e.g., have an NGO Board member or a local politician talk to the media on your behalf and say positive things about your local Community Involvement)
- Develop targeted articles or opinion pieces in relevant publications (e.g., education magazines, sustainability magazines)
- Online via: individual program website (micro site); coverage on your NGO partner's website; coverage on your local company website
- Community Involvement one-pagers or program brochures in company press folders at conferences and events; get short program videos running on flat screens in the foyer at an event
- Use any other company communication channels, e.g., customer newsletters, to include your news
- Enter your community project for some awards. Win one and tell everyone about it!

Tip for choosing a good time to approach the media

A lot of media people will caution that "good news doesn't sell." For news about your Community Involvement, consider times like the summer, when other news tends to be thinner, or around seasonal holidays, e.g., Christmas, when newspapers like to report on charitable activities. If you know there are other big events coming up, try to avoid fighting to be the most newsworthy (you'll always lose out to "Man bites dog").

There may be a relevant date to tie into: e.g., December 5 is International Volunteer Day. News about your Employee Volunteering activities will be more welcome around this day. Or what about Earth Day in April? It's getting bigger each year and plays well both internally and externally.

5. Budget

Although much communication is inexpensive compared to advertising or sponsorship, some money is still needed. Plan some funding separate from your core community project budget for the following items. This way you ensure higher quality and greater reach for your communication upfront and less last-minute stress in getting something good together when you urgently need it:

- Good photography

- Quality project information

- Quality press materials

- For larger projects, consider PR or design agency support

If the money is coming from your project budget, then you also control it and can factor in that cost when reviewing your program's overall investment.

6. Measurement and evaluation

Wherever possible, track and report on stakeholder feedback and media coverage. If you don't do this, all that you've just read and much of the effort you, your Communications team or PR agency have put in will be wasted. Make sure you collect and share feedback and coverage.

For all online and offline media coverage look out for:

- Copy of the original article

- Name and date of publication

- Summary translation into English

- Tone of the article (positive/negative; mention of program, NGO partner)

- Publication details (daily/weekly/monthly, general interest, business, trade, youth, other)

- Distribution (local, regional, national)

- Circulation

- Was there a call to action? How many readers responded? In what way?

7. Reporting

Share it! Positive reactions to your communication – from the media, stakeholders, or your employees – demonstrate the value of your project and how it is enhancing your company's reputation. Consider which of your internal stakeholders should know about what feedback and coverage your communication receives. Coverage that enhances your company's reputation is a good reason for your business to get you to do more good work.

Internal Community Involvement communications

All of your company's employees should be aware of your Community Involvement activities, want to take part in them as volunteers, and act as multipliers in sharing stories with colleagues, business partners, family, friends, and acquaintances.

You can follow the same approach as with external communications to develop your internal communications plan using the same elements:

- Communications objectives

- Target audiences

- Key messages

- Communications strategies and tactics

- Budget

- Measurement and evaluation

- Reporting

Some golden rules for internal communications:

- Always communicate to your employees before or, at worst, at the same time as you announce externally. Nothing is worse than your own people not knowing what's going on.

- Make it relevant. Why should employees care about what's happening? What's it got to do with them? What's in it for them? And, of course, what do you want them to do about what you've just told them?

- Keep it simple. Love 'em or hate 'em, popular national papers such as the *Sun* in the UK or *Bild* in Germany have editorial policies to write so that an eight-year-old can understand them. It's a good principle to check that what you want to get across to people doesn't go over their heads.

- Use both stories and facts and figures. One without the other is either intangible or impersonal.

Appendix 10.1 on pages 229ff. is a tried-and-tested internal communications checklist with ten simple questions you can use to check if your internal communications are up to scratch.

Inform, engage, involve

As with working with NGOs or building relationships with external stakeholders, one communication rarely clinches the deal. Here's a simple three-step principle:

- **Inform.** First, communicate it and make sure they understand it.

- **Engage.** Next, get them passionate about it. What makes different people tick? (Chapter 11 covers this in more detail.)

- **Involve.** The final stage: They understand it. They like it. So put them to use and get them to help make your project even better.

Using employee influencers

While you need buy-in from senior management generally, think strategically about how you can get support from different groups of employees around the company. Get a Board-level sponsor. Are there different groups who can take part in your program, e.g., graduates or new employees? Identify key influencers in the business – how can you involve them?

Internal communications tools

As with external communications, the only limit to your tools is your imagination.
  There will often be traditional company channels you can use:

- Online employee news, including the CR Intranet and Community Involvement pages

- Employee magazines

- Company-internal TV

- Conference calls

- Internal events

- Your own regular status updates to senior management – at least every three to six months

As in the rest of the world, so in a company. Employees are increasingly overloaded with information. Their jobs are also getting harder and their time more limited. So you may have as much, if not more, success with some more innovative direct approaches such as:

- Employee community roadshows: market your community work to employees. Set out information stands where people come together, e.g., the canteen. Make sure you have a call to action so, besides obtaining information, they can get involved if they want.

- Use unusual media and locations to place your information: balloons with messages on; news on the back of toilet doors; creative flyers; singing actors.

- Employees' first-hand experience of your Community Involvement program can be enhanced with visits to program sites to interact with program participants. "Seeing is believing" is a powerful approach and will motivate employees to volunteer in the programs. It is also very effective to take Board members on "Seeing is believing" visits.

- Wherever possible, promote Employee Volunteering in your Community Involvement program (see Chapter 8). Employees who have volunteered will communicate enthusiastically about their experience to colleagues, family, friends, and acquaintances, even customers.

- Use recognition to celebrate employees who are so passionate about getting involved that they are ambassadors for the company in the community. Anything from a letter from the CEO thanking Employee Volunteers to a more formal celebration event is great for both motivating people and promoting your community work.

Tactics for launching a key program to employees

You may want to bring a number of tactics together such as:

- A senior company representative talking about Community Involvement
- A presentation about your Community Involvement, both the particular project you're introducing and the overall approach
- A representative from your NGO partner introducing your joint local program activities
- Program beneficiaries telling employees about their personal experience
- Promotional materials: banners, posters both for decoration and information, maybe giveaways for employees, e.g., baseball caps, keyrings, coffee mugs, or t-shirts
- Finding a way for employees to experience part of the program, e.g., through the NGOs and beneficiaries acting it out, or by giving employees a chance to get involved

Budget

Engaging employees should be low-cost. You can usually jump on the back of a range of existing communications channels. Your best investment may be taking the Internal/Employee Communications Manager to lunch.

Besides existing publications, conferences, etc., create a few innovative tools that help you stand out. This will require some money for design and production costs. While it varies by market, this can still be done pretty cheaply – usually significantly less than €5,000 (about $7,500). But as with external communications, when it comes to annual budgeting, make sure you set some money aside for it.

Measurement

Finally, test what you have communicated. Did it "stick" in employees' minds? Find out what your colleagues think. Some simple questions to ask:

- Did they understand it?

- What did they think of it?

- What else do they want to know?

- How often do they want to be kept informed?

- Do they think their company should do this?

- Would they want to get involved?

If you're nervous about doing this, try it out on some of your closer colleagues first, but ask them for honesty in their feedback!

You may have traditional employee surveys in which you can include these kinds of M&E questions. Alternatively, you may want to go out and ask people yourself. It doesn't matter what you do, just make sure you get feedback so you know what works and how to do it better in the future.

Appendix 10.1. Overview of communications plan for external Community Involvement communications

Sample list of contents:

1. Current State Analysis, external Community Involvement communications

    1.1   Achievements to date:

        1.1.1   Global communications

        1.1.2   Local communications

    1.2   Challenges and risks

    1.3   Opportunities

2. Communications objectives

3. Key messages

4. Key audiences

5. Communications strategies and tactics

- Stakeholder communication
- Media outreach
  - Contacts/relationships with relevant journalists
  - Press conferences and press release distribution
  - Selected one-on-one interviews for key spokespeople
  - Identified speaking engagements
  - Targeted articles in relevant publications
- Communications tools development

6. Budget

7. Measurement and evaluation

8. Reporting

Appendix 10.2. Corporate Responsibility/Community Involvement internal communications checklist[1]

This document is designed as a simple step-by-step process to follow for any Community Involvement internal communication. You can use it as either a ten-minute "sanity check" or follow it in detail as a planning tool.

Checklist for internal communication of CR/Community Involvement

Step 0
Hygiene check. Check alignment with internal stakeholder groups:

✓ Before going into action, make sure the activity is known and endorsed (or acknowledged) by relevant internal stakeholder groups. Typical departments/ management levels you may want to sanity-check with are: top management, Communications, HR, Marketing.

✓ Is the timing right? Does it collide with one/many other projects targeting the same audiences? Does it contradict any other internal communication content coming out?

Step 1
Be clear on your overall objective behind your CR/Community Involvement communication:

✓ What is the target for the community issue you're covering? Make sure your internal communication has the size and impact required to reach the objective, e.g., compare a target like: "50% of all employees to donate funds for company charity" with "involve a minimum 20% of the company's engineers in giving classes at university in the next two years." Different internal communication measures are needed for each goal.

Step 2
Define your CR/Community Involvement internal communications goals:

✓ Set results that you would like to see as an output of the internal communication activity, e.g., reach all target groups X times within Y weeks/months. This will help you choose the right tools to obtain results.

Beware: Issuing information about the activity should not be a communication goal in itself.

→

---

1 Adapted from E.ON Hungary communications tool.

Step 3
Define and cluster your target audiences:

✓   Cluster internal audiences in groups, not just "all employees." This will make sure you tailor your message to the relevant ones and do not bother with those that aren't your real targets. (Think of target groups, e.g., operations, middle management, office, top management, home-based.)

Step 4
Develop the core communication message:

✓   Besides keeping an eye on the information about the Community Involvement activity, formulate it from the perspective of "What's in it for them?"

Step 5
Check out communication platforms that reach each target group:

✓   Explore existing internal communication channels for targeted audiences – what will work best? Also consider creating alternative/innovative ways to reach them.

Step 6
Tailor communication key messages for target audiences:

✓   Be sure you consciously develop and adopt a communication content, style, and tone that fits your target groups. You might want to tailor it to certain groups or feature people from their peer group.

Note: For new and major Community Involvement issues, make sure you inform your most important internal stakeholders first. Get their support for the main points of the message, and allow them time to feed back if necessary before going to mass employee communication.

Step 7
Health check:

✓   Evaluate Steps 3–6, and, if there are inconsistencies or too many questions, repeat from Step 3 to make sure you are still fully aligned with your overall communications and internal communications objectives from Steps 1 and 2.

Step 8
Develop communication materials and tools for target audiences and finalize timing:

✓   See earlier for suggested tools/methods.

✓   Make sure look and feel is consistent with your company style.

✓   Besides direct communication materials/tools for each target audience, think of "supporting materials." Maybe additional communication for special audiences, e.g., middle management, may need a message/letter from top management that encourages them to bring the information to their teams.

→

Step 9
Production and launch of internal communication

Step 10
Measure and evaluate success of initiatives:

✓ Get feedback from target audiences (formally or informally – just ask). Feedback could also be online registration numbers or response to offline materials. In case of any major discrepancies from goals, an amendment/correction may be needed, or further communication activity should be adjusted or strengthened.

✓ Evaluate. Have the communication goals been delivered and the overall Community Involvement objective achieved? Where not achieved, analyze carefully: Where do the deficiencies come from? Wrong/unattractive content? Too much disturbance in or an overcrowding of communication channels? Other factors?

✓ The right conclusions are crucial for your next project (and next communication!).

11

'I knew it would be worthwhile'
Overcoming challenges and instigating change

Why do we have a chapter on change in this book?

In some corporate cultures, adopting strategic Corporate Responsibility and Community Involvement as essential to business and a competitive advantage has been an easy and natural process, with people "getting it" and supporting initiatives from the start. In other companies, it has been more challenging, with practitioners experiencing difficulties in engaging people. They sometimes feel they work on the margins, and are less recognized than some of their colleagues in more "institutionalized" functions such as Marketing, or in more profit-oriented functions such as Manufacturing. They wonder about the best approach to bringing sustainable development thinking and practices into their organizations.

In this final chapter, we offer some inspiration for you to go and "win your cause" inside the company. Our featured guest talks about approaches and experiences that have worked for him during a long, successful career. The interview is followed with advice on understanding and overcoming obstacles, influencing without authority, relying on your own inner resources, and getting external support.

Interview with Dr. Mark Wade: Being right is not enough[1]

Dr. Mark Wade joined Shell in 1979 as a research biochemist, moving in 1997 to the Corporate Center as a founder member of the Sustainable Development Group. Until early 2003 he was Head of Sustainable Development Policy, Strategy & Reporting. Then he moved on to Shell Learning's Leadership Development group: here he led the Sustainable Development Learning program, incorporating sustainable development learning into all stages of the talent pipeline from graduate attraction to senior executive development. Until his retirement from

---

1 Graphs illustrating the conceptual models referred to in this interview can be found in Appendix 11.1 on pages 248f.

Shell in 2006, he was Shell's Liaison Delegate to the World Business Council for Sustainable Development and Chairman of the Business Network of the European Academy for Business in Society (EABIS). He is now a member of the Supervisory Board of EABIS. Mark is also Chairman of the consultancy Future Considerations, a member of the Board of Trustees of Tomorrow's Company and Sustainability advisor to New Zealand Trade and Enterprise.

During his time with Shell, Mark was recognized internally and externally as a key player and architect of Shell's Sustainability journey. He now works with senior executives in major organizations, helping them understand the strategic and operational importance of sustainable development. Mark offers a unique range of experiences and competencies to bring sustainable development thinking into the mainstream of major corporations and institutions.

How can managers go about integrating Community Involvement throughout the company? Where do you start when you need to do it all?

MW: "In my case, it is not so much Community Involvement per se, but the wider concept of sustainable development I've wrestled with, which includes Social and Community Involvement. But the dynamics of the change challenge are essentially the same. As an important first step, you need Board commitment. Any effective change process has to start at the top if you want whole-company, systemic change. Otherwise the odds will be stacked against you.

"You need senior-level buy-in to the strategic and operational importance of the drivers of change to the company. If the CEO and the Board don't 'buy it,' the company will fail to articulate a compelling case for change. You need the official legitimacy that says 'It's okay to do this' or, better still, 'It's vital we do this,' or else you'll be battling against the system and you risk being lost in the noise. The top then needs to support and empower you and people at all levels in driving change."

How do you best approach the Board?

MW: "When working with the Board, first engage individuals, and only then the whole Board. Individuals all have different roles, and each will look at the proposed change from their own remit. So, talk to the CFO about how the change will mitigate risk and identify opportunities, to the head of Manufacturing about license to operate, to the head of Marketing about the impact on brand and customer satisfaction, to the Head of HR on morale and motivation in attracting and retaining the best people, etc. Have customized conversations – to show how the change advocated can benefit each in addressing their particular challenges in a new way. Through these conversations, you will enlist support and build up a portfolio of reasons why it makes sense. When you come to engage the Board as a whole, the job will be that much easier. You can then bring the commonalities together to make a compelling case for change that makes sense to the parts and the whole.

"Once you have CEO and Board approval, kick off the whole-company change process, build awareness, and manage the integration with strategy and operations."

How do you then engage the next level down? How do you get different functions to interact in implementing change?

MW: "It's actually about having the same sorts of conversation that you have had with the Board members. Talk to the senior leaders of each of the main departments. Engage people both intellectually and emotionally. Start by asking: 'What are your priorities in your part of the business? What keeps you awake at night?' Help them see that the change proposition can help them do what's important to them better. Work with them to explore how taking a wider look at things (through a Sustainability or Community Involvement lens, whichever is the focus) can help identify risks and opportunities and be a source of innovation.

"There is sound psychology behind this approach. The case for change is objective and logical, but individuals react to change from a very subjective, personal perspective: 'How will it affect me?' So you need to show the benefit to the individual and how this will help, not hinder, him or her. Connecting in a positive way to their priorities and allaying their fears is key.

"Don't avoid the difficult conversations. Change usually takes investment in time, effort, and money. Be honest about this. Help people see that this is a worthwhile investment that will be more than repaid by lasting benefits.

"Praise those who are already doing what you are advocating and encourage them to do more in a systematic way. Often people may not realize that what they are doing locally is in line with the wider change objectives. Use the innovators and early adopters to reach the early majority. This way you will achieve a critical mass of like-minded thinkers capable of building a company-wide culture and competence around the desired change. When you start, you will be up against incomprehension by most, tolerance by some, and buy-in by only a minority."

How do you then go about helping the whole company become truly supporting?

MW: "Be systematic. Manage this transformation as you would manage any other business project: professionally, with the right governance, planning, and resources.

"Start with a good governance structure. Appoint people who will make it happen. Have representatives from all functions and business groups. Ideally the steering committee – or whatever you want to call it – should be chaired by the CEO or a Board member. The role of this group is to bring commonality to the approach and make sure it is embedded into what I call the 'hard-wiring' of policies, standards, systems, and processes, as well as the 'soft-wiring' of the hearts and minds of people.

"The first job of this group is to help establish a common language for change in simple words that are meaningful within your company. The terms themselves (such as Sustainability versus Corporate Citizenship or, in the social context, Community Involvement versus Social Performance) are not that important. What matters most is that the words resonate with your culture and values.

"Once you have a simple, clear, concise logic and a set of defined words, you must be rigorous in the consistent use of them. If you don't do this upfront, then people will invent their own interpretations of what they might mean, and you end up with 'a tower of Babel,' with conversations that never join up. Once you have established this basic literacy, you can use it as the foundation on which to have more sophisticated conversations on what it means for different parts of the company.

"The next thing is to start to communicate the change proposition through as many media as possible and to engage people in these conversations."

Is mere communication enough to achieve more than basic understanding?

MW: "No. Communication is a great way of reaching lots of people quickly, but all it can ever do is raise a basic awareness and understanding of generic messages. You have to continuously repeat and reinforce them, and even then they won't stick. To make the change meaningful to individuals and to help them understand what they need to do differently on a Monday morning, you have to get more intimate.

"To understand this better, it is useful to look at this in terms of a competency hierarchy and then to deploy the appropriate tools to the tasks. At Shell we developed the Sustainable Development Learning Framework[2] for this purpose.

"To achieve systemic change, you need to move people up from 'basic awareness and understanding' to 'working knowledge', 'skilled', and finally to 'mastery and advocacy.' As you move up the hierarchy, the level of personal engagement goes up and the types of learning become more focused. The most efficient way of doing this is to infuse the learning elements into existing training and leadership development programs. Specialized offering may also be developed, such as Sustainability workshops for finance managers or engineers to make the change meaningful to their everyday roles and challenges. E-learning tools can also be useful, reaching a lot of people in an intimate way if properly designed.

"The best ways of really engaging people in new ways of doing things are interventions based on self-discovered and experiential learning. This is so much more effective than 'teaching.'

"Programs built around Jaworski and Scharmer's 'U' process[3] offer a powerful way of equipping people with new insights and competencies. This is particularly useful for building the mind-sets and skills necessary to deal with complexity and multi-stakeholder interactions."

Do you have concrete examples for that?

MW: "For example, you can design training for refinery managers and their teams on Community Involvement to support their license to operate. Fundamental to this is developing the right mind-set and competencies to engage meaningfully with the community on their hopes, fears, and expectations. The 'U' process encourages people not to jump to conclusions, and to learn how to understand complex situations in a holistic way. People get to visit sites and situations on the ground, outside of their normal experience. They learn how to sense and see things differently, and then use that to create plans for innovative action in their own spheres of influence. This brings new perspectives and wiser decision-making.

---

2 See Appendix 11.1, Figure 11.5, page 248.

3 See Appendix 11.1, Figure 11.6, page 248. Joseph Jaworski is co-founder of the Global Leadership Initiative and author of *Synchronicity: The Inner Path of Leadership*. Dr. C. Otto Scharmer is a Senior Lecturer at MIT, the founding chair of the Presencing Institute, and a founding member of the MIT Green Hub.

"The approach is equally valid for all leaders needing to cope with the complex, fast-changing demands of modern business, where Sustainability considerations are increasingly relevant. I believe it should be central to all leadership development."

Can you say a bit more about why you need to bring the "hard-wiring" and "soft-wiring" together?

MW: "Like many Sustainable Development or Community managers I was not an expert in change. My early approaches were those of an enthusiastic amateur. I came to realize that bringing Sustainability into the 'hard-wiring' of policies, standards, systems, and processes, Key Performance Indicators, etc. had to be balanced with reaching the 'hearts and minds' of people through touching their inner values and business sense – the 'soft-wiring.' If all you do is write the rule book, you will get, at best, a culture of compliance or, worse, avoidance. Why? Because people will not have understood the reason for the rules. Likewise, if all you do is kick up a froth of enthusiasm, without the rigor of aligned governance, then it will evaporate. People will see that they are not supported by the system. I came to this empirically, but it is reinforced by theory in the integral model of change as defined by Wilber.[4]

"This shows, rather more elegantly than my shorthand, the interdependency of the internal and external dimensions of individuals and organizations. I now apply this integral model of change, paying attention to getting all four quadrants right."

So what happens next in implementing change?

MW: "Although you aim to be systematic about change, you also need to let go and allow 'a thousand flowers to bloom.' It is critical to support employee initiatives and unleash the potential for innovation in the company. The company as a whole needs to be prepared to experiment and learn. It takes courageous leadership to do that, especially in a command-and-control culture, where management can be quite frightened of what kind of challenges to the status quo and innovative thinking could emerge.

"It's important to understand that this is manageable chaos, and that it is beneficial to stimulate change thinking and innovation, both strategic and organizational. You can bring discipline to it, and manage the creative chaos of what happens to emerge in a structured way. Capture and spread emerging best practice. Consolidate this into new standards. If you can master that, then you will reap the benefits."

How can Sustainability and Community managers address the internal challenges that often accompany change and transformation processes?

MW: "First, don't go into this with your eyes shut! Once you set off there is no turning back. You will have raised expectations – internally and externally. Better not to start than to give up half way.

---

4 See Appendix 11.1, Figure 11.7, page 249. Kenneth Earl Wilber II is an American philosopher who has written about adult development, developmental psychology, philosophy, and ecology. His work formulates what he calls Integral Theory. In 1998, he founded the Integral Institute, for teaching and applications of his Integral Theory.

"Be flexible. There will always be times when you hit the buffers. You don't have to win every battle. Sometimes it is best to retreat and try a different approach. With limited resources, go for the quick wins and where change is welcomed. The difficult parts then become the minority. Sometimes it can be useful to 'fly under the radar' and work with people and through existing processes without making a song and dance about the change.

"Even with a top-level mandate you will rarely have 'power.' There are many times when I have had the mandate, but still had to work through influencing.

"There are also right and wrong times. If the company is not ready, perhaps because it is very conservative, then be content to keep the idea alive until it is. Be wise. Pick the right moment and tactics. Use all your political and influencing skills. Remember, 'being right' is not enough! There is a real danger that change agents who are too impatient or too idealistic just become an irritant who risk getting kicked out. You need to find the balance between 'tearing the house down' and infusing new ways into the system. There are lots of subtleties to this game.

"Although it is not necessary for a company to go through a crisis to change, crisis can provide a great opportunity. It is at such times that the organization is prepared to admit that old ways of doing things have not worked and people will be more willing to look at alternatives."

That sounds complex . . . how do you then know what to do when, and how?

MW: "It is complex and often messy. Embedding Sustainability, or even just Community Involvement, is a journey. It's difficult and takes a long time. It is a process of continuous learning. That's the reality. Being systematic and courageous in the way I've described will help. I find that companies with strong values, good governance, and a culture of innovation will manage this more easily. Companies lacking these will find it much harder."

How come you can speak in such a definite and determined way about all this?

MW: "I speak with passion and confidence, because these are exactly the challenges I've dealt with in my roles at Shell and subsequently as an advisor. Most of what I've learned has come from my successes and failures while doing it. To my delight, I found that the theory of organizational change in the Wilber model matches precisely my empirical experience, giving weight to the advice offered."

Would you like to give a final message to those people who work with Sustainability or Community Involvement as a change initiative?

MW: "You have the hardest and the most rewarding job in the world. You have the privilege of being an arbiter of change that can enhance the competitiveness of your company and its power to be a force for good. Get it right and you will add value to your company and value to the communities and society it serves."

Overcoming challenges and instigating change

Old habits die hard. People tend to stick to the comfort of what they are used to. Thinking differently, doing something differently, requires them to be open and let go of familiar habits – in short, to change.

It is because of this context that we consider Corporate Responsibility, Sustainability, and Community Involvement to be about whole-organization, long-term change. Some companies still see themselves as outside of society, rather than as an interdependent part of it. Some companies still "keep their cards close to their chests," rather than perceiving the "boundaries" of their company as open and permeable, and being open and actively engaged in exchange with their stakeholders.

We will introduce here a few final concepts and models that you might find helpful. We'll tell you about the needs of the people around you, and we'll point to what you need in terms of confidence, inner authority, and external support so you can achieve your goals in Community Involvement.

There's always change

Change is nothing new – it is actually the one constant in our lives. Change happens all the time, in our private as well as in our professional lives, and in society around us. Our own body changes every day; our children grow up. Change is about growth and development.

It's not uncommon for people to say, "The world is changing faster and faster – faster than ever." In reality, people have been saying this throughout history. Just think back to when the telephone was invented, or the automobile, or television. Changes always seemed to be about speeding up.

Companies go through change as well – and business theorists argue that they need to, in order to remain competitive. "Change or die," goes the popular aphorism. Just think about products that became redundant, like the typewriter. If the market around a company changes, it has to change its product line, its business model, and its way of doing things – or "die."

Be it in their private or their professional lives, some people thrive on change. They are curious about new things, open to new opportunities, highly flexible, and happy to change. Others prefer constancy and value tradition. They feel easily unsettled by complexity and uncertainty. They like a predictable, steady pace and a sense of security. Change can feel threatening to them.

What is it that those people dislike in change situations? Change interrupts "the way we do things around here." That's what you often hear from people: "We've always done it like that." Try signing your name with your other hand – it feels awkward and uncomfortable, doesn't it? You need to concentrate on it, and it takes more energy than signing your name the way you're used to. You need to go through a psychological transition. That's what change brings about. You're not very good at it at first. You have to practice. It has to become a new habit, and that transition takes time.

How, as a manager, do you enthuse everybody in the company about something that they are unfamiliar with and know little about?

Common obstacles and how to address them

First of all, it is important to understand your own and other people's typical reactions to change, and to acknowledge those.

The psychologist Claes Janssen developed the "Four Rooms of Change" theory (see Figure 11.1). According to this theory, when confronted with change, we all move through the four rooms of contentment, denial, confusion/chaos, and then inspiration. None of us can take a "Tarzan swing" to go straight from contentment to inspiration! For some people, the periods of denial and confusion are shorter, for others they last longer. Once you have gone through inspiration and reach contentment again, you know that you can't stay there forever – the next change will come along, and the whole cycle will start all over. If you think back to situations of change in your personal or professional life, can you see how you may have moved through the four rooms of change?

Figure 11.1 The 'Four Rooms of Change' by Claes Janssen, PhD

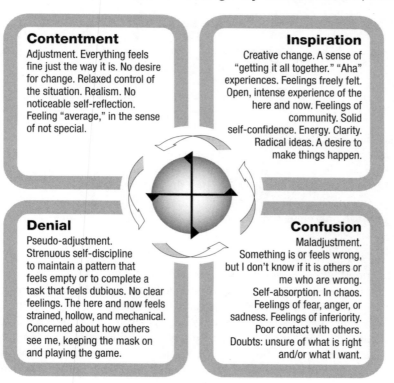

Contentment
Adjustment. Everything feels fine just the way it is. No desire for change. Relaxed control of the situation. Realism. No noticeable self-reflection. Feeling "average," in the sense of not special.

Inspiration
Creative change. A sense of "getting it all together." "Aha" experiences. Feelings freely felt. Open, intense experience of the here and now. Feelings of community. Solid self-confidence. Energy. Clarity. Radical ideas. A desire to make things happen.

Denial
Pseudo-adjustment. Strenuous self-discipline to maintain a pattern that feels empty or to complete a task that feels dubious. No clear feelings. The here and now feels strained, hollow, and mechanical. Concerned about how others see me, keeping the mask on and playing the game.

Confusion
Maladjustment. Something is or feels wrong, but I don't know if it is others or me who are wrong. Self-absorption. In chaos. Feelings of fear, anger, or sadness. Feelings of inferiority. Poor contact with others. Doubts: unsure of what is right and/or what I want.

Source: Ander & Lindström AB; www.fourrooms.com

Note: This is the authorized version of the "Four Rooms of Change" (numerous plagiarisms exist).

Then, for those of you who read Saint-Exupéry's *The Little Prince*[5] when you were younger, do you remember the image of the serpent that swallowed the elephant? That's what the adoption cycle for new trends and new technologies looks like (Figure 11.2):

Figure 11.2 **The technology adoption life cycle**

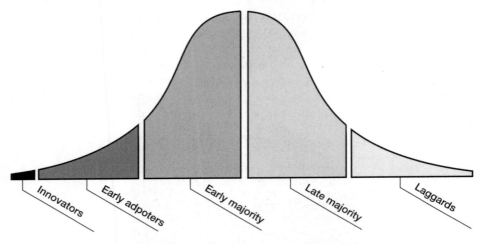

Source: G. A. Moore, *Crossing the Chasm* (New York: Harper Business, 1991). Copyright © 1991 by Geoffrey A. Moore. Reprinted by permission of HarperCollins Publishers.

This is a bell curve, and each group in it has its own psychology. Understanding their way of seeing and their preferences will help you to work with them. As a Community Involvement practitioner, you might be an innovator or an early adopter in your company – and those two groups tend to mobilize the early majority.

The late majority tends to wait until something has become an established standard. The laggards will only come around once they can't avoid it any longer.

Habitual ways of seeing

Our motivation for change and whether we perceive the need for urgency in making changes are tied to our ways of seeing. We tend to see things from within our "paradigm," from within the way we explain the world to ourselves. Often that habitual way of seeing needs to be "disturbed," so we don't get stuck in it. To help people see differently, you often have to disrupt their accepted view. When you manage to do that, you may hear them say, "Now I get it!" You can try experiencing a shift in seeing by looking at the famous "young girl–old woman" perceptual illusion[6] (see Figure 11.3). It might take you

---

5 A. de Saint-Exupéry, *The Little Prince* (1943).

6 The creator of the image displayed here was British cartoonist W. E. Hill, who published it in 1915 in *Puck* humor magazine as "My Wife and My Mother-in-Law." Hill almost certainly adapted the figure from an original concept that was popular throughout the world on trading and puzzle cards: an anonymous German postcard from 1888 depicted the image in its earliest known form (mathworld.wolfram.com/YoungGirl-OldWomanIllusion.html, accessed December 2009).

Figure 11.3 **'Young girl–old woman' perceptual illusion**

30 seconds or longer to see alternately a young girl or an old woman. Some people will see both very quickly; others will need help with being able to see more than one image – and that's how it may be for your colleagues, superiors, or Board members, too.

For many years, companies perceived themselves as "closed systems," separate from society. Although this view has been outdated for years, some people still subconsciously act based on such a deep-seated belief. A more timely way of seeing is that of a company as an "open system," part of society, interrelated and in exchange with its stakeholders. Once you can see it that way, how do you act accordingly? What needs to change in the company's way of doing things? What are the consequences?

As an internal influencer and "change agent" you can help people with how they deal with change. You can help them see differently, help them understand, and help them to work through their denial and confusion and to start exploring options. You can support them when they start new activities.

Understanding what motivates people

People aren't the same. They're motivated in a variety of ways. Figure 11.4 shows five different motivation types:

- **Inspiration.** "What's the greater purpose?"

- **Task.** "If it's not tangible, I won't be engaged."

- **Personal.** "I want to be appreciated for what I contribute."

- **Position.** "Is it good for me?" "Is it good for the business?"

- **Relationship.** "Can I work with people that I like?" "Can I have a good time?"

Each of us will have one primary form of motivation. This can often lead to miscommunication if we don't understand what motivates the other person. How often do you find yourself in a situation thinking "I'm not sure they're getting this"? You then try to communicate from a new angle. Maybe you stop talking about the goal of the project and start talking about some of the people involved. Suddenly the other person gets excited. You've found their primary motivation is relational, not inspirational.

Figure 11.4 **Effective influencing – understanding motivation**

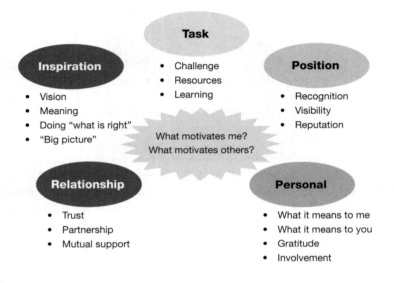

Source: A. R. Cohen and D. L. Bradford, *Influence without Authority* (Hoboken, NJ: Wiley, 2nd edn, 2005).

Power, control, and project focus

Another common obstacle in a company is that people fear losing control, or their power position. If something else becomes important, will their area of influence become less important? As Mark Wade explains at the beginning of this chapter, it's important to appreciate people for their contribution, and to help them understand how Corporate Responsibility and Community Involvement are relevant to their particular area.

What might also get in the way is people's desire to finish a project so they can go back to life as normal. The tricky thing about Community Involvement, as with all areas of Corporate Responsibility and Sustainability, is that it is an ongoing process and represents a new way of doing things in the long run. It is about a different attitude, and it needs to become part of the corporate culture. Those companies that have been recognized as leaders in Corporate Responsibility and Sustainability have all ingrained this thinking into their corporate culture and corporate values.

Working with the corporate culture takes time, and it demands engaging with all levels of the organization. As Mark Wade says, you need to engage both "the system" (your company's official structure with its policies) and the individuals who make up the organization (the employees with their hearts and minds). For the "system" to support Community Involvement, you definitely need your Board members' support, and you need HR and Internal Communications to talk about it to employees. You will also need the Brand people from Marketing to connect Community Involvement to the social brand dimension: for example, to the "human and trusted" perspective. When it comes to individuals, you need employees to live this thinking as part of corporate culture and values. Changing the culture is not about one or the other odd event – it's an ongoing process. Culture is about what people want to be and what they live every day. You cannot force it on them; they need to live it out of their own motivation and commitment.

Espoused theory and enacted behavior

A tricky thing on the "system" level can be if your company has "officially" embraced a commitment to CR, including Community Involvement, as an "espoused theory"[7] – yet has not integrated these elements into the company's "way of doing things" and into official governance principles, policies, and management systems. Without effective systemic integration, you will need to rely on people's goodwill to support you, and you might get that from some, but not from others. People's resistant behavior may still be based on outdated underlying beliefs and ways of seeing. We explain this here so you can better understand the frustrations you might experience. Beyond initial lip service, you will need to get full commitment from the Board toward comprehensive systemic integration, so you can hold people in various functions responsible for supporting you.

Internal fragmentation

You may also hear "Well, why don't you deal with that? It's your job – I have other pressing priorities." That's how CR and Community Involvement end up as marginal functions, somewhere behind closed doors at the end of the corridor. People feel it is easier to outsource something than to take ownership and change direction and behavior. The common understanding these days is that CR and Community Involvement should become so mainstream, so much a part of the way things are done, that CR and Community Involvement people should aim to almost put themselves out of a job, other than that of facilitating and coordinating activities.

For that to happen, it is important that relevant functions understand what the benefits are for their own area. You cannot do the work for people in the long run – you need to "mainstream" CR and Community Involvement, so they become integrated into the business, and business functions take ownership.

---

7 C. Argyris and D. Schön, *Organizational Learning II* (Reading, MA: Addison-Wesley, 1996).

The 'sandwich position' of middle management

Middle management is often "sandwiched" between top management and employees. They receive orders from top management and need to meet three- or six-month targets, and they also need to keep their employees motivated. When you work to engage middle management staff, listen to their concerns, find out what they are busy with, and what their current priorities are. How do your issues relate to theirs? Can you find a connection? Can you establish relevance?

Next, they might say: "Well, I can only support you on this if my superior approves." That superior might be somebody in top management. You will need to talk to her or him, or get your own boss to do so.

Overcoming 'Yet another change initiative' or 'Not invented here'

People can become cynical. They have seen so many change initiatives come and go, evaporate or fail. They may also have been disappointed in trying to change things themselves, having experienced a lack of support. It will be important to keep people's spirits up, on the one hand, and show them real results, on the other.

What may also play a role is "not invented here" thinking and skepticism towards anything that people feel is forced upon them from above. This can result in rejection. That's why it helps to pursue CR and Community Involvement through a participatory approach, engaging people throughout the company from the outset in thinking together about what it means to them and what they think the company should do. This approach tends to be more successful because it allows people to feel involved from the start and to develop a sense of ownership for solutions.

To give you an example: Nokia runs annual internal quality awards, and employees are invited to submit proposals for improvement. The year the company first made Corporate Responsibility a topic for the quality awards, submissions rose by 30%, and a quarter of all submissions made were about Corporate Responsibility.

It is a good idea to engage people throughout the organization in conversations: for example, in cross-functional focus groups. You might ask: What does the topic mean to them? What ideas do they have for the company? This way, people feel involved and take ownership.

New technologies also offer ways to engage employees in large-scale conversations, without the limitations of geography. For example, IBM uses Achordus[8] as a tool to engage groups of up to 10,000 people in facilitated online conversations on issues related to culture, values, and Corporate Responsibility.

Influencing without authority

With all the convincing and persuading you will bring to overcoming the obstacles explained earlier, you will be influencing. This is your main internal role. We talk about influencing without authority, as you will probably not be in a position simply to "tell" people what to do. Your job will not be about giving orders. It will be about engaging people. Ros Tennyson, in Chapter 7, speaks of influencers and change agents as "invis-

---

8 www.achordus.com

Individual qualities needed to promote your cause

As also explained in Chapter 2, it helps if you bring:

- Excellent communication skills, both internally and externally, and beyond your own area of expertise
- The ability to bring people together, create good relations, and foster trust
- Openness to and an understanding of issues beyond the core business
- Listening skills and the ability to see multiple points of view
- Team orientation
- Passion, motivation, and enthusiasm
- Patience, staying power, and frustration tolerance

ible leaders." The art of leadership here is about engaging, involving, and motivating people.

> "The wicked leader is he who the people despise. The good leader is he who the people revere. The great leader is he who the people say, 'We did it ourselves.' " — Lao Tzu, Chinese Taoist philosopher

Your work is really all about relationships: building them up, maintaining them, and creating a network of collaborators and supporters. From that kind of "connectivity," a lot of change and innovation can emerge.

You will need to change hearts and minds one person at a time – so be prepared to engage in a lot of listening, a lot of dialogue, and a lot of influencing and persuasion (in that order). Stephen Covey[9] recommends trying first to understand, and only then aim to be understood. As we have emphasized several times in this chapter, people want to feel understood about their own issues first, so if you can ask them questions about those and hear them out, they will then be more willing to hear about your cause. To encourage positive dialogue, avoid telling them what you want from them. Instead, ask them about their own thoughts and ideas. If they can actively contribute, they will develop a sense of ownership.

Your work involves the art of being persistent without being pushy. As Mark Wade explained, know when to retreat and come back another way.

Good inner resources and external support

You probably won't effect change within your company overnight: it will take a lot of time, and a lot of patience. In terms of your own resources, you will need to build your inner confidence and find your own grounding. Our authority tends to grow with age, training, reflection, and experience. The more you work with this, the more mature and confident you will become. Manage your own authority well.

---

9 S. R. Covey, *The 7 Habits of Highly Effective People* (New York: Free Press, rev. edn, 2004).

Get external support: Five approaches

You don't need to do it all alone, and you don't need to have all the answers. You can strengthen your inner resources through connecting to an external support network, and it is good professional practice to do so. We suggest five approaches you can take:

1. If your company has an Organization Development function within HR, and people in it specialized in change processes, don't be shy about talking to them. They will be just as important to you as your colleagues from the strategy department. A great example for us was O$_2$ Germany. Their head of Corporate Responsibility at the time formed a CR steering committee involving the heads of various corporate functions. He made sure the "change people" from Organization Development were always with them at the table when they met.

2. Make sure you join a peer network. Have exchanges with peers from other companies about their successes and challenges. There may be such a network already in your country. You can also meet peers at Corporate Responsibility conferences,[10] or you can join corporate membership organizations such as the Boston College Center for Corporate Citizenship or Business for Social Responsibility in the US, Business in the Community in the UK, or CSR Europe in Brussels. If you want to stay tuned in to the very latest thinking on Corporate Responsibility and Sustainability in the context of organizational change, consider joining the European Academy for Business in Society.[11]

3. Look for your own role models, inside and outside your company. How would they approach what you are attempting to do? You can also consider finding a mentor or a coach.

4. Get good training. What is out there? You can get training on your communication, rhetoric, and presentation skills; voice and body language; facilitation; influencing and persuasion; managing difficult conversations; internal consulting; and conflict resolution. Your company might have some courses as part of its own learning and development portfolio, or you can search on the Internet for what's offered by external providers.

5. Last, but not least, you can get individual support or help with internal convincing and facilitation from qualified external consultants. Ask around to find out whom other people have worked with and whom they recommend.

Your job: Sometimes tough, but a rewarding and fantastic journey

You will find that your job as an internal influencer is both complex and tough some-

---

10 For example, those run by Ethical Corporation in the UK, or by the Conference Board, Boston College Center for Corporate Citizenship or Business for Social Responsibility in the US.

11 Website addresses for all of these organizations are given on pages 250-51.

Books about change

If you want to help people understand what change is about, two quick and easy books we recommend are Spencer Johnson's *Who Moved My Cheese?** and John Kotter's *Our Iceberg Is Melting*.† Both are quick and fun reads that offer simple fables about doing well in an ever-changing world. You can read these yourself and give them to colleagues as conversation starters.

If you are interested in reading more about how other people did it, we recommend Sandra Waddock's *The Difference Makers: How Social and Institutional Entrepreneurs Created the Social Responsibility Movement*.‡

* S. Johnson, *Who Moved My Cheese?* (New York: Putnam, 1998).
† J. Kotter, *Our Iceberg Is Melting: Changing and Succeeding Under Any Conditions* (New York: St. Martin's Press, 2006).
‡ S. Waddock, *The Difference Makers: How Social and Institutional Entrepreneurs Created the Social Responsibility Movement* (Sheffield, UK: Greenleaf Publishing, 2008).

times and fantastic at other times. It's a long journey. All our colleagues in this field have said the one thing they first had to "unlearn" in their jobs was impatience. Nevertheless, if you look back after your first year of work, and then after three years, you will see that you have created change, and you will have built a network of enthusiastic collaborators and supporters. Programs will be in place, people will be committed, and outcomes will have been achieved in the community. Ultimately, the outcomes of your work will benefit both society and your company, and stakeholders internally and externally will appreciate your contributions.

Appendix 11.1. Figures illustrating conceptual models referred to in the interview with Dr. Mark Wade

Figure 11.5 **Shell's Sustainable Development Learning framework**

Objective	Activity	Medium	Agent
Awareness and understanding	**Communicating** Key messages Latest updates Best-practice examples	SD ePortal Newsletters, e-letters Shell Report Resource library	Corporate center Businesses Functions

Working knowledge
 	
 Skilled
	Training/Learning
	 SD presentation packs
	 SD case studies
	 SD best-practice guides
	 SD modules/events
	 SD e-learning tools
		SD workshops
		 SD masterclasses
		 Chronos (e-learning)
		 Leadership assessment
		   and development
		 Training/coaching
		   interventions
			SD advisors
			 Subject experts
			 Self-directed
			   program
			   managers

Mastery and advocacy	**Beyond Training** Active learning Experienced people Functional leadership Competency profiling	SD networks Cross-postings Career planning Competencies	Businesses HR planners SD/HSE advisors SD practitioners

Shell Learning

© Royal Dutch Shell plc

Figure 11.6 **The 'U' Process approach of Jaworski and Scharmer**

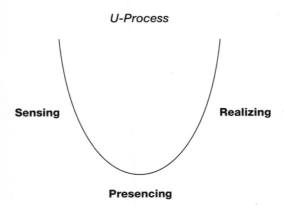

U-Process

Sensing

Realizing

Presencing

Sensing. Participants visit other sites and organizations, develop fresh insights into those organizations – and begin to question some of their own assumptions.

Presencing. Participants integrate all of their "sensing" and together reach a shared sense of the possible way forward and their own deep, personal commitment to this.

Realizing. Together, participants create plans for prototyping and action that represent new, innovative thinking.

Source: O. Scharmer; www.presencing.com

Figure 11.7 **Wilber's integral model of change**

Useful organizations

We have referred to these organizations throughout the book as they provide a wealth of useful information for people working in Community Involvement and Corporate Responsibility. This list is not exhaustive; it is the authors' list.

Organizations for Corporate Responsibility and Corporate Community Involvement

AccountAbility	www.accountability21.net
Boston College Center for Corporate Citizenship (BCCCC)	www.bcccc.net
Business for Social Responsibility (BSR)	www.bsr.org
Business in the Community (BITC)	www.bitc.org.uk
CSR Europe	www.csreurope.org
European Academy of Business in Society (EABIS)	www.eabis.org
Global Business Coalition on HIV/AIDS, Tuberculosis and Malaria (GBC)	www.gbcimpact.org
International Business Leaders Forum (IBLF)	www.iblf.org
International Finance Corporation (IFC)	www.ifc.org
LBG	www.lbg-online.net
Transparency International (TI)	www.transparency.org
World Business Council for Sustainable Development (WBCSD)	www.wbcsd.org
World Economic Forum	www.weforum.org
United Nations Global Compact	www.unglobalcompact.org

Advice on cross-sector collaboration

The Partnering Initiative (TPI)	www.thepartneringinitiative.org

Membership organization for Employee Involvement

ENGAGE	www.engageyouremployees.org

International NGO partners for Disaster Relief

CARE International	www.care.org
Center for International Disaster Information	www.cidi.org
International Federation of Red Cross and Red Crescent Societies	www.ifrc.org
World Food Programme	www.wfp.org

Guidance on Corporate Responsibility reporting

Global Reporting Initiative (GRI)	www.globalreporting.org

Glossary of relevant terms: Corporate Community Involvement

Added Value from cross-sector collaboration – Added value from cross-sector collaboration/partnering is understood as the outcomes and impact achieved together for beneficiaries, stakeholders, and society that none of the partners could have achieved alone.

Business indicators – Part of measurement and evaluation. Measures of business benefits realized through leveraging the results of a company's Community Involvement internally and externally. *See Chapter 9.*

Business Integration of Community Involvement – *See Chapter 5.*

Cause-related marketing (CRM) – A product or a corporate brand is linked to a relevant social cause, promising consumers/customers that, for every item of a product bought, a certain percentage will be donated by the company, on behalf of the consumer, to the company's chosen cause. *See Chapter 5.*

Civil society – A generic term comprising all not-for-profit and non-governmental organizations, including community-based organizations.

Community – Commonly understood as the regions, cities, towns, and villages in which the company does business, and where its employees, customers, or other stakeholders work and live.

Core competencies – The core strengths of the company, e.g., corporate-wide scientific or technology expertise, production skills, or management competence. A core competency can be any combination of business-inherent knowledge and skills. Increasingly, in their **Corporate Community Involvement**, companies are expected to contribute their core competencies to solving relevant societal issues.

Corporate Citizenship – A company is a fully participating member of society, with both rights and participatory responsibilities to give back to society and contribute meaningfully. Some companies use the term to describe their **philanthropy**, their **Corporate Community Involvement**, or all of their **Corporate Responsibility** activities.

Corporate Community Involvement – Active community partnership in projects between a company (or a platform of companies) and/or governments and/or NGOs in the countries/regions/communities where the company operates. The company contributes project funding, co-designs and co-manages the project, and its employees get involved as volunteers. The focus is on creating positive *impact* for society and, as a result, business benefits. Often also called: **Corporate Citizenship**, Corporate Community Engagement, Corporate Community Investment, Corporate Community Relations, Community Partnerships or **Social Performance**.

Corporate Giving – Also known as corporate **philanthropy**, corporate **donations**, or "the writing of checks to charity." The act of corporations donating some of their profits, or their resources, to non-profit organizations. *See Chapter 4.*

Corporate Responsibility (CR) – Corporate Responsibility is complex: it is about your company's responsible and sustainable behavior in *all* company matters, including all financial, environmental, employee, and societal issues. Corporate Community Involvement is one sub-section of a company's overall Corporate *Social* Responsibility, also called Social Performance.

CR/Sustainability council or steering group – A group in a company, typically consisting of senior managers and often external stakeholders, that makes recommendations to the company's Executive Board on the planning, monitoring, implementation, and reporting of CR/Sustainability objectives, including a company's Community Involvement.

Cross-sector collaboration/partnership – Collaboration or partnership between the private sector and/or government and/or the third sector (also called civil society). Depending on the constellation, can also be called "public–private partnership," "tri-sector," or "multi-sector collaboration." Increasingly, academia is considered a relevant sector for collaboration as well. Cross-sector partnerships are increasingly seen as the development approach of the 21st century. By sharing the skills, resources, and expertise of each sector, and working in collaboration at local, national, and/or international levels, cross-sector partnerships have a real potential to drive innovative solutions to societal challenges in an integrated and sustainable way. *See Chapter 7.*

Disaster relief – Money and/or services made available as a fast response to human suffering to individuals and communities that have experienced losses owing to disasters. The term *disaster* is applied to mean both human-made and natural catastrophes. *See Chapter 4.*

Donations – see **Corporate Giving** and *Chapter 4*.

Employee Involvement – How a company supports its employees' engagement in society. Employee Involvement consists of **three core elements**: **Employee Volunteering**, **Matched Time**, and **Matched Funding**. *See Chapter 8.*

Employee Volunteering – Part of **Employee Involvement**. Voluntary contribution of time, energy, and skills by a company's employees to causes in the communities where employees work and live. Organized by the company, employees volunteer as individuals or as teams, often with paid time off for volunteering, e.g., two days' paid leave per year. *See Chapter 8.*

Foundation – A foundation is a non-profit organization that supports charitable activities in order to serve the common good. Foundations are often created with endowments – money given by individuals, families, or corporations. With the income earned from investing the endowments, they generally make grants to unrelated organizations or institutions or to individuals for scientific, educational, cultural, religious, or other charitable purposes; or they operate their own programs. *See Chapter 4.*

Global Reporting Initiative (GRI) – A multi-stakeholder initiative whose mission is to develop and disseminate a global framework of sustainability reporting guidelines for voluntary use by organizations and encompassing the economic, environmental, and social dimensions of their activities, products, and services. The GRI framework for reporting includes reporting principles and specific content indicators to guide the preparation of organization-level sustainability reports (www.globalreporting.org).

In-kind Donation – see **non-monetary giving**.

Input – Part of measurement and evaluation. The resources (e.g., staff, financial resources, management resources, networking connections, space, and equipment) used to accomplish a project's objectives. *See Chapter 9.*

Key Performance Indicators (KPIs) – Part of measurement and evaluation. Key Performance Indicators are financial and non-financial metrics used to help (an) organization(s) define and measure progress toward organizational goals. KPIs are used to assess the present state of a project and/or a partnership and to prescribe a future course of action based on insights gained from the assessment. KPIs are typically tied to an organization's or a partnership's strategy. *See Chapter 9.*

Matched Funding – Part of **Employee Involvement**. Employees raise funds for charitable causes of their choice. The company matches the amounts raised, up to a certain amount annually per employee. *See Chapter 8.*

Matched Time – Part of **Employee Involvement**. Employees volunteer for charitable causes during their own free time. The company contributes a certain amount per hour volunteered to the charities concerned, up to a certain number of hours volunteered per employee and up to a financial limit. *See Chapter 8.*

Memorandum of Understanding (MoU) – A document formalizing a commitment by all parties to a collaboration and summarizing the outline of its terms. Usually an MoU is agreed before a project is developed.

Millennium Development Goals (MDGs) – The eight MDGs, which range from halving extreme poverty to halting the spread of HIV/AIDS and providing universal primary education, form a blueprint agreed to by all the world's countries and all the world's leading development institutions (www.un.org/millenniumgoals).

Non-monetary giving – An alternative form of **Corporate Giving**. A non-cash gift, also called an **In-kind Donation**, is a non-monetary contribution of equipment, supplies, or other property by a company to the community.

Outcomes – Part of measurement and evaluation. The long-term results of a program or initiative. These are qualitative and often difficult to measure. *See Chapter 9.*

Outputs – Part of measurement and evaluation. Tangible short-term results that come from the combination of inputs available and processes (activities) completed. Usually quantitative. *See Chapter 9.*

Partnering Agreement – A document outlining the objectives of a partnership and detailing planned activities, resource commitments as well as roles, responsibilities, and decision-making procedures. *See Chapter 7.*

Philanthropy — see **Corporate Giving**.

Private sector – An umbrella term for the business/corporate/for-profit sector.

Public–private partnership – see **cross-sector collaboration/partnership**.

Public sector – An umbrella term comprising government (at national, regional, and local levels), intergovernmental agencies, and public service organizations.

Social entrepreneurship – Recognizing a social problem and using entrepreneurial principles to organize, create, and manage a venture to create *social change*. Whereas business entrepreneurs typically measure performance in *profit and return*, social entrepreneurs assess their success in terms of the *impact* their programs have on society.

Social Impact Assessment – A form of assessment undertaken by companies or governments at the project planning stage of major infrastructure developments to consider a project's social or societal effects. *See Chapter 5.*

Social Performance – A company's measured performance towards its employees and in society, and the impact of that performance.

Social Performance Management System – An in-company framework for managing the company's social and societal issues, consisting of policies, standards, guidelines, and reporting and review processes. *See Chapter 5.*

Socially Responsible Investment (SRI) – An increasing number of investors – both private and institutional – are demanding more accurate information on companies' environmental and social performance to help guide their investment decisions. An increasing number of pension funds also invest part of their money according to socially responsible criteria. SRI combines investors' financial objectives with their concerns about social, environmental, and ethical issues. Green, social, and ethical funds use ethical, social, and environmental screens for portfolio selection.

Social sponsoring – Similar to companies sponsoring the arts, cultural events, or sports, social sponsoring is about a company sponsoring a social initiative: for example, a charitable event. Now seen as historically preceding **Corporate Community Involvement**, social sponsoring is driven by a strong marketing motivation, typically that of having the company brand clearly identified with a charitable cause. See *Introduction*.

Societal indicators – Part of measurement and evaluation. Measures of performance for a company's **Community Involvement**, focusing on output, outcomes, and impact of programs in society. See *Chapter 9*.

Stakeholders – In 1984, Professor R. Edward Freeman introduced the term *stakeholder*,[1] which he defined as anyone who is affected by or can affect an organization. Stakeholders include consumers, employees, business partners, investors, suppliers, unions, governments and regulators, educational institutions, the media, and opinion leaders, NGOs, and local communities. Increasingly, the environment and future generations are considered stakeholders as well.

Strategic philanthropy – Companies seek to align their previously random **Corporate Giving** and focus it on a strategic cause that connects to their core business. In making their contributions, they are looking for at least a small return through reputation benefit.

Sustainability – The degree to which activities are capable of continuing, contributing effectively to their purpose, while not compromising the environmental, economic, or social balance for future generations.

Sustainability indices – A corporation's responsible performance is measured in a number of global sustainability indices, e.g.

- Dow Jones Sustainability Index (www.sustainability-indexes.com)

- FTSE4Good (www.ftse.com/Indices/FTSE4Good_Index_Series/index.jsp)

---

1   R. Edward Freeman, *Strategic Management: A Stakeholder Approach* (Boston: Pitman, 1984).

Index

Page numbers in *italic figures* refer to tables and figures